PDM

Piano for the Developing Musician

Sixth Edition

PDM

Piano for the Developing Musician

Sixth Edition,
Media Update

Martha Hilley
The University of Texas at Austin

Lynn Freeman Olson
Composer

SCHIRMER
CENGAGE Learning™

Australia • Brazil • Japan • Korea • Mexico • Singapore • Spain • United Kingdom • United States

SCHIRMER
CENGAGE Learning™

Piano for the Developing Musician, Sixth Edition, Media Update
Martha Hilley and Lynn Freeman Olson

Publisher: Clark Baxter

Development Editor: Kimberly Apfelbaum

Assistant Editor: Nell Pepper

Editorial Assistant: Rebekah Matthews

Technology Project Manager: Wendy Constantine

Marketing Manager: Mark Haynes

Marketing Communications Manager: Heather Baxley

Content Project Manager: Georgia Young

Art Director: Faith Brosnan

Print Buyer: Justin Palmeiro

Image Permissions Editor: Amanda Groszko

Text Permissions Editor: Bob Kauser

Production Service: Newgen

Cover Designer: Cambraia Fernandez

Cover Image: The Metropolitan Museum of Art, Frank Lloyd Wright, window triptych from the Avery Coonley Playhouse. Purchase, Edward C. Moore, Jr. Gift and Edgar J. Kaufman Charitable Foundation Gift. 1967 (67 213 1-3)

Compositor: Newgen

Library of Congress Control Number: 2004116868

ISBN-13: 978-0-495-57218-3

ISBN-10: 0-495-57218-7

Schirmer, Cengage Learning
20 Channel Center Street
Boston, MA 02210
USA

Cengage Learning is a leading provider of customized learning solutions with office locations around the globe, including Singapore, the United Kingdom, Australia, Mexico, Brazil, and Japan. Locate your local office at: **www.cengage.com/global**

Cengage Learning products are represented in Canada by Nelson Education, Ltd.

For your course and learning solutions, visit **www.cengage.com**.

Purchase any of our products at your local college store or at our preferred online store **www.ichapters.com**

Printed in United States
5 6 7 8 9 10 11 22 21 20 19 18

Contents

The Web icon ( ) indicates additional content and practice suggestions that appear in the Online Tutorials at http://www.cengage.com/login The Note icon ( ) indicates that mp3s related to the material are available for download at the PDM Web site.The Disk icon ( ) refers to aural backgrounds and recordings on the MIDI disks that accompany the text.

2. Pentascales

3. Root Position Triads

SKILLS AND ACTIVITIES

SUBSEQUENT REPERTOIRE

4. Extended Use of Intervals, Pentascales, and Triads/ Dominant Seventh

EXEMPLARY REPERTOIRE

TOPICS TO EXPLORE AND DISCUSS

SKILLS AND ACTIVITIES

9. The ii–V7–I Progression

10. Secondary Dominants/Styles of Accompanying

11. Harmonic Implications of Common Modes

EXEMPLARY REPERTOIRE

TOPICS TO EXPLORE AND DISCUSS

SKILLS AND ACTIVITIES

SUBSEQUENT REPERTOIRE

12. Diatonic Seventh Chords in Major and Minor/ Secondary Seventh Chords

13. Altered/Borrowed Triads

14. Altered Seventh Chords/Extended Harmonies (Ninth, Thirteenth)

TOPICS TO EXPLORE AND DISCUSS

SKILLS AND ACTIVITIES

SUBSEQUENT REPERTOIRE

Preface to the Sixth Edition

Piano for the Developing Musician, Sixth Edition Media Update, is the only text strictly focused on the music major who must pass a piano proficiency before graduating. In a diverse collection of repertoire tightly structured around the skills these students must know, I have designed this single volume to fill the needs of a four-semester curriculum and coordinate with your theory curriculum. I have listened to your requests and increased the number of ensembles, brought back some of the repertoire favorites from previous editions, revised harmonization exercises with an eye to students' capabilities, added scale fingerings in technique exercises, and developed a more sequenced program of improvisation throughout the fourteen chapters.

ONLINE TUTORIALS

Virtually a second book residing on the PDM Web site at *http://www.cengage.com/login*—the PDM Online Tutorials continue with the sixth edition. Watch for the Web icon ( ) that appears often in the text. It tells you that additional content and practice suggestions appear online, where the student will be able to see, hear, and practice additional material. (As before you will need to have specific plug-ins to view the majority of the tutorials—the latest version of Shockwave Player from Macromedia as well as QuickTime. The plug-ins will need to reside within your Netscape and/or Internet Explorer folders.)

In each chapter of the Online Tutorials, you will find new examples, more practical advice on playing the repertoire in the text, more selections that tackle those same concepts, and additional practice drills. And you will find student compositions for each chapter—in some instances with Web movie performances. In my classes, student peers vote "Best In Show" to the composition(s) that they think should appear on the Web site. You will notice other student compositions included in the text. I encourage instructors to send me your students' compositions after their own peer review for possible inclusion online or in future editions of PDM—and I welcome receiving compositions directly from students as well. Send the composition as a Finale "Tiff" file or the equivalent format for Sibelius. Email the compositions directly to *mfhilley@mail.utexas.edu*. I am sorry but I am unable to accept hand-written manuscripts.

THE TEXT

The Preliminary Chapter on Rudiments contains those basic music rudiments we feel are essential to the successful study of piano. For those students who have had no previous piano background and also for those students with no theory background, time spent in the Preliminary Chapter on Rudiments will be time well spent.

CHAPTER FORMAT

Each numbered chapter of PDM follows a consistent structural outline:

EXEMPLARY REPERTOIRE

Every chapter opens with a composition that forms the basis for learning the concepts and skills introduced in the chapter. MIDI recordings (free to the instructor) for digital keyboards with disk drive, hardware sequencers, or computers with sound cards provide an aural representation of the repertoire. These standard MIDI files are recorded on Tracks 3 and 4 so students can mute a track and work hands separately as needed.

TOPICS TO EXPLORE AND DISCUSS

Selected names and terms follow the keynote composition. Use this section to integrate music history and performance practices into the piano classroom. Elaboration appears in the online Instructor's Manual.

SKILLS AND ACTIVITIES

Technique
A series of drills and études stress finger and hand development with hands working independently and together. MIDI files contain non-pitched percussion backgrounds to promote rhythmic security and support ease in transposing. Additional exercises or practice suggestions for many of the text items appear in the Online Tutorials on the PDM Web site.

Reading
Compositions and excerpts address the challenge of reading and sight-playing music at the keyboard in a variety of styles, keys, score configurations, and clefs. MIDI recordings support the majority of text items. Be certain to take advantage of the additional reading materials for each chapter and/or study suggestions that appear in the PDM Online Tutorials.

Keyboard Theory
In many instances the heart of the chapter, drills and exercises stress a full understanding of the subject matter. The structure of PDM is designed to closely correlate with the student's two-year theory sequence. MIDI backgrounds support many of the items and extra help appears in the Online Tutorials.

Harmonization
Melodies from folk, older popular standards, keyboard literature, and original compositions (in many instances, short excerpts of melodies to provide more variety) help students understand and *use* harmonic concepts. As with other skills areas, check the Online Tutorials for steps to follow when choosing harmonies and practice suggestions.

Transposition
Exercises and assignments ask students to practice this skill of musicianship and application of theoretical understanding *through regular execution*. As before, I have honored your requests for shorter examples and students themselves have created many of the items. MIDI recordings of transposition items *in the transposed key* will give students a helpful audio guide for self-assessment.

Improvisation
You will find many more step-by-step examples of improvisation to help students with their own creations in this important skill. The exercises have been created to help students build a genuine understanding of the melodic and harmonic components of music while encouraging a certain level of freedom at the keyboard. Nevertheless, any meaningful *freedom* must originate from some level of *structure*. MIDI backgrounds as well as material in the Online Tutorials support this skill.

Ensemble
You will find an even greater number of duet and multi-keyboard scores for the pleasure of students and teachers alike. MIDI recordings of individual parts support both practice and performance.

Composition
A wonderful tool for assessing understanding, compositional assignments act to reinforce historical style, genre, form, and theoretical concepts. Examples of student work appear in the Online Tutorials on the PDM Web site.

Subsequent Repertoire
Every chapter ends with additional keyboard repertoire that reinforces the goals of the chapter and offers the opportunity to go further with an idea. Combined with the Exemplary Repertoire that opens each chapter, PDM 6 offers selections from the Baroque through the 21st century. MIDI recordings provide an aural representation of the subsequent repertoire.

It is an exciting time to be a part of higher education and the study of music. Using the piano keyboard as our medium through the ever-changing world of functional skills and musical understanding, we are happy to welcome a full integration of the Internet. The Online Tutorials allow the computer to act not only as a Practice Supervisor but also as a conduit for a large variety of additional practice materials. From the PDM Web site, instructors and students can access instructional aid, practice suggestions, or find additional drills, exercises, and compositions to fill your course beyond capacity. *Enjoy*!

Dedication

In 1985 when *Piano for the Developing Musician* first became a reality, the following acknowledgments were in the front matter of the books:

> "Our editor, Clark Baxter, calms our world with confident smiles and his commitment to our project is total. His wonderful wife, Abigail Sterne Baxter, is our editorial consultant and great friend."

I am now about the business of dedicating the sixth edition of PDM and can think of no two more deserving people than Clark and Abbie Baxter. No longer "my editor," Clark is now "my publisher" and he remains my "pillar." His commitment to PDM continues. Abbie is now my editor and my stability in the demanding world of revision. Her expertise, her fine eye, attention to detail, and her gentle persuasion all have made this edition possible.

It is for these reasons that I dedicate this edition of PDM to Clark and Abigail Baxter. You have been there from the beginning. A dedication seems so little but it is what I want, and it is what Lynn would want.

Acknowledgments

There are many to acknowledge. I want to thank those students from the University of Texas at Austin who graciously agreed to have their compositions included. When you go to the Web site you will see more student compositions. Thank you to these students as well.

Once again I thank the reviewers who took time from their hectic schedules: Cynthia Benson, Bowling Green University; Marsha K. Green, McLennan Community College; Janet Palmberg Lyman, Indiana State University; Pamela D. Pike, University of Arkansas, Little Rock; Anita Renfroe, Millersville University; Lori Rhoden, Ball State University; Terrie Shires, University of Central Arkansas; Richard Smith, Central Missouri State University; Joan Reist, University of Nebraska, Lincoln; Susanna Garcia, University of Louisiana at Lafayette; Nancy Matesky, Shoreline Community College; David Cartledge, Indiana University.

I was thrilled, too, that I would be able to work with Bonnie Balke at A-R Editions again. She is still "the rock."

And I must thank David Hainsworth, Systems Analyst at the School of Music, for his guidance and his patience with my many changes creating the new version of the Web site.

Preliminary Chapter on Rudiments

PIANO FOR THE DEVELOPING MUSICIAN assumes some previous musical knowledge. Not every music major, however, has rudimentary skills. To make it possible to begin Chapter 1 in a class setting, we offer some "entrance level" review here.

COMMON METER SIGNATURES

$\frac{2}{4}$ $\frac{3}{4}$ $\frac{4}{4}$ $\frac{6}{4}$ $\frac{3}{8}$ $\frac{6}{8}$ $\frac{2}{2}$

The top number indicates total basic pulses per measure. The bottom number indicates what type of note will receive one pulse (beat).

TABLE OF COMMON NOTE VALUES

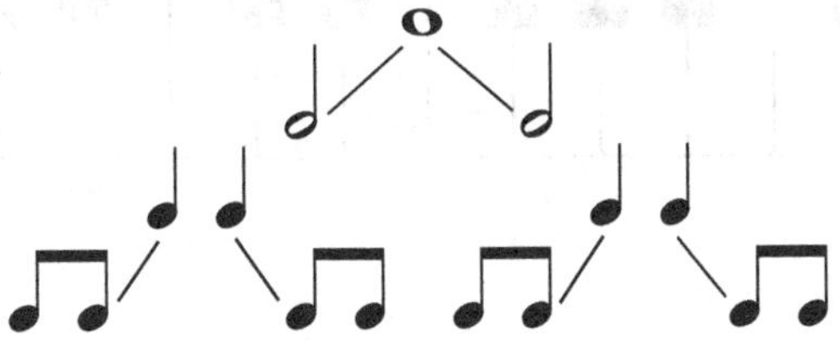

TABLE OF COMMON REST VALUES*

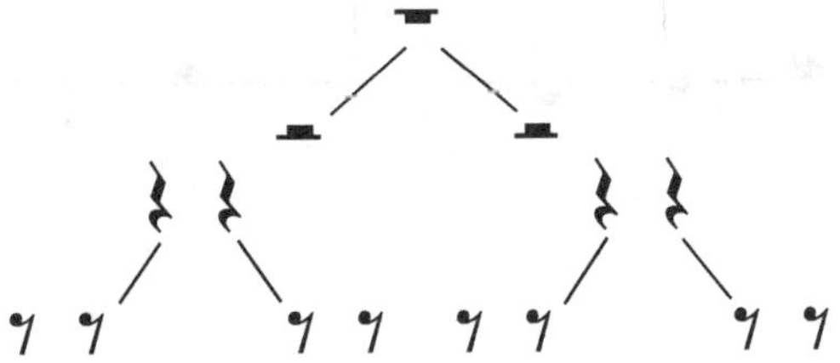

* In many editions a whole rest is used to indicate a measure of silence, regardless of the meter.

KEYS AND NOTE NAMES

1. As you know, the musical alphabet involves seven letter names. As a drill, say the given letter name and then recite the missing ones in order. If the noteheads move upward, go forward in the alphabet; if the noteheads move downward, go in reverse. Recite in rhythm.

   a. ♩ = 60

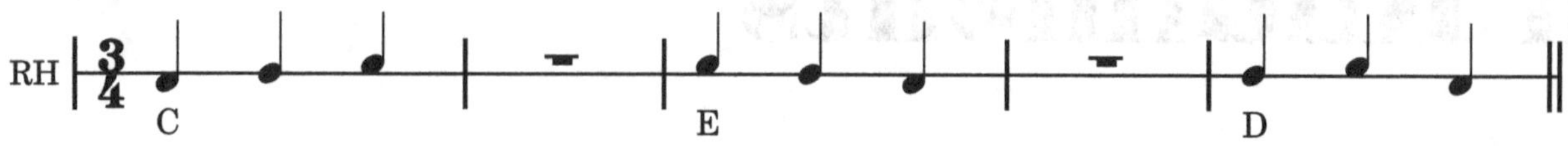

   b. ♩ = 60

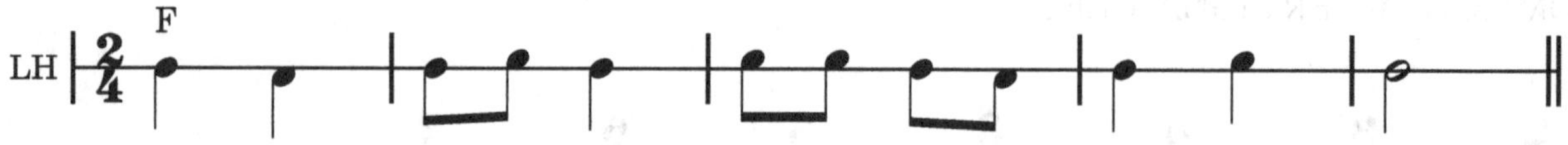

2. White keys relate directly to the musical alphabet. What visual cues quickly help you identify with the names of the white keys?

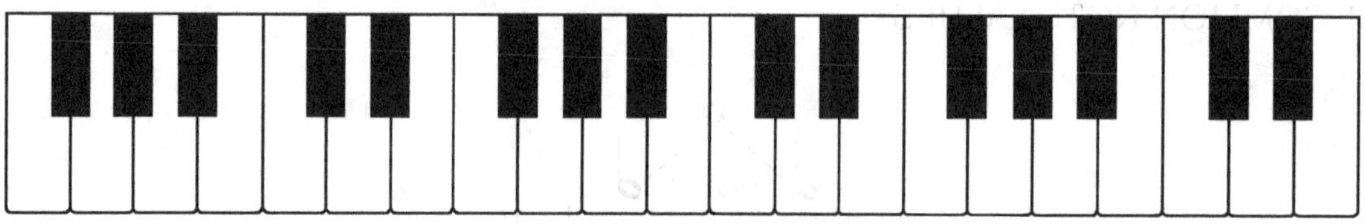

3. Now play the naming drills in item 1 above. Use a pointer finger, anywhere on the keyboard. Continue to *name while you play*.

4. Simultaneously play and name these similar exercises. Occasionally change hands but continue to use only a pointer finger.

   a.

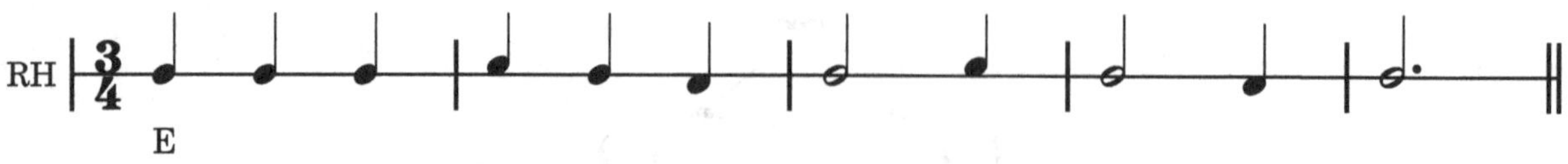

   b.

c.

Go to the PDM Web site for additional examples.

5. In keyboard work, fingers are numbered like this:

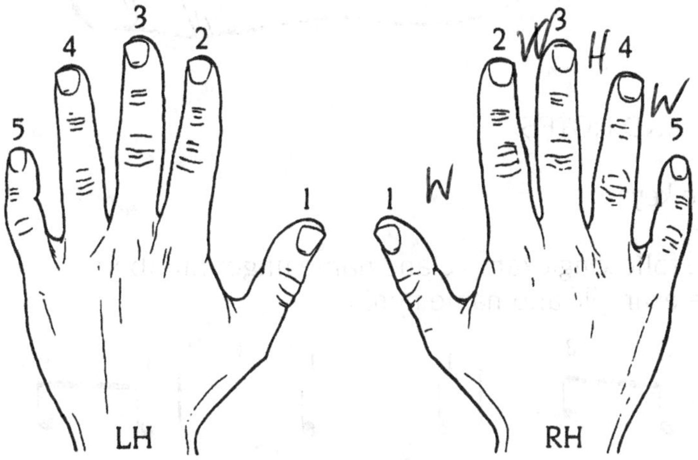

WWWH

You can see that if you have a three-note pattern of adjacent keys to play, you have three different finger groups to choose from (adjacent keys are generally played by adjacent fingers).

RH: 1 2 3 (or 3 2 1); 2 3 4 (or 4 3 2); 3 4 5 (or 5 4 3). WWWHW

LH: 3 2 1 (or 1 2 3); etc.

What will be true of four adjacent keys? Five adjacent keys?

GOOD HAND SHAPE

Let your arms hang at your sides. Notice how the fingers are slightly curved at the middle joint. This is a natural, unforced, relaxed hand position. Place both hands on a flat surface in front of you. Maintain the natural shape of your hand. Notice the slightly "rounded" condition of your fingers and overall hand shape; this is the most natural and best position for your hands in playing the piano.

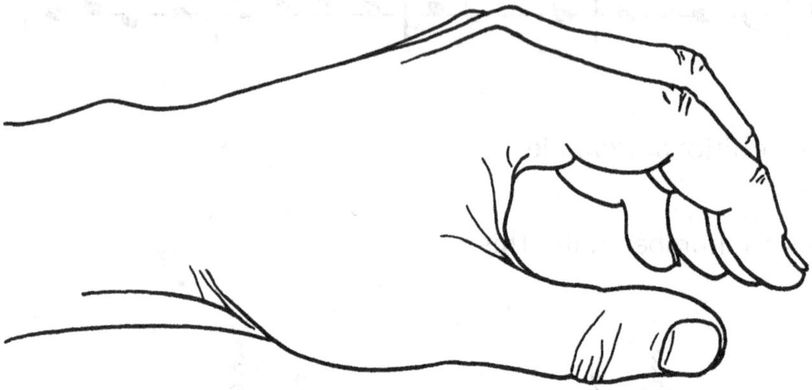

FINGER PATTERNS AND NOTES

1. Using all white keys,

   - play the following example and name finger numbers
   - play the example and name notes

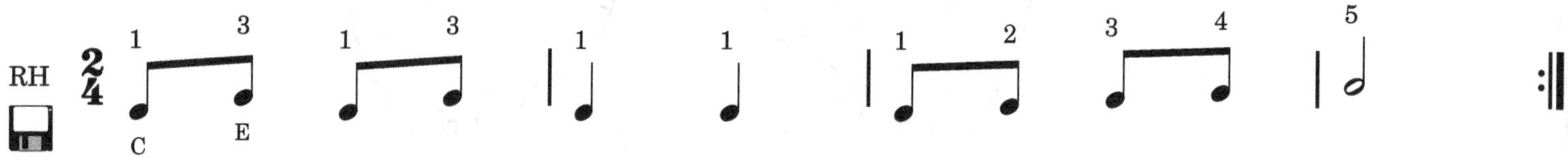

2. Play the following examples and name fingers. Then play and name notes.

a.

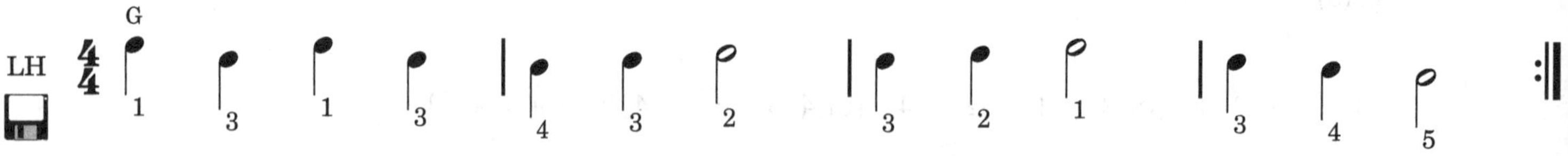

b.

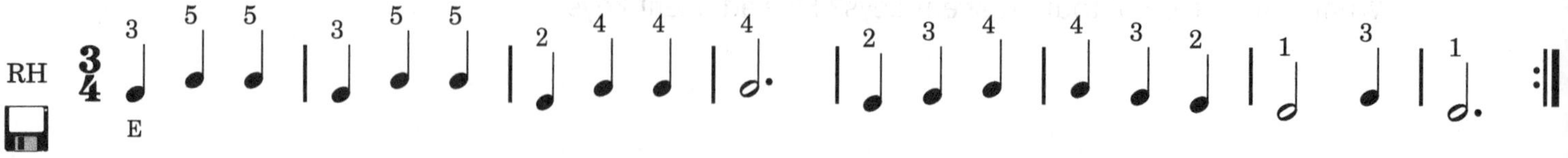

c.

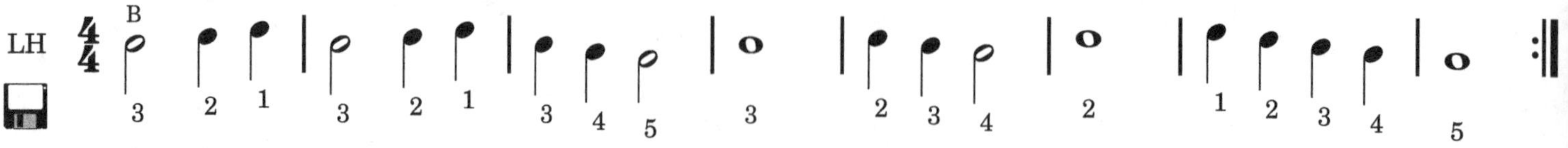

When you played 1–3, you skipped a white key. In keyboard positions using adjacent keys, to skip a finger is to skip a key and a note name.

THE STAFF AS RELATED TO THE KEYBOARD

1. The majority of keyboard music appears on a double staff joined by a brace. This arrangement accommodates the two hands.

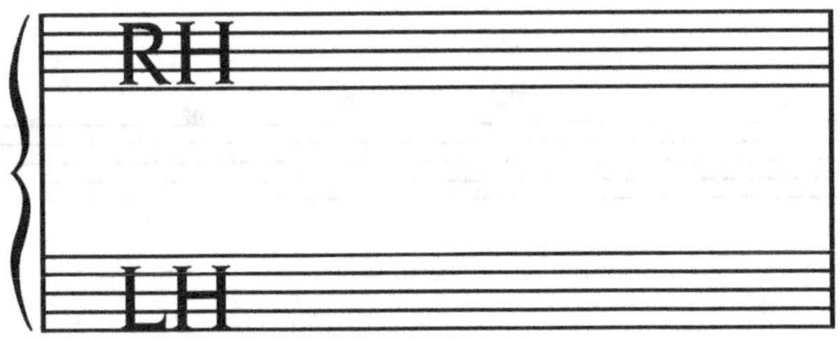

2. Play the following "five finger" melodies.

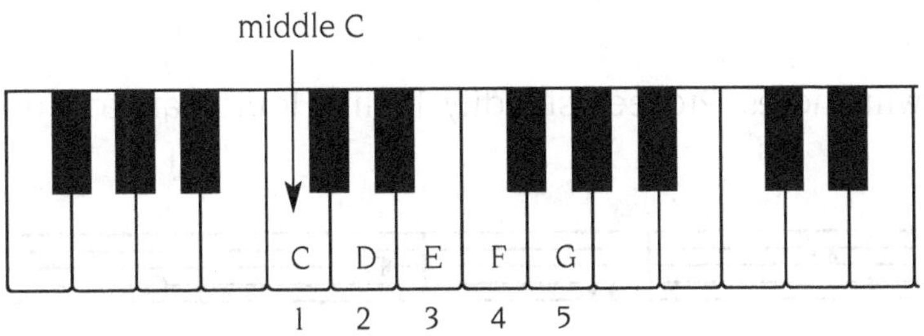

a.

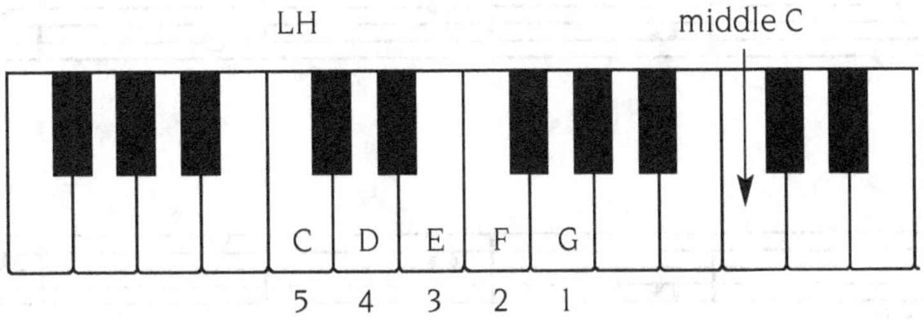

b.

c.

d. Determine position before playing.

3. Verbally name the following notes. Proceed steadily, feeling four beats to a note. Think treble clef.

Name the same notes again, this time allowing only three beats per note. If you have no trouble doing this, turn your book upside down and do it once again. Think treble clef the first time and bass clef on the repeat.

Go to the PDM Web site for additional "random whole note reading."

4. Return to the notes in item 3. *Play* each note, four beats to a note. This time think bass clef. Place a mark by the notes on which you hesitate. Practice the ones you marked.

   If you have no trouble with four beats to a note, repeat the exercise using two beats for each note.

5. The end goal for item 3 will be to *play* through twice, ***one beat to a note***, treble clef first time and bass clef on the repeat. Tempo should be approximately one beat = 60.

6. Keyboard music most often employs the *Grand Staff*, a combination of a *Treble Staff* (G clef) in the upper position and a *Bass Staff* (F clef) in the lower position.

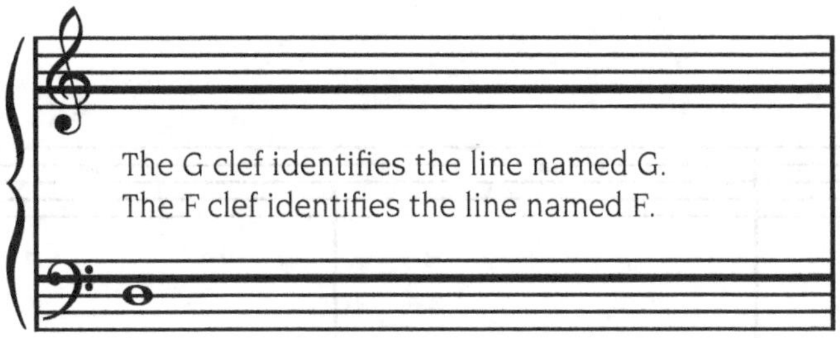

The G and the F represent specific keys close to the center of the keyboard, thus establishing the following permanent relationship. Notice that, on the staff, adjacent notes move from line to space, space to line.

7. Play the following, all based on five-finger patterns. Notice the direction of upward, downward, and repeating.

a.

b.

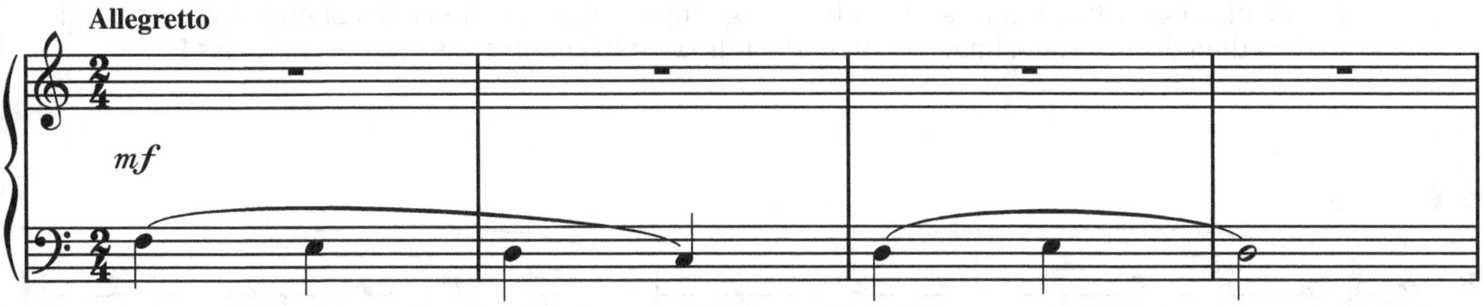

c.

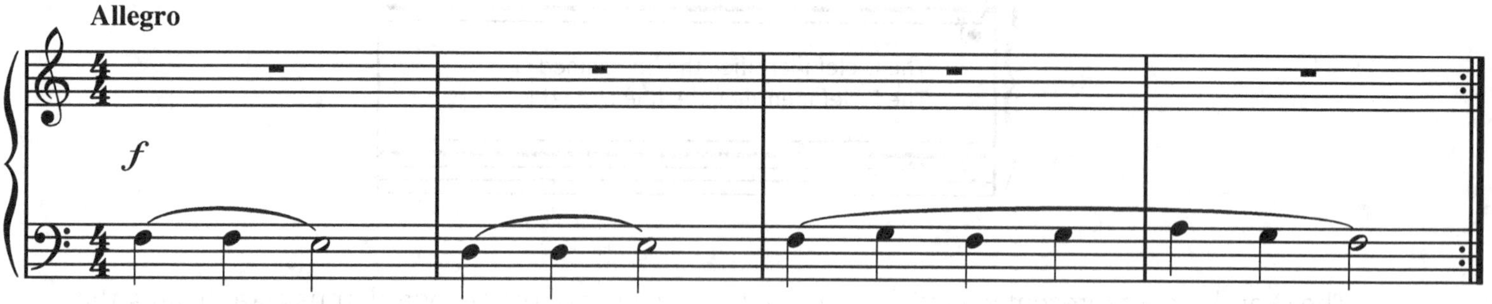

d.

Go to the PDM Web site for more examples in alternate five-finger patterns.

MASTERING THE COMMON CLEFS AND VARIOUS INTERVALS IN FIVE-FINGER POSITIONS

1. To focus on individual clefs (as well as to save space), we will now show only one staff. However, you will always know which hand to use.

   Before playing each example, scan for fingering range. Recall the principles of fingering discussed earlier, then decide which fingers to use. The following begin on either Treble G or Bass F.

a.

b.

c.

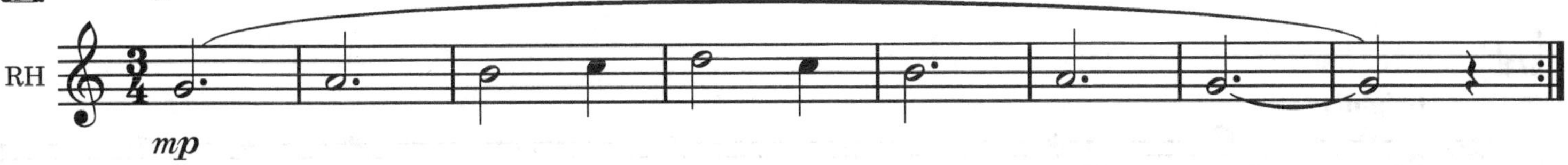

Go to the PDM Web site for more examples in alternate five-finger patterns.

2. The following exercises begin *a step away* from G or F

a.

b.

c.

d.

Go to the PDM Web site for more examples in alternate five-finger patterns.

3. The following begin *a skip away* from G or F.

a.

b.

c.

d.

Go to the PDM web site for additional examples using alternate clefs.

4. The distance relationship between two notes is called an *interval*. In five-finger positions of adjacent notes, the visual and tactile relationship to the keyboard is very clear. Play and listen:

a.

b.

5. Play the following single-staff examples after determining fingering and scanning the intervals. Notice that some examples begin *on the clef line*, whereas others do not.

a.

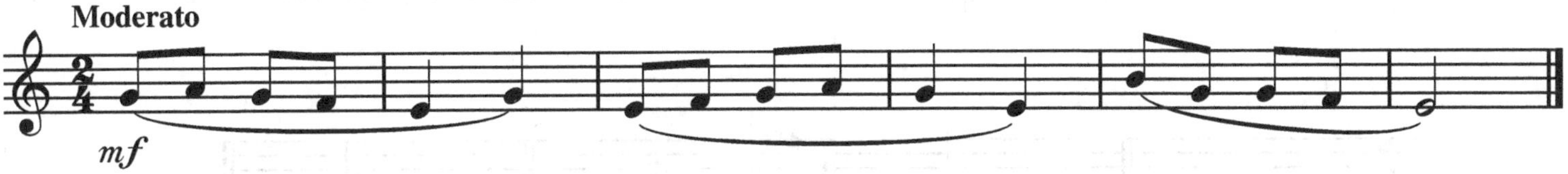

b.

c.

d.

Go to the PDM Web site for additional examples using alternate clefs.

6. Within a five-finger position, various intervals can be used. They are named for their total compass:

As you can see, 3rds and 5ths appear on two lines or two spaces; 2nds and 4ths appear on a space and a line. Intervals also may appear in "blocked" fashion, the tones to be sounded simultaneously.

7. Name the intervals shown in each measure:

8. In five-finger positions, a 4th is played by skipping two fingers; a 5th will use only fingers 1 and 5.

9. Play these reading drills after scanning quickly for fingering range and interval patterns.

Begin on G or F.

a.

Cheerfully

b.

Robustly

c.

Liltingly

d.

Sorrowfully

Go to the PDM Web site for additional examples using alternate clefs.

10. Begin an interval *away* from G or F.

a.

Brassy

b.

c.

ADDING SHARPS AND FLATS TO FIVE-FINGER POSITIONS

1. Because sharps and flats most often use black keys, a different keyboard "feel" results. The hand adjusts on the keyboard, forming a natural shape to accommodate the black key or keys.

   On the keyboard, a *sharp* indicates a move to the very next key *upward*, black or white; a *flat* indicates a move to the very next key *downward*, black or white.

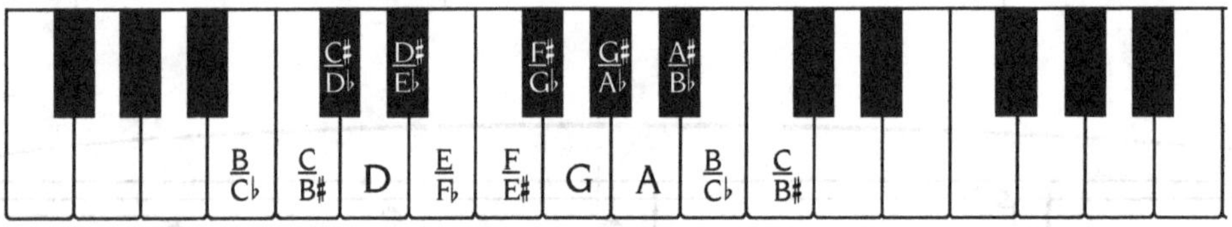

2. Play the following examples using sharps and flats.

a.

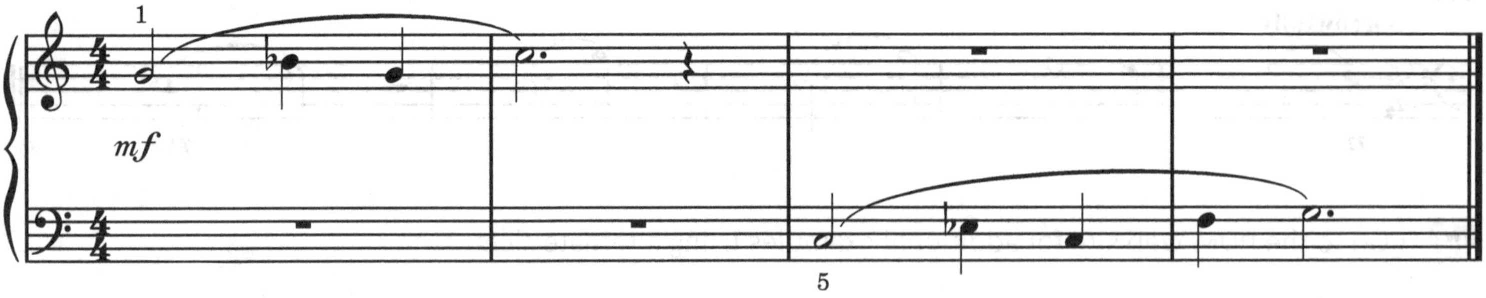

b.

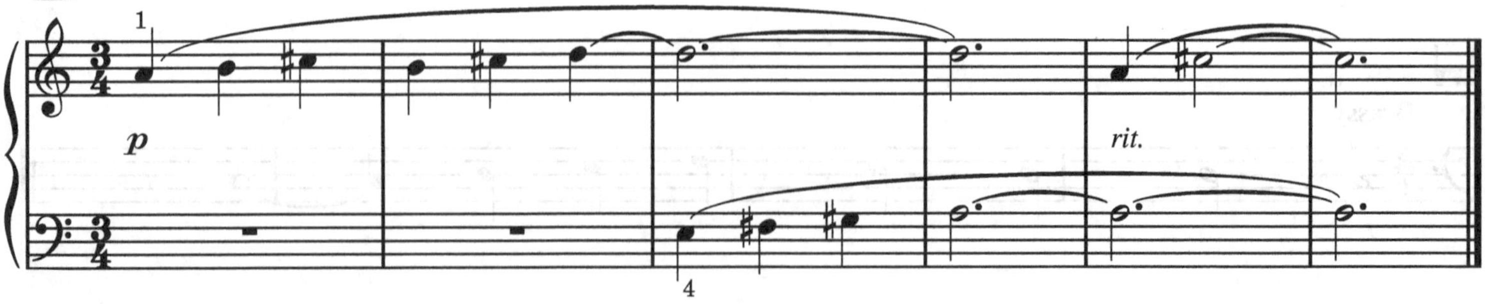

Go to the PDM Web site for more examples in alternate five-finger patterns.

OTHER USEFUL STAFF LOCATORS

1. In addition to the clef lines for G and F, it is helpful to memorize certain other "landmark" notes and know where they are on the keyboard. Learn these notes and related keys.

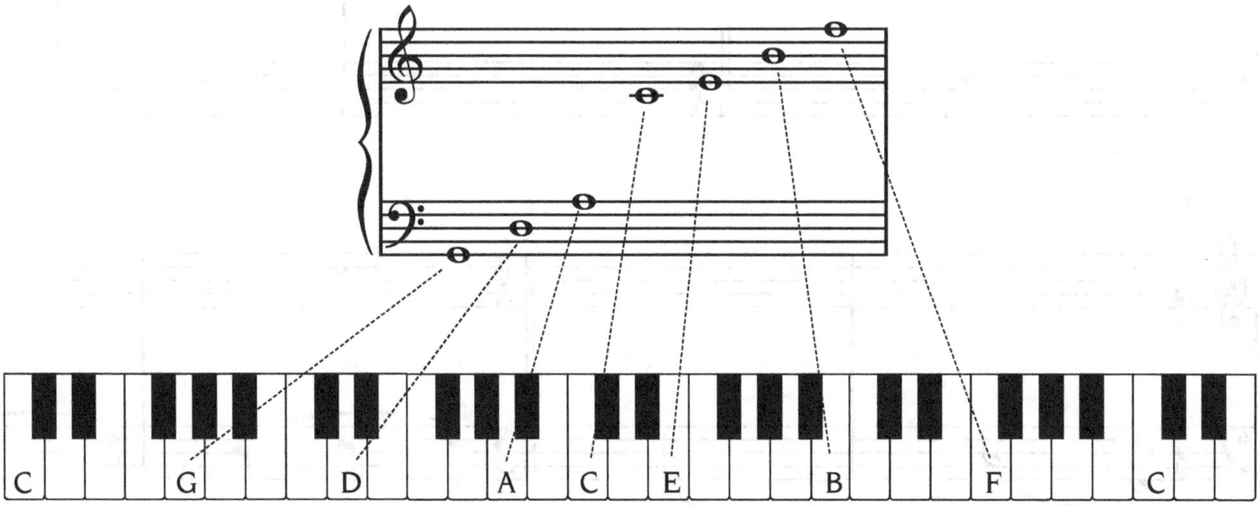

2. Each of these brief examples begins on one of the staff locators. Remember to check for fingering range, then play. You may pause and get your bearings at each double bar.

a. b.

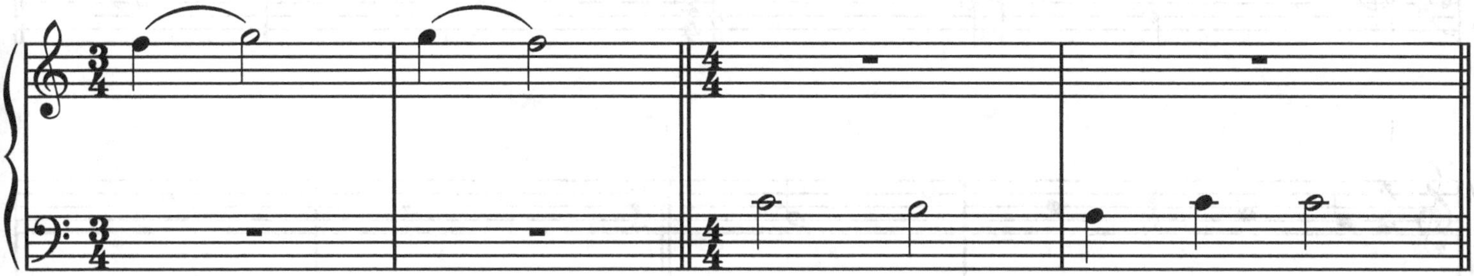

c. d.

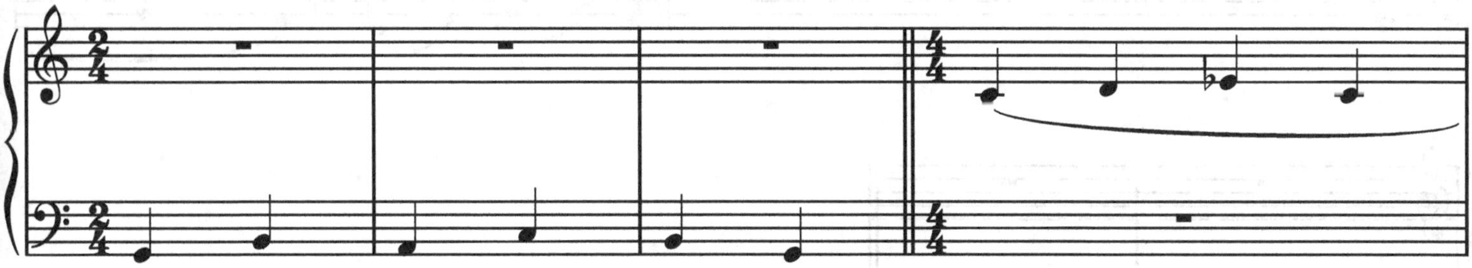

e.

f.

g.

h.

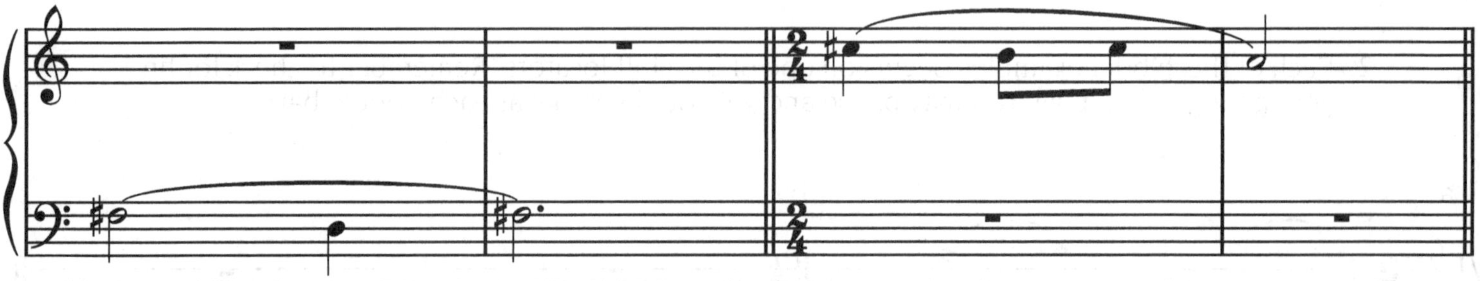

i.

j.

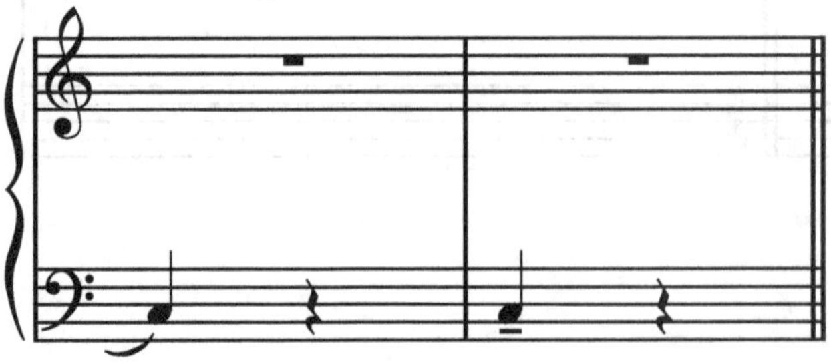

OTHER HAND POSITIONS

1. In keyboard music, the hands often expand to cover positions larger than five keys. As you go on, you will gain a tactile sense of many such expansions (as well as contractions). One common expansion covers a 6th:

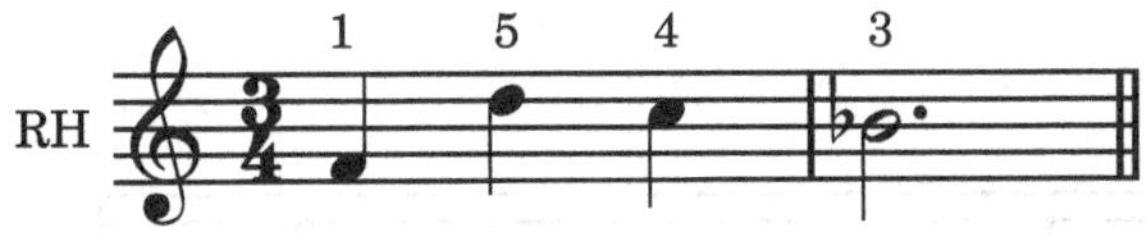

2. Notes too high or too low for the five-line staves appear on small *leger lines* or in their spaces.

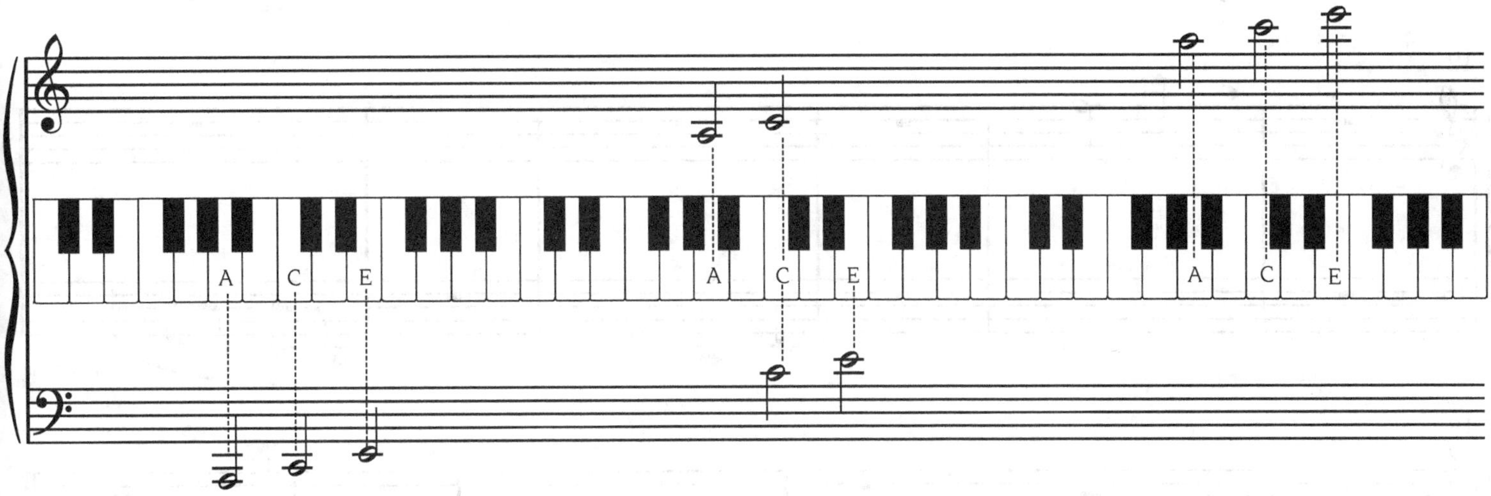

Play and name the keys and notes you see above, just to fix them in your ears and mind as a keyboard/staff relationship. Remember the RH/LH rule.

3. Notice the range of each measure of music. During the open measures, locate the next position.

KEY SIGNATURES

1. Key signatures can be viewed as lists of flats or sharps occurring throughout the example, section, or composition and affecting all notes of the same name no matter where they appear on the staff.

   a. How many different positions occur in this example? Check the PDM Web site to confirm your answer and see additional examples.

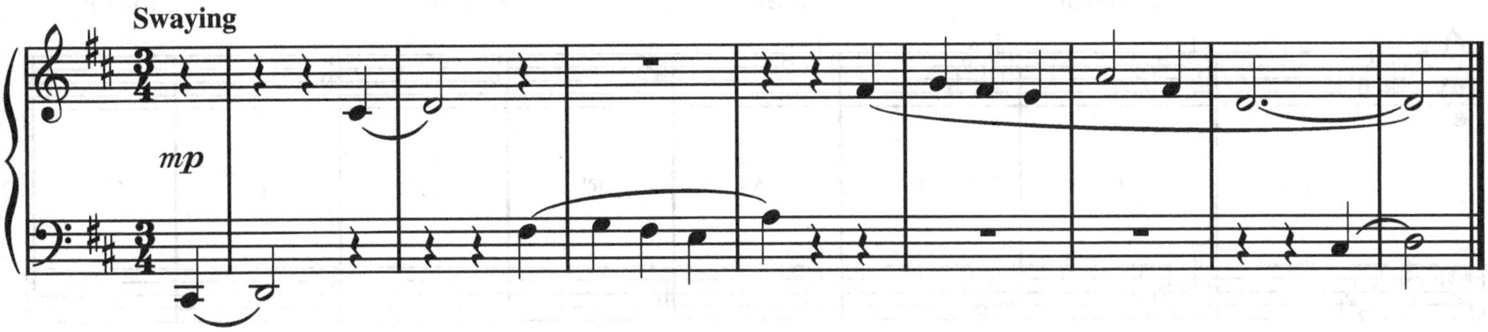

   b. This is a study in "5ths and 4ths." Prepare carefully for the hands-together ending.

2. Key signatures, of course, are much more than lists; they help summarize and remind us of tonalities.

   - In major sharp signatures, the last sharp (farthest to the right) is a half step below the *key name*.

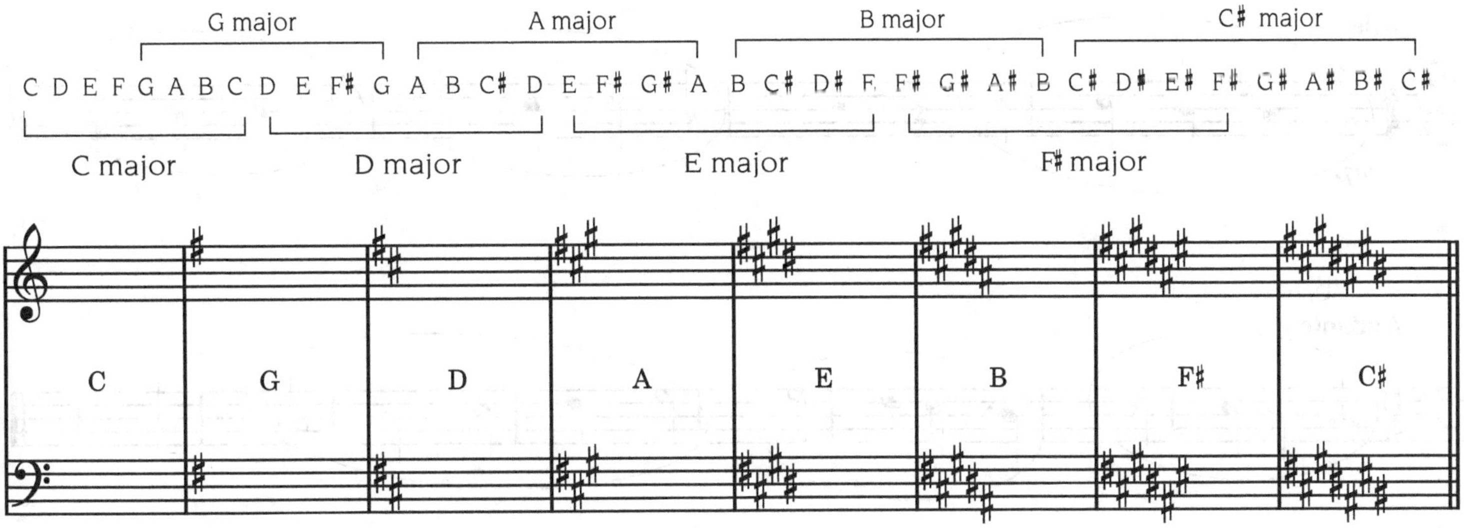

- In major flat signatures, the next-to-last flat names the key (F major has one flat).

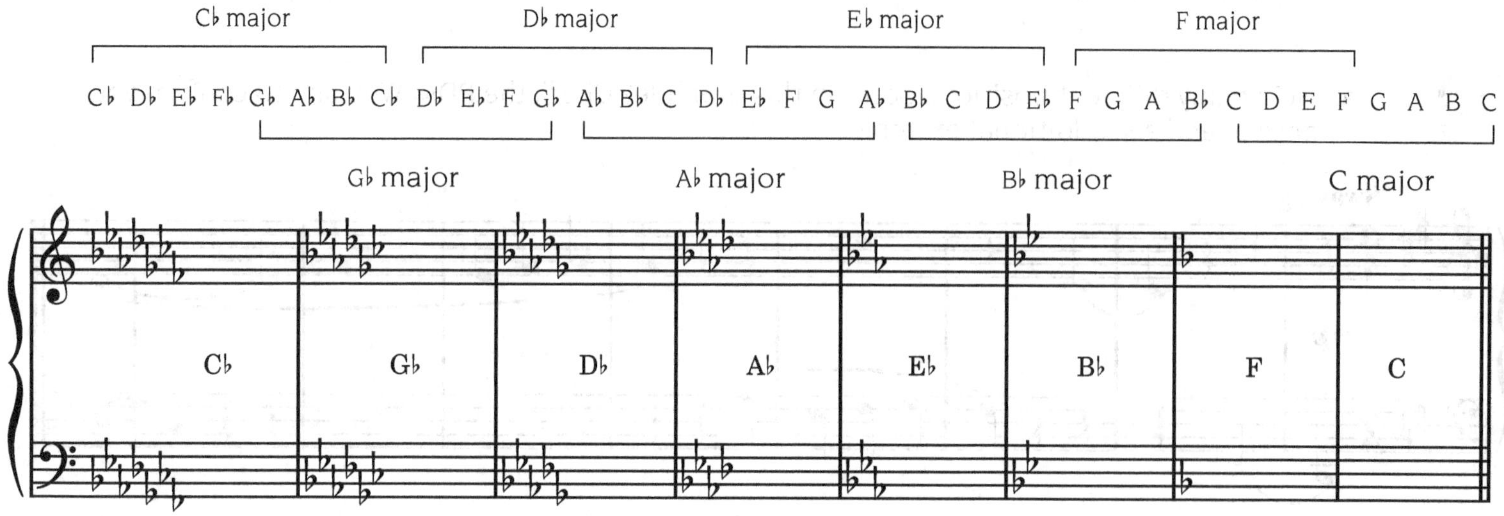

SUGGESTIONS FOR GOOD READING

1. As quickly and as much as possible, eyes should be off the keys and focusing on the notes.

2. Sit at the center of the keyboard and maintain this position no matter how low or high the music goes. This way, you will gain a physical memory for key location without looking too much at the keys.

3. Scan all music for fingering range, position changes, intervals, sharps, and/or flats.

4. Train yourself to see groups of notes rather than just one note at a time. The circles in the following indicate some natural groupings. What makes each one "natural"? (Sometimes a parallel or related feature between patterns makes a kind of "natural" reading symmetry.)

   Play each example after planning fingering:

a.
Allegro

b.
Andante

c.
Vivace

d.
Moderato

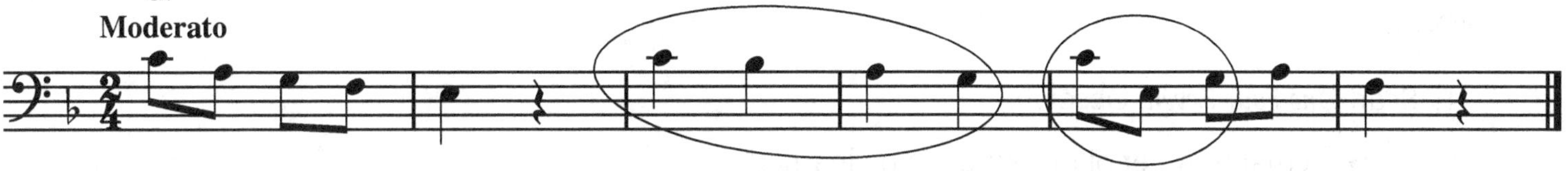

e.
Allegretto

f.
Allegro

g.
Eagerly

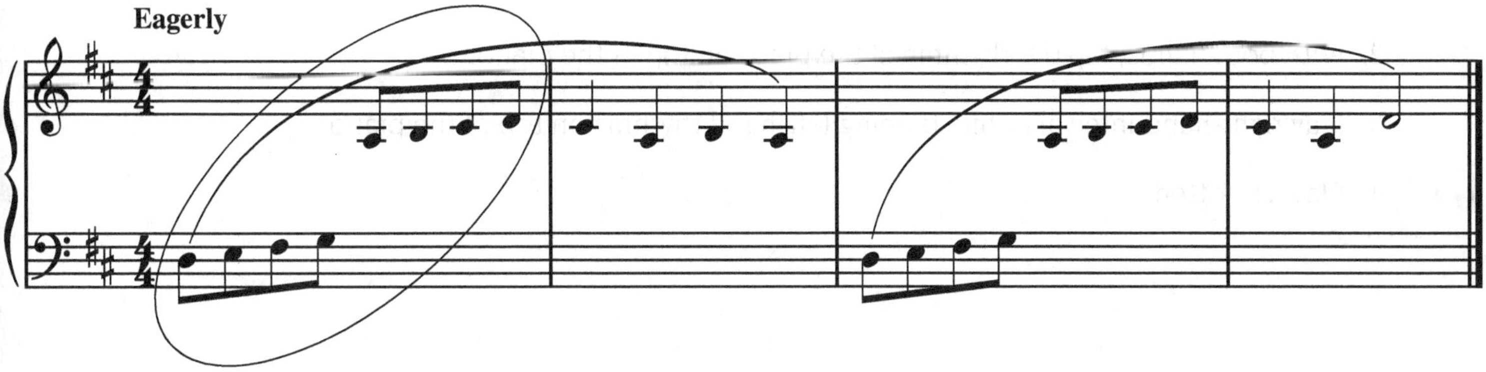

Go to the PDM Web site for more examples in alternate five-finger patterns. There are also suggested tempi with voice-over counting.

Intervals

EXEMPLARY REPERTOIRE **One Four Seven** Lynn Freeman Olson

INQUIRY

1. Scan *One Four Seven*. Observe:
   - actual number of measures to be learned
   - pattern of intervallic change
2. Determine logical fingering.
3. Given the meter, determine a tempo.
4. Given the overall character, determine dynamics.
5. What does the title mean?

PERFORMANCE

1. Block the right- and left-hand intervals, hands together, restriking only when the intervals change.

2. With both hands, tap the rhythms of the piece on top of the piano.
3. Play right-hand intervals while tapping left-hand rhythms on top of the piano.
4. Play as written.

One Four Seven

LYNN FREEMAN OLSON

TOPICS TO EXPLORE AND DISCUSS

- Alternating meters versus variable meters
- Intervals: melodic and harmonic

SKILLS AND ACTIVITIES

TECHNIQUE

1. The following exercises use harmonic and melodic intervals. Determine a logical fingering for each example before playing.

a.

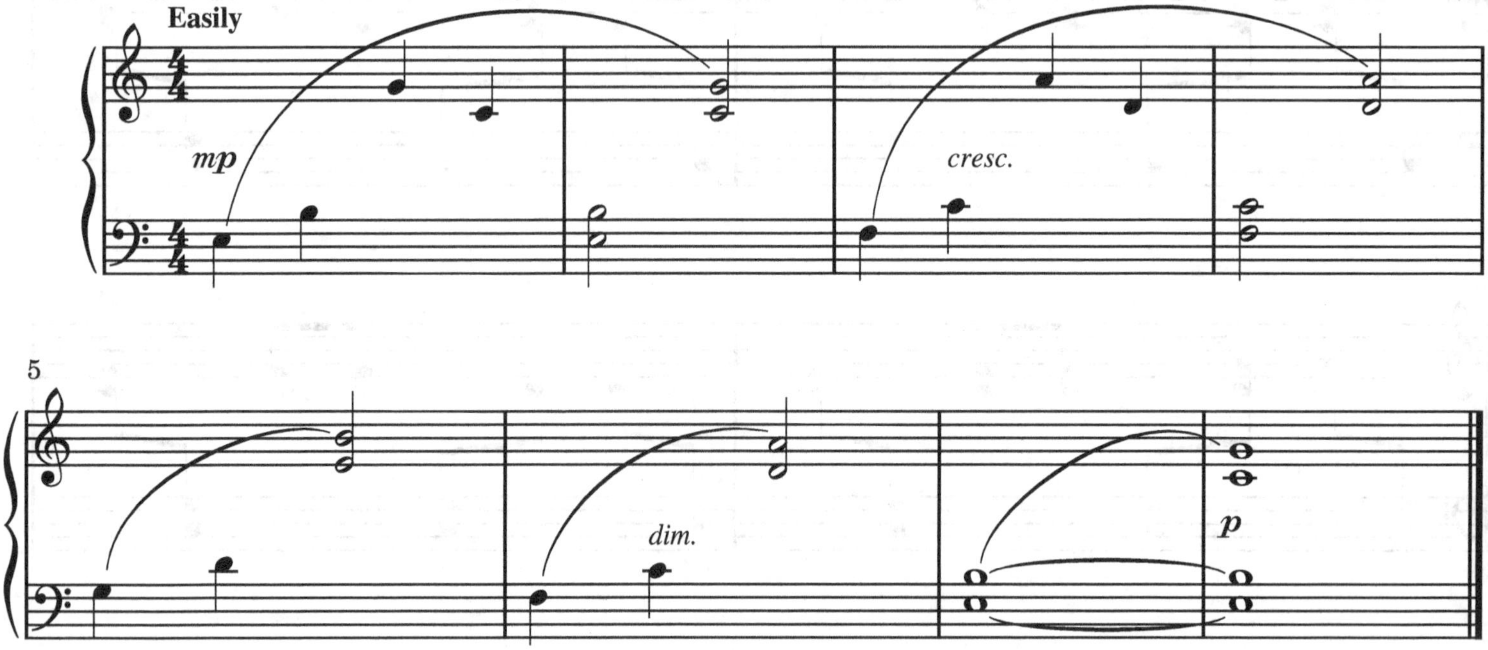

b.

c.

d.

e.

f.

g.

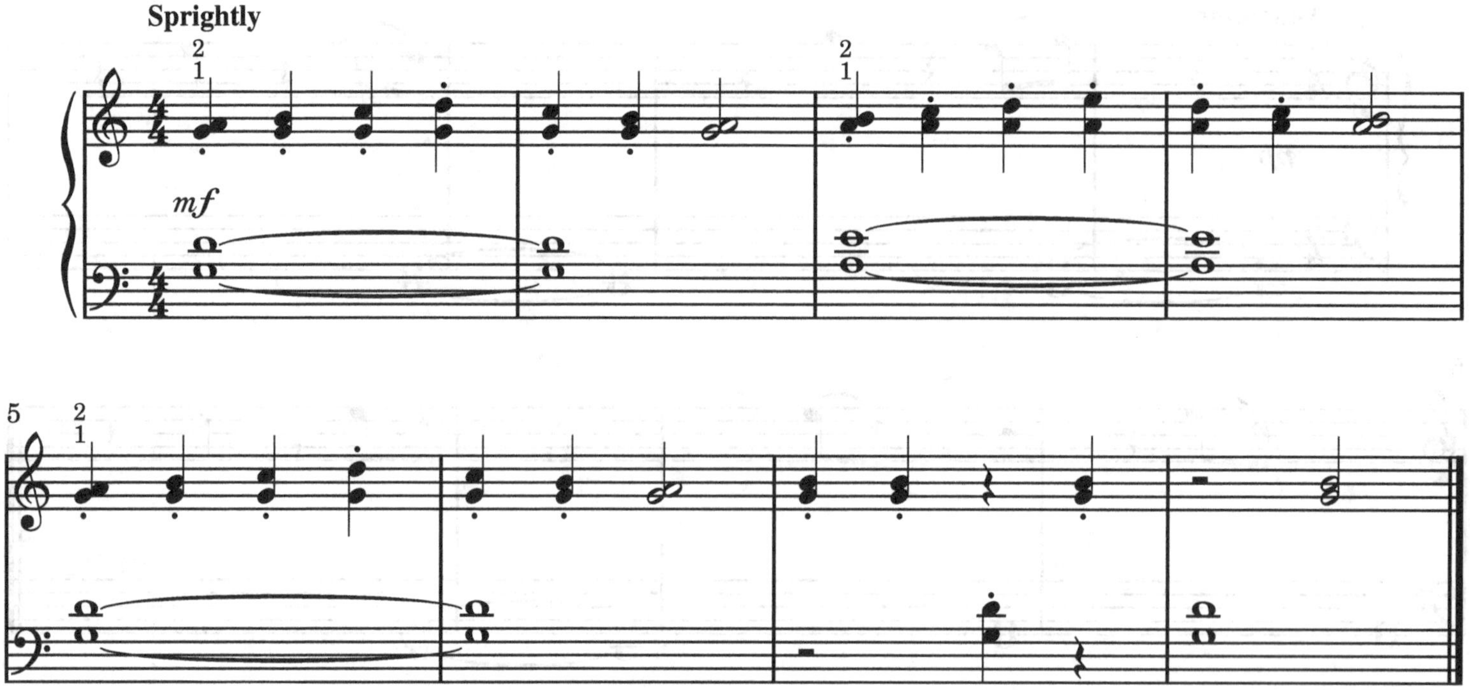

h.

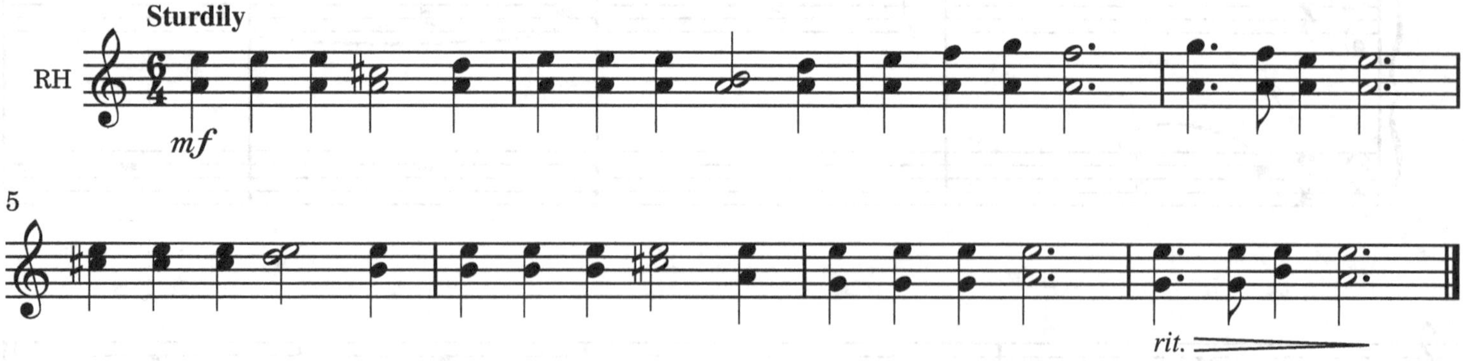

Go to the PDM Web site for additional examples using alternate keys and clefs.

READING

1. *Intervallic reading*. With hand in lap, think:

   - interval
   - keyboard location
   - fingering

   Then play with a measure of rest between each interval.

LH
RH

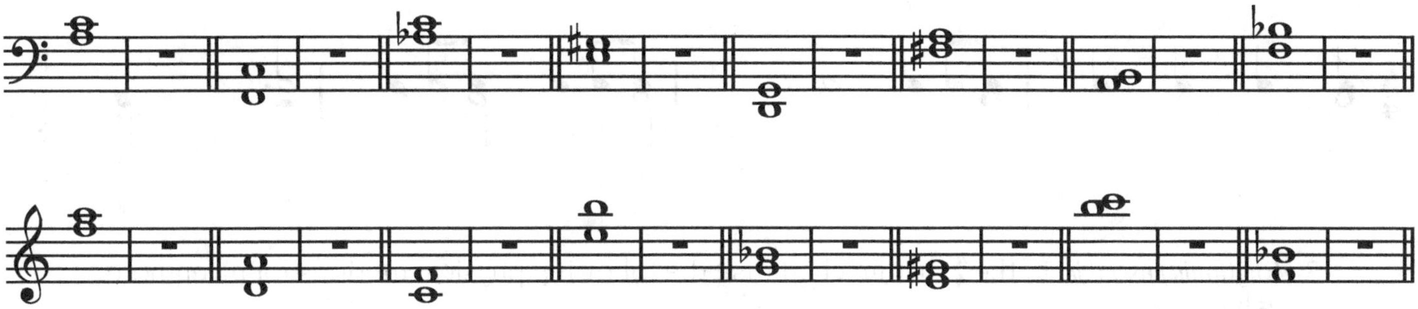

Go to the PDM Web site for additional intervallic reading.

2. *Rhythmic reading*. Tap the following while counting the beat.

a.

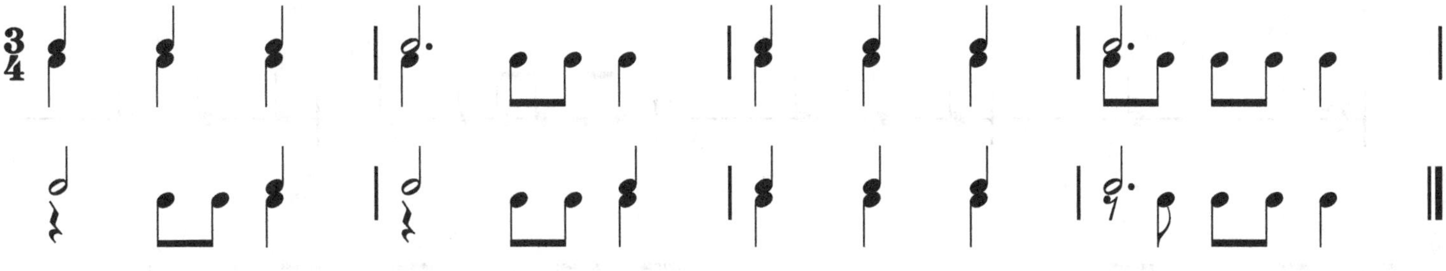

b.

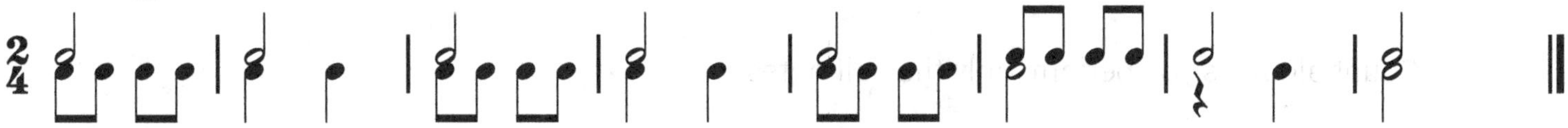

c.

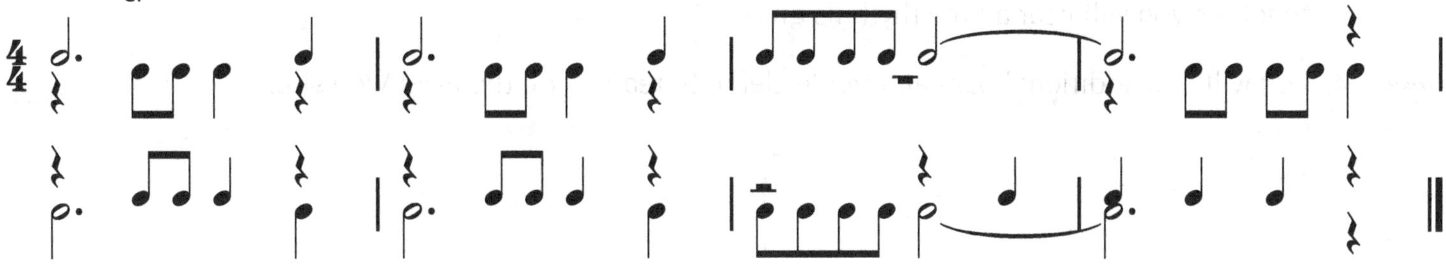

d.

e.

3. *Rhythmic ensemble*. In the $\frac{4}{4}$ rhythm chart, use the following physical motions for given note values:

— CLAP

— SNAP

— TAP

Count aloud as you perform only the quarter notes.

Count aloud as you perform only the half notes.

Count aloud as you perform only the eighth notes.

Form a rhythm ensemble by assigning certain note values to certain students. When you perform together, you will hear all the rhythms given.

4. You will find additional bass and treble clef note reading on the PDM Web site.

KEYBOARD THEORY

1. Play the indicated intervals above and below the following pitches. Use white keys only. Play one interval for each pitch.

a.

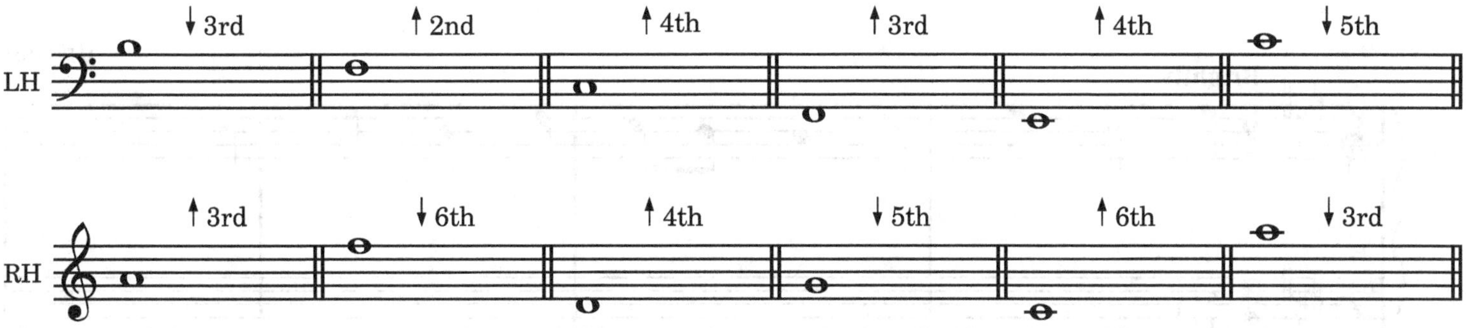

b.

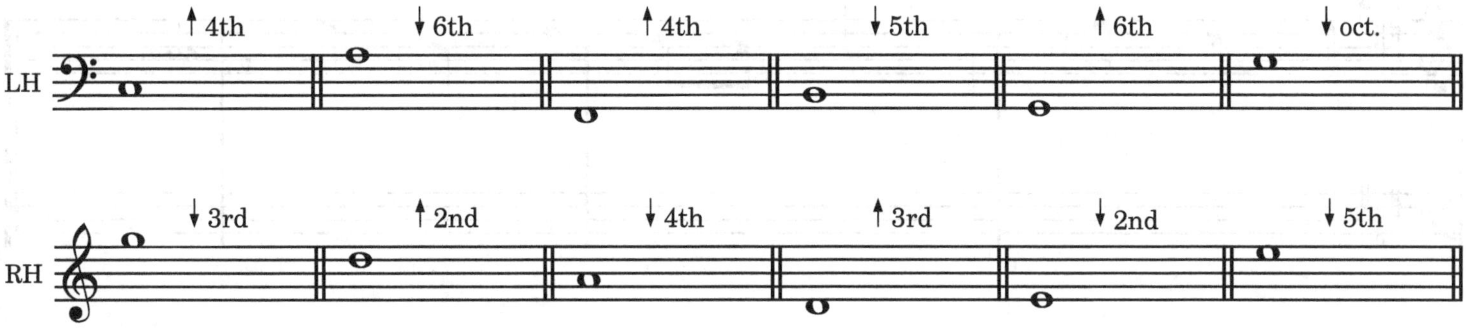

Go to the PDM Web site for additional work with interval recognition.

HARMONIZATION

1. Harmonize each of the following melodies with the 5th indicated in parentheses. Play the 5th blocked (in long or short values) and/or broken. Select an accompaniment style to enhance the mood.

a.

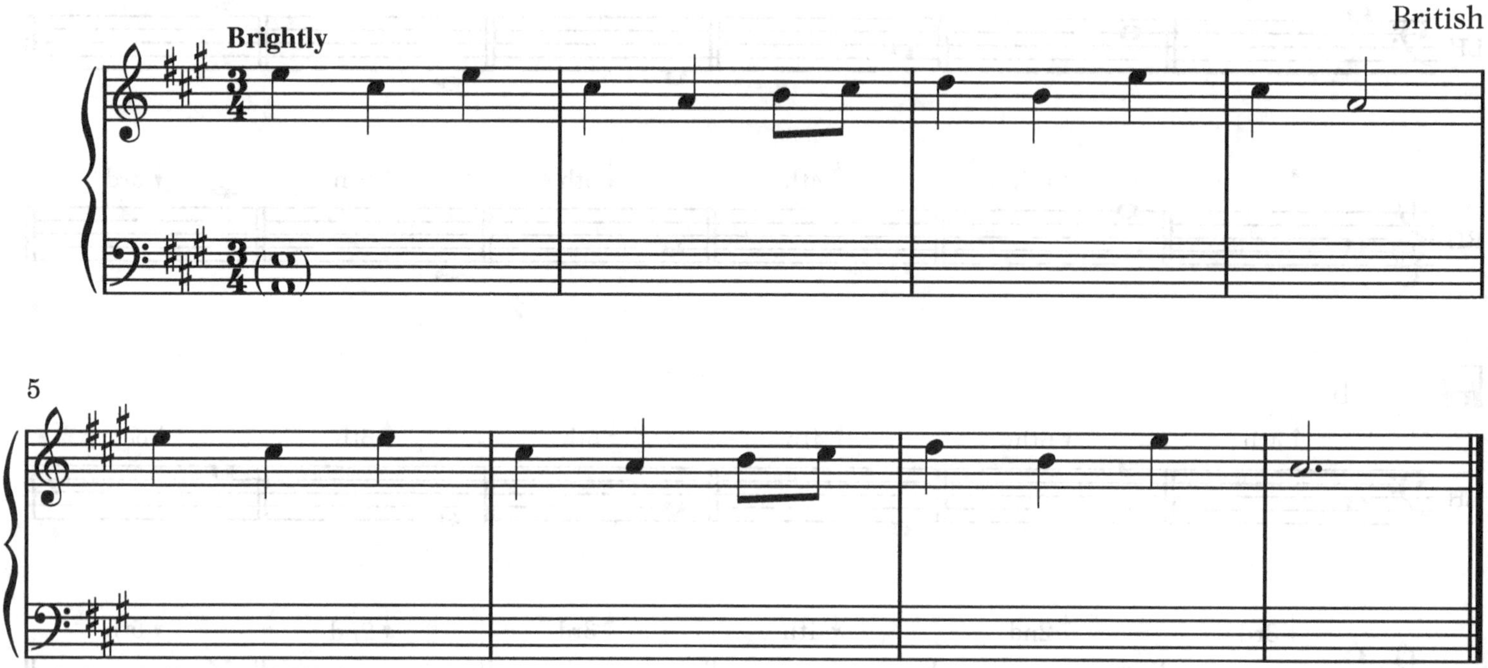

b.

c.

d.

American

e.

American

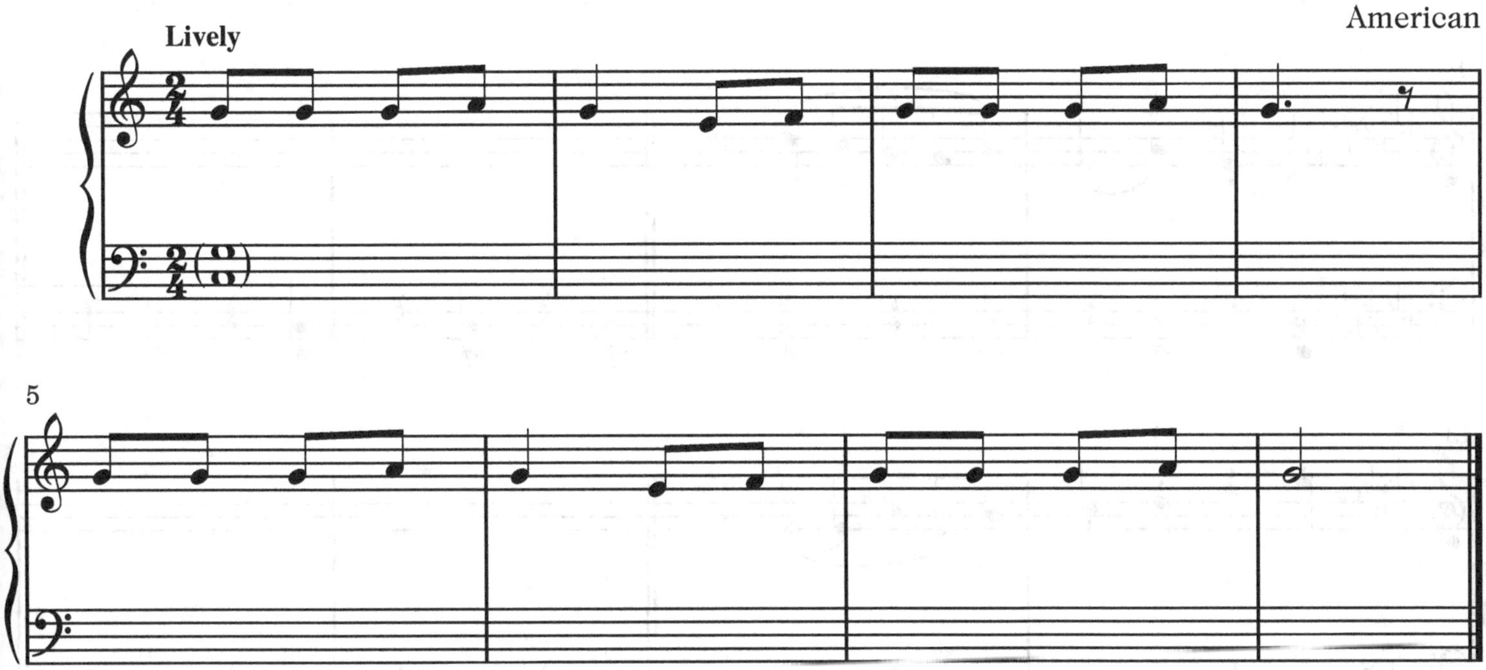

Go to the PDM Web site for additional harmonization examples with ostinato accompaniment.

TRANSPOSITION

1. Transpose each of the Harmonization examples to at least three other major keys.
2. Play *One Four Seven* with the first interval based on G, transposing the rest of the piece accordingly.

Go to the PDM Web site for additional transposition examples.

IMPROVISATION

1. Use the two- and three-black-key groups to play answers to your teacher's musical questions. These are improvised answers, not melodic echoes.

Go to the PDM Web site for additional improvisation work.

(This page has been left blank to avoid a difficult page turn.)

ENSEMBLE

1. The following is a "spoken invention." Discuss as a class the musical meaning of the word *invention*. Perform as a three-part chant with clapping. Additional directions follow the score.

My Dog Treed a Rabbit

American
Arr. Lynn Freeman Olson

Improvise on black keys to match the rhythm. "Rabbit" is always played on E♭ and G♭. The clapping part plays a bass ostinato throughout.

2. Play with the recorded disk example.

Hoo Doo

(In a Hollywood Bazaar)

LYNN FREEMAN OLSON

9
13
f
mf
p

18
1
2
3
4
5
6
mp
p
mp
pp
p
mp
22
1
2
3
4
5
6
cresc.

COMPOSITION

Create a piece in the style of *One Four Seven* using variable meter. Refer to observations in the Inquiry section (page 22).

List some of the style characteristics of *One Four Seven*. One example has been given:

- alternating hands
-
-
-
-
-

Trade compositions with your classmates and prepare for class performances.

Go to the PDM Web site to see representative student compositions.

SUBSEQUENT REPERTOIRE

1. *Seaview, After Turner* uses 5ths and tone clusters that cover the span of a 5th. Determine the pattern of motion throughout the piece from one position to another. What did you discover?

Notice the sign for pedal: *down* *hold* *up*

Go to the PDM Web site for additional reading suggestions.

Seaview, After Turner

LYNN FREEMAN OLSON

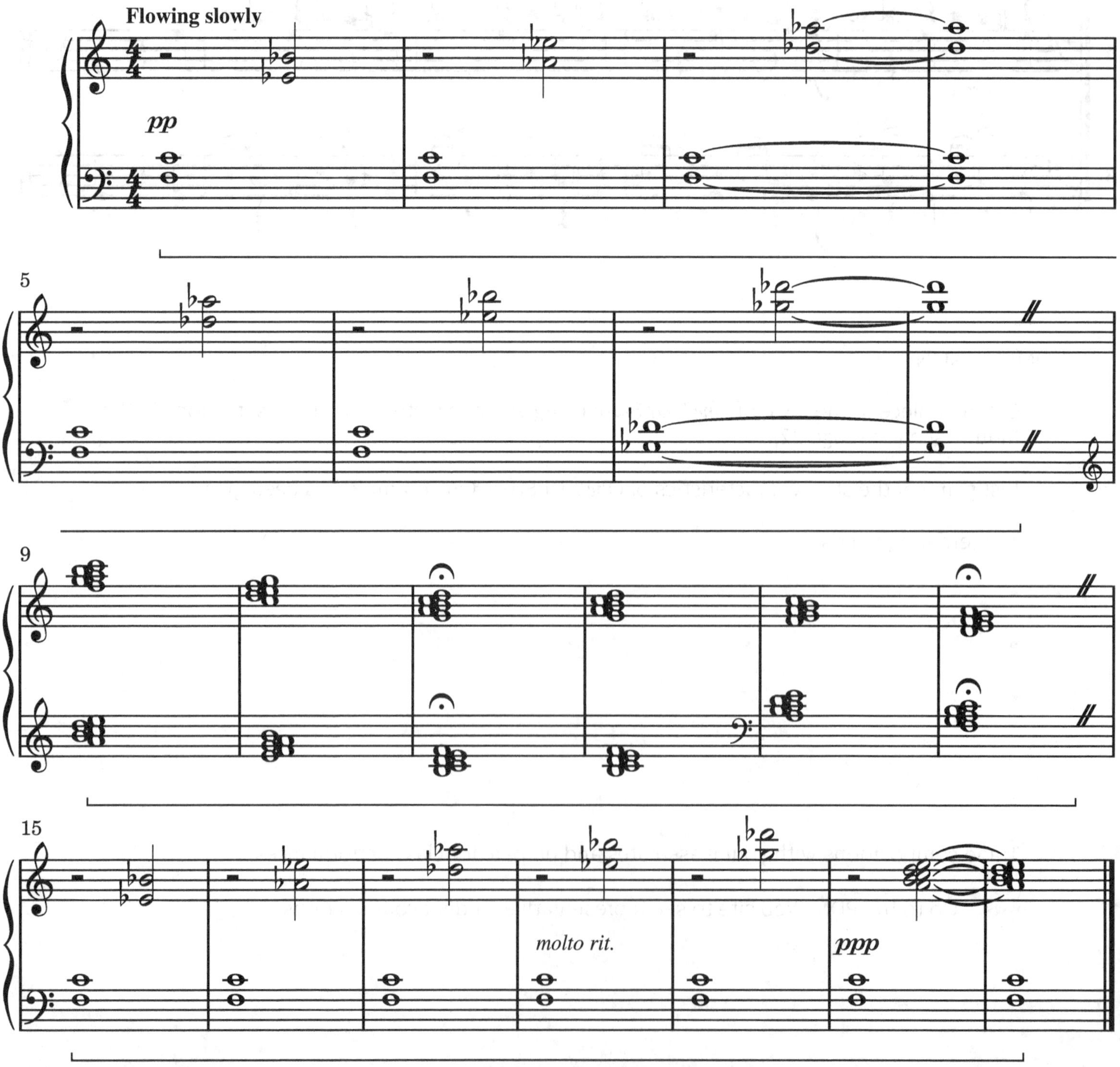

2. Block each interval position in *Saturday Smile*, keeping a steady beat.

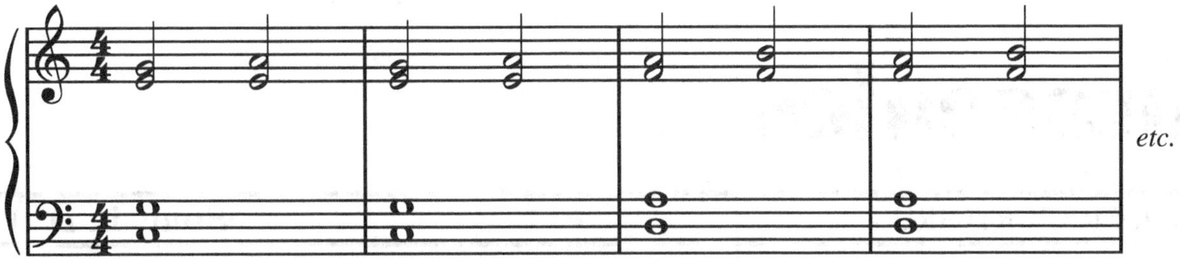

Experiment to find a tempo that feels right for the piece. Then perform as written.

Go to the PDM Web site for additional reading suggestions.

Saturday Smile

LYNN FREEMAN OLSON

So casual

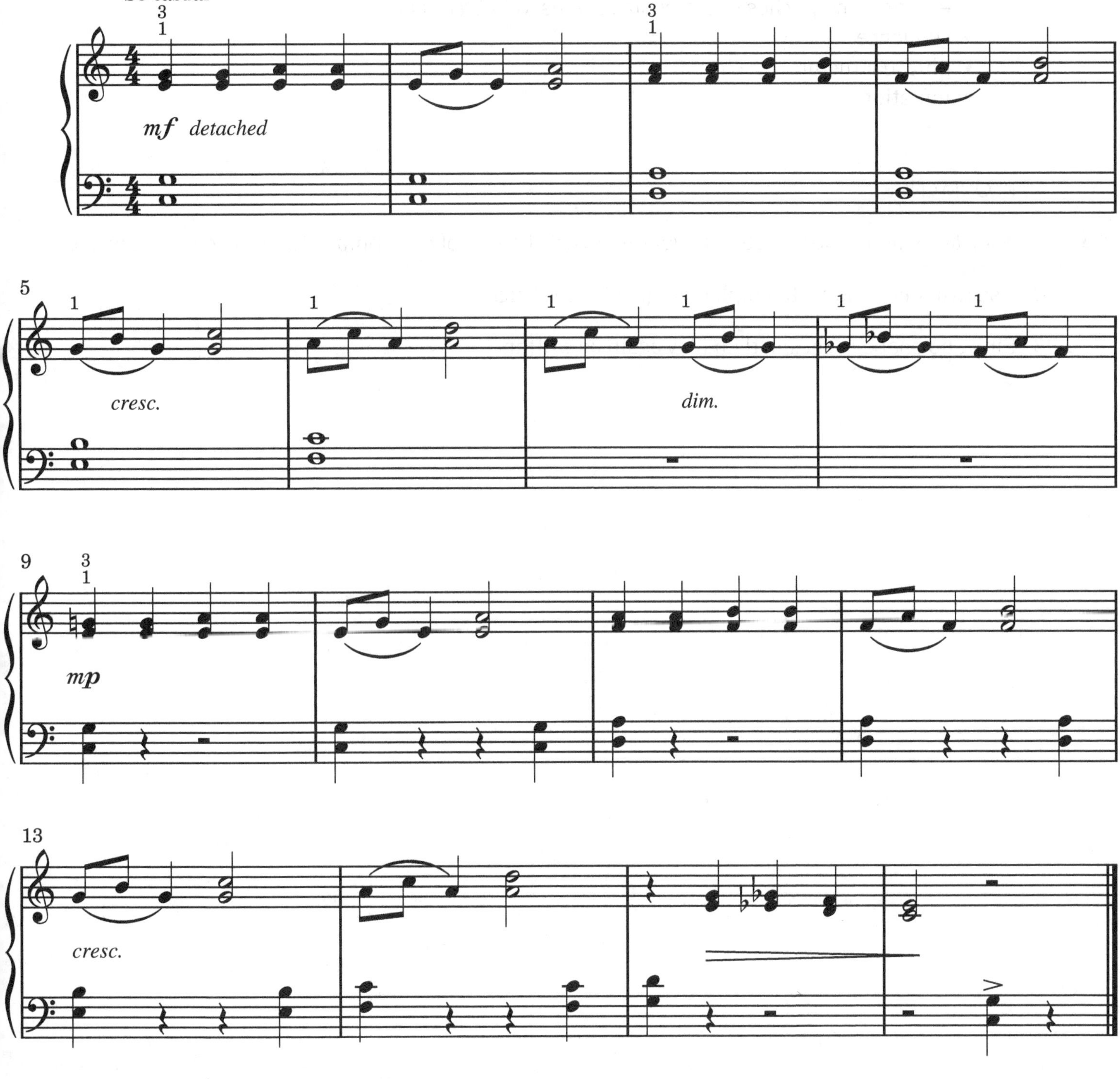

Pentascales

EXEMPLARY REPERTOIRE

Study in D Béla Bartók

INQUIRY

1. Scan *Study in* D. Observe:
   - type of motion between hands
   - melodic direction
   - melodic range
     — A pentascale is a pattern of five consecutive stepwise pitches.
     — Name the pitches of the pentascale used in *Study in* D.
   - sequence
   - phrase structure
   - imitation

PERFORMANCE

1. A *legato* sound is appropriate. Lift your hands at the end of each phrase to prepare for the next one.
2. Use dynamic shading to emphasize the phrase structure.
3. Sing and shape in the air, then play again as written.

Study in D

BÉLA BARTÓK
(1881–1945)

TOPICS TO EXPLORE AND DISCUSS

- Béla Bartók
- Louis Köhler
- Cornelius Gurlitt
- Legato
- Sound: Describe the musical effects of parallel, contrary, and oblique motion.
  Describe the musical effect of one octave versus two octaves apart. What is the visual effect?

SKILLS AND ACTIVITIES

TECHNIQUE

1. The pentascale used in the Bartók *Study in* D is major.

D E F♯ G A

1 1 ½ 1

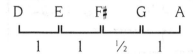

All major pentascales use the same pattern of whole and half steps.

The Italian *staccato* derives from a word meaning to "pull apart" or detach. In playing *staccato*, you do not punch the keys or jump away from them; you simply shorten each sound by releasing the key. You will feel your hand "release" easily. A dot above or below the notehead indicates staccato. Play each example.

a.

b.

A special sign is not always necessary to show a legato sound.

2. Perform the following legato major pentascale phrases.

a.

and so on, upward, on every white-key pentascale pattern

b.

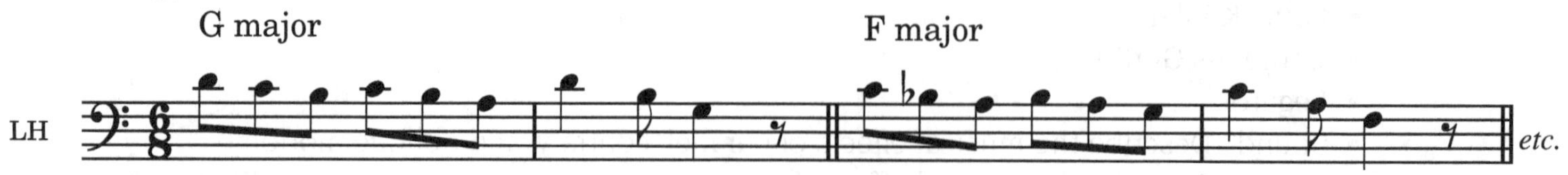

and so on, downward, on every white-key major pentascale pattern

Repeat:

- finger staccato, ***mp***
- wrist staccato, ***f***

Go to the PDM Web site for additional pentascale technique examples.

3. Play the 5th. Feel the shoulder, elbow, and wrist relax; then play the other notes with finger staccato.

a.

b.

4. *One-handed exercises*. Play with the nondominant hand; tap the beat with the other hand.

a.

b.

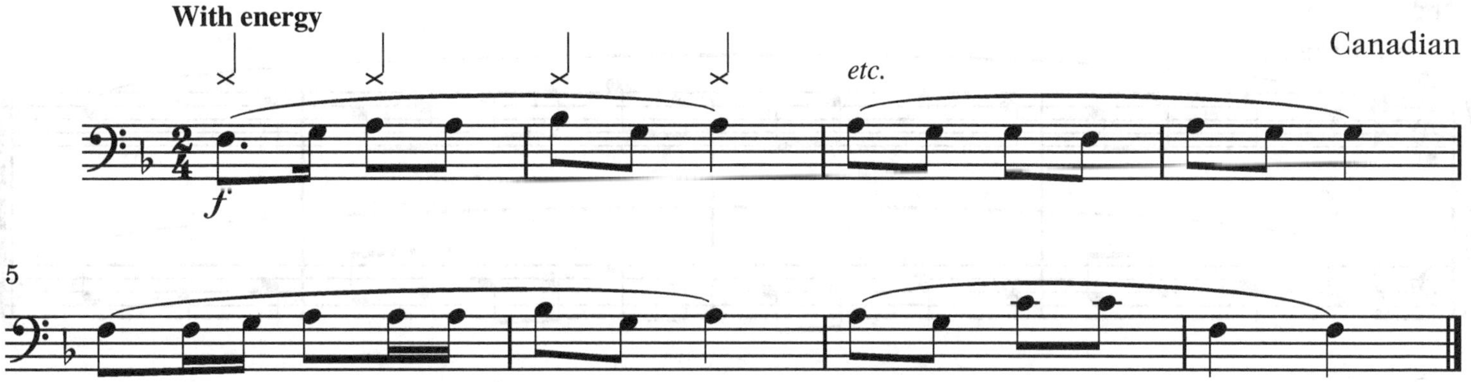

READING

1. How many different types of motion (parallel, contrary, oblique) are used in *Con Moto*?

Con Moto

(Original in C)

CORNELIUS GURLITT, Op. 117, No. 4
(1829–1901)

2. Play the following pentascale melodies. Consider:

- indicated articulation
- evenness of touch
- phrasing
- dynamics
- distance between hands

a.

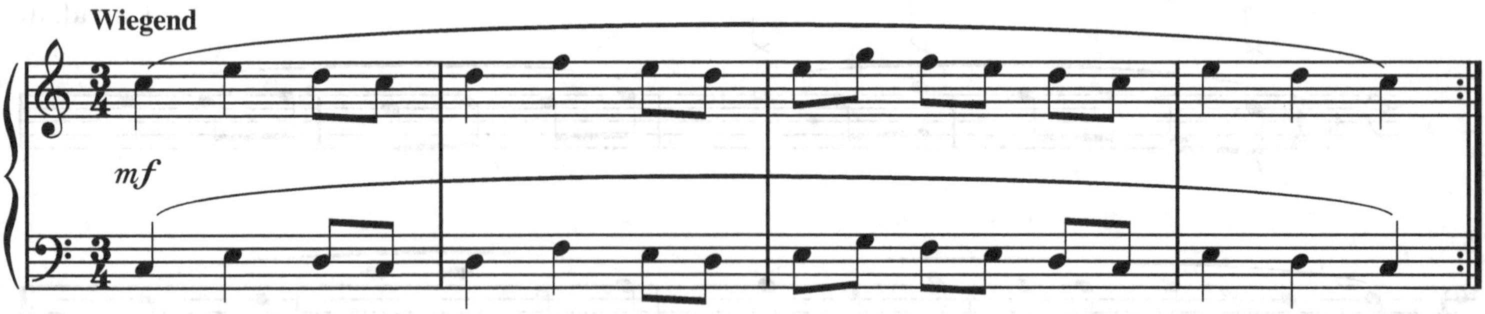

b.

c.

d.

3. The following examples were composed by group piano students.

a.

SCOTT HERRICK

b.

TRAVIS MUELLER

c.

CASEY THOMPSON

d.

Lively

LISA LEHMAN

e.

Allegro moderato

KEVIN YOUNG

f.

Gemächlich

JOSEPH SMITH

g.

Lustig

MEGAN PACHECANO

Go to the PDM Web site for additional examples.

4. In the $\frac{4}{4}$ rhythm chart, use the following physical motions for given note values:

 — TAP

 — CLAP

 — SNAP

Count aloud as you perform only the quarter notes.

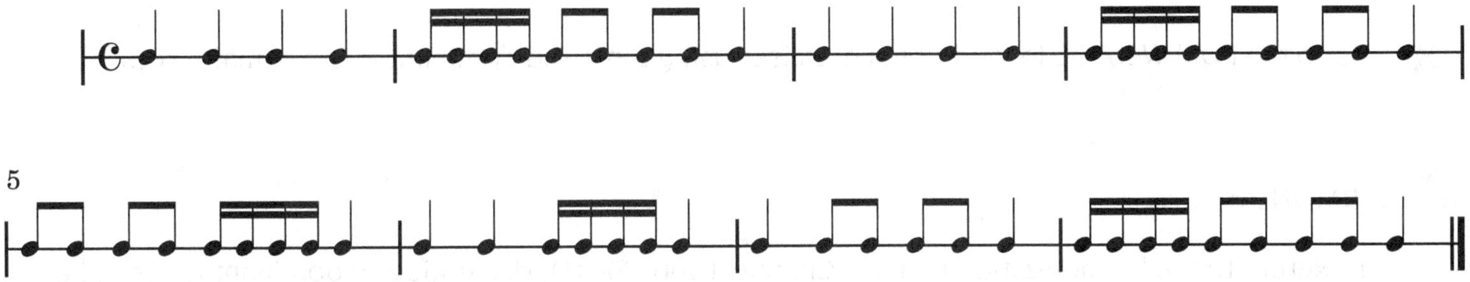

Count aloud as you perform only the sixteenth notes, then count aloud as you perform only the eighth notes,

Form a rhythm ensemble by assigning certain note values to certain students. When you perform together, you will hear all the rhythms given.

KEYBOARD THEORY

1. In a major pentascale, the bottom tone is called *tonic* (I) and the top tone *dominant* (V). Pentascale melodies may be accompanied by these single tones.

   Generally, when the melody is made mostly of tones 1, 3, and 5, accompany with the tonic (I); when the melody is made mostly of 2 and 4, accompany with the dominant (V). Your ear will always be the final test of appropriate accompaniment.

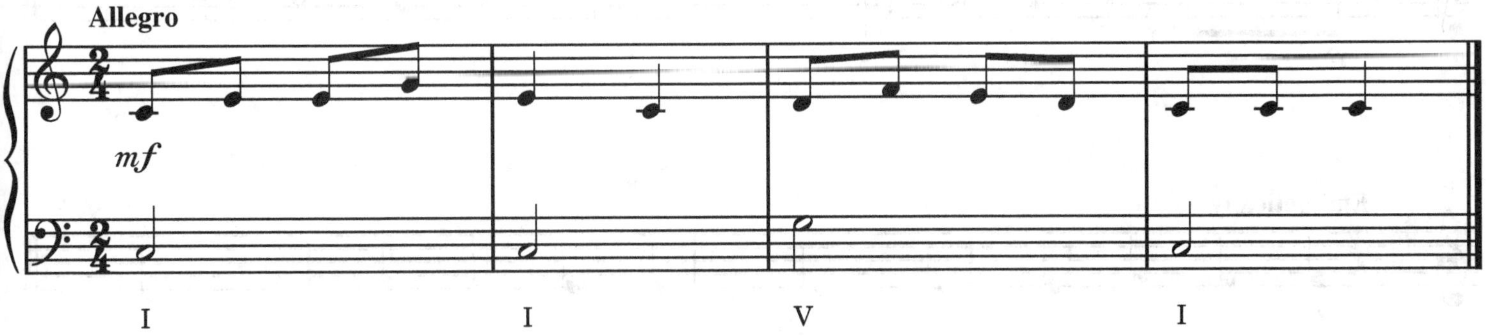

For right-hand melodies, you may choose to place the left hand in pentascale position as illustrated. We also encourage the frequent use of dominant *below* tonic. This is easy when you place your left-hand thumb on a white-key tonic.

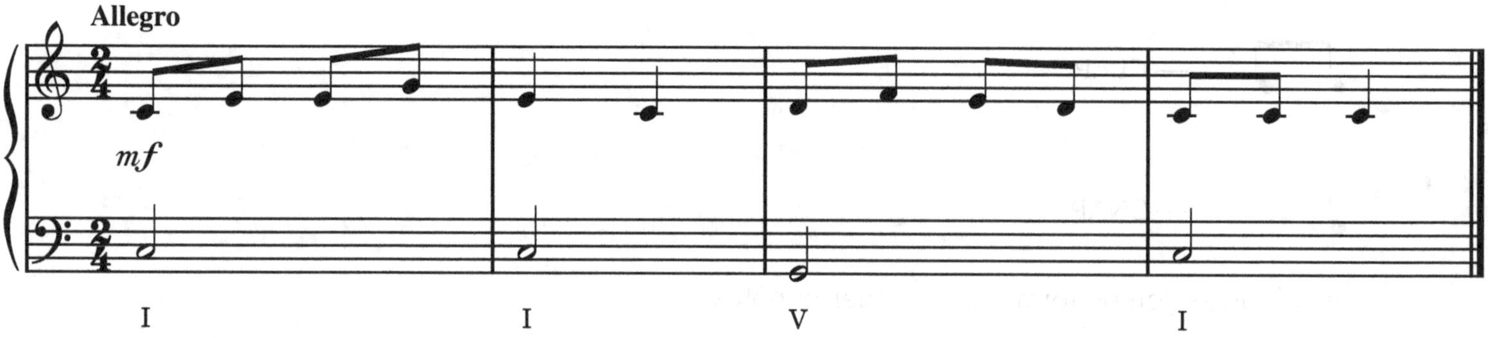

Go to the PDM Web site for additional exercises using tonic and dominant tones of major keys.

HARMONIZATION

1. Return to the harmonization items in Chapter 1 (pp. 30–31). Use tonic and dominant tones to harmonize these melodies.
2. Accompany the following melodies with tonic and dominant tones. Try both the "dominant above" and the "dominant below" left-hand positions. Place Roman numerals under each melody with an arrow designation for the dominant (↓ or ↑).

a.

b.

c.

d.

Vivace

e.

Dreamily **American**

Go to the PDM Web site for additional examples.

TRANSPOSITION

1. Transpose each melody and tonic/dominant accompaniment from item 1 in Harmonization on page 49 to two other major pentascales.

2. Transpose the following examples the interval of a tritone (aug 4th / dim 5th). To do so one note at a time is a difficult task. Follow the steps listed to ensure success.

    - Do not play in the written key
    - Determine melodic range
    - Observe melodic contour
    - Determine beginning scale degree and appropriate starting fingering

    a. Transpose *up* to the key of G major.

Moderato **HILLEY**

b. Transpose *down* to the key of F major.

Wiegend **HILLEY**

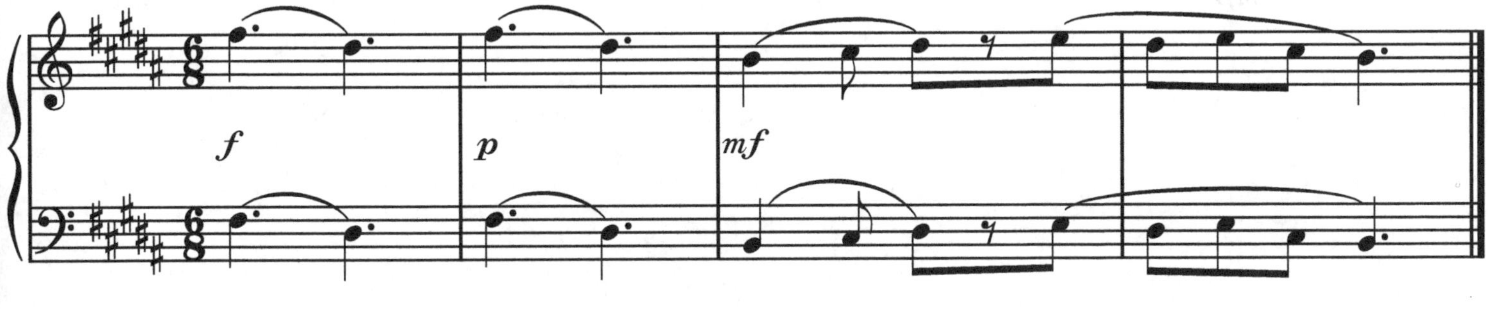

c. Transpose *down* to the key of C major.

Go to PDM the Web site for additional examples.

IMPROVISATION

1. Improvise melodically within a major pentascale using the rhythms of item 4 (page 48). Also improvise with the person next to you — take turns doing the first four bars as the other does the second four bars. The student improvising the first four bars sets the tempo.

Go to the PDM Web site for additional examples.

ENSEMBLE

1. Perform twice without stopping. Switch parts the second time through.

Lullaby

(adapted)

2. Discuss the dynamic levels before performing *Tap It Out*.

Tap It Out

LYNN FREEMAN OLSON

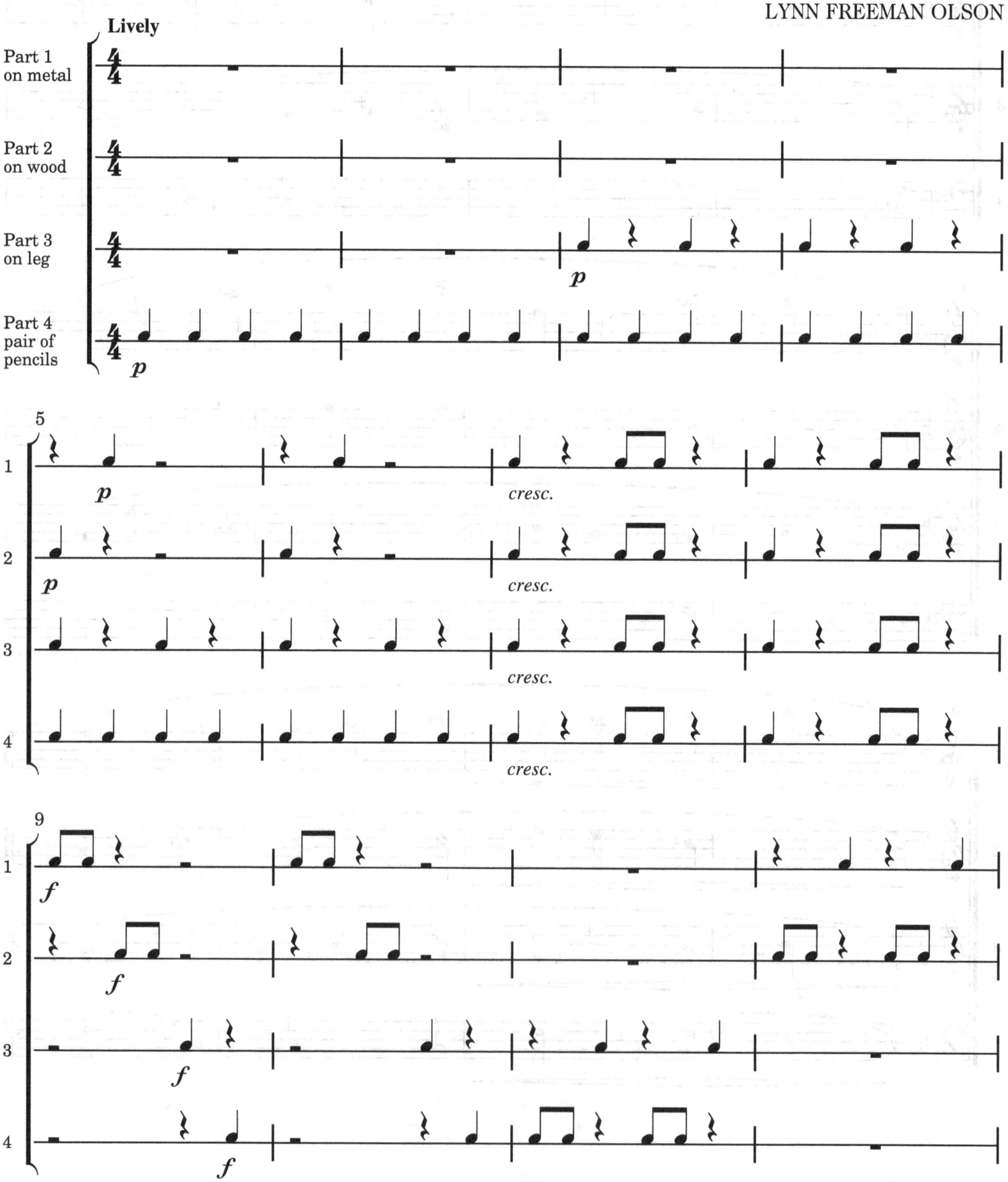

13
1
2
3
4
17
p
p
p
p
21
cresc.
cresc.
cresc.
cresc.
f
f
f
f

SUBSEQUENT REPERTOIRE

1. Look carefully at the "accompaniment" hand and the use of ties and slurs. Your fingering should be determined by looking at the *entire* phrase. A legato sound is appropriate. Notice the use of imitation, sequence, and repetition.

Etude

(Original in C)

CORNELIUS GURLITT, Op. 117, No. 3
(1820–1901)

Go to the PDM Web site for tutorial.

2. Improvise on all boxed pitches in *Inner View*.

Inner View

LYNN FREEMAN OLSON

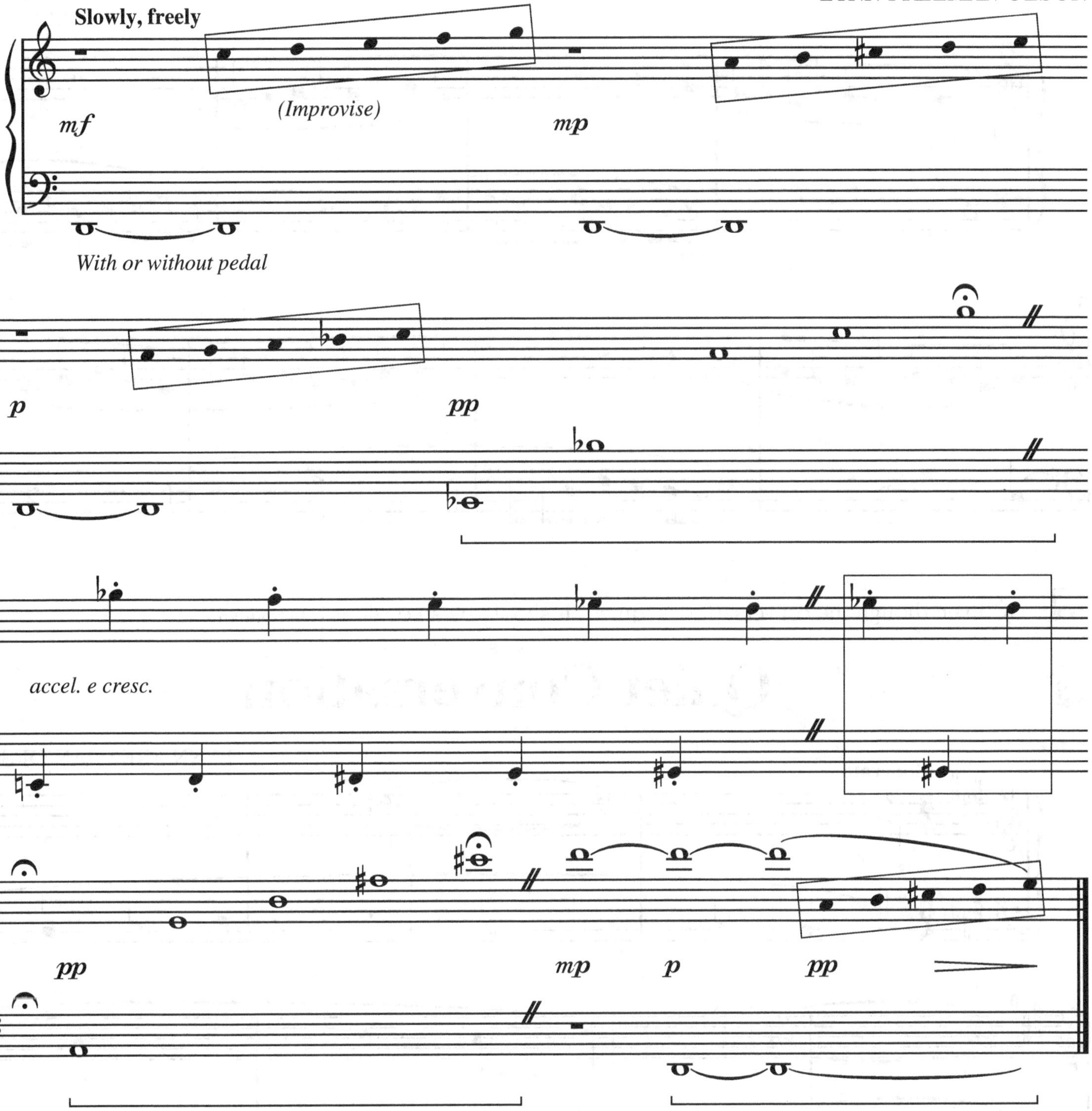

3. E*choing* employs imitation. Where in the piece does exact imitation cease?

Echoing

LOUIS KÖHLER, Op. 218
(1820–1886)

4. Even though the conversation is "quiet," it should be an obvious *conversation*.

Quiet Conversation

LYNN FREEMAN OLSON

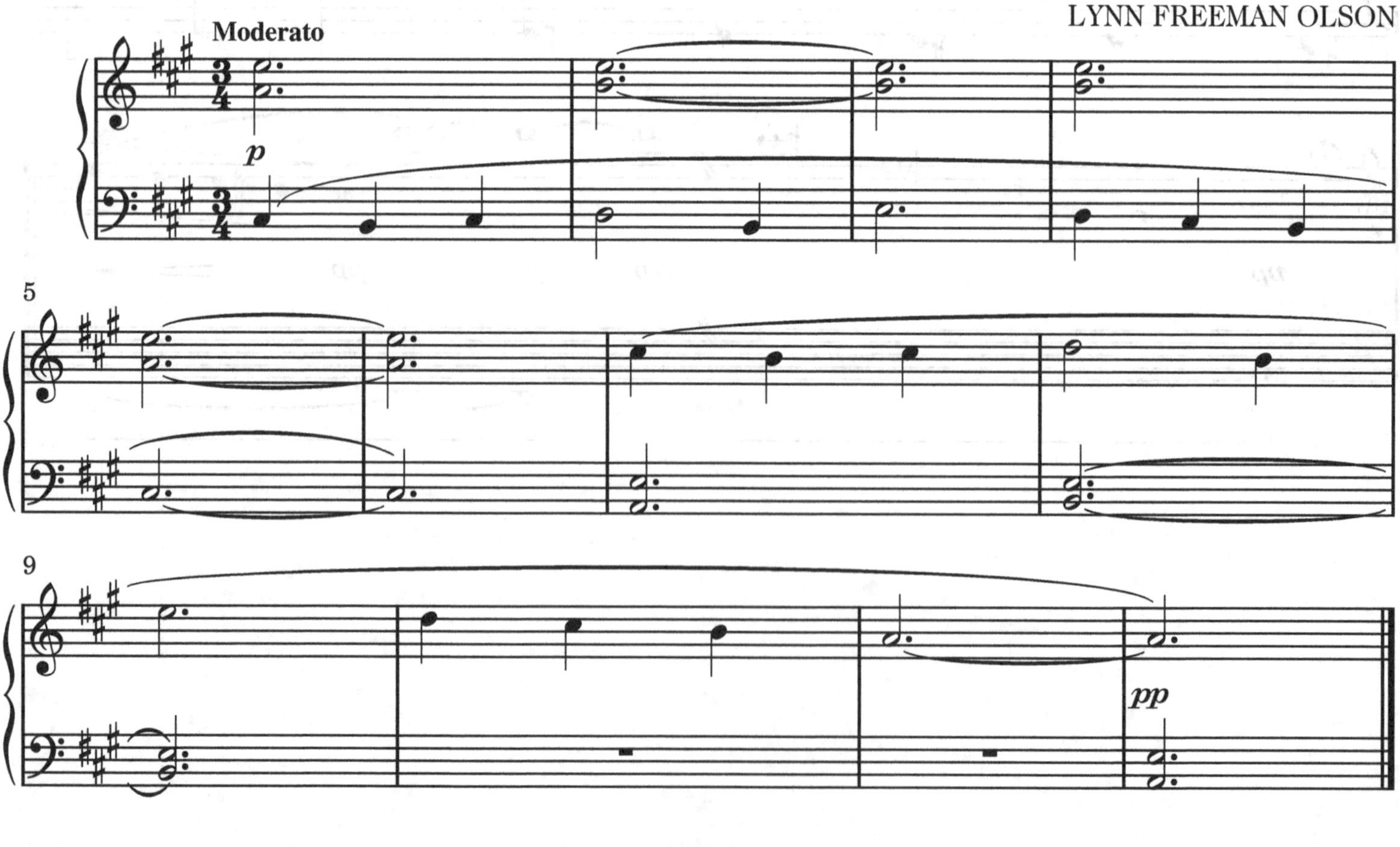

Root Position Triads

EXEMPLARY REPERTOIRE **Scherzo, Op. 39, No. 12** Dmitri Kabalevsky

INQUIRY

1. Scan *Scherzo*. Observe:

    - repetitious shapes and their relationships
    - sequential patterns and direction
      — tones 1, 3, and 5 of a pentascale form a triad
      — the tones of a triad may be played singly or in various groupings
    - hand position shifts
    - contrasting articulations
    - unity and variety

2. Determine logical fingering.

PERFORMANCE

1. Play hands together as blocked triads with two pulses to each position.

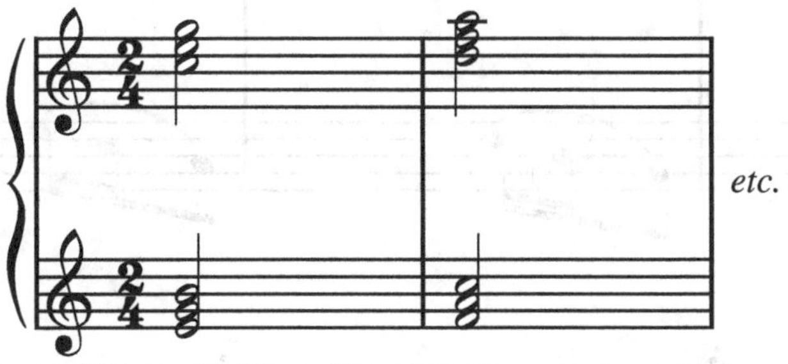

2. Play as written.

Scherzo

from 24 *Pieces for Children*

DMITRI KABALEVSKY, Op. 39, No. 12
(1904–1987)

TOPICS TO EXPLORE AND DISCUSS

- Dmitri Kabalevsky: identify several musical contemporaries
- Vincent Persichetti

SKILLS AND ACTIVITIES

TECHNIQUE

1. Play each example as written. Then play again using two hands, two octaves apart. Pay close attention to the indicated articulation.

a.

b.

c. RYAN McGUIRE

d.

2. Play with the indicated hand; conduct with the other.

a.

b.

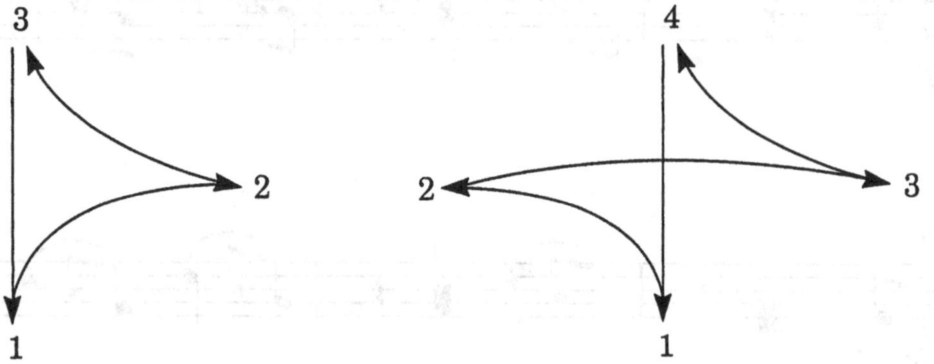

3. The following graphic shows the use of the pedal that sustains sounds (a "damper pedal" on acoustic pianos). It indicates foot action. Pedal with your heel on the floor; lower and raise the pedal with the ball of the foot. Use your right foot.

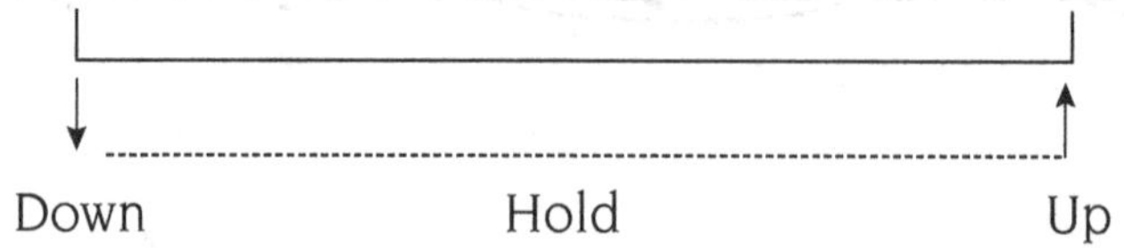

The graphic below shows connection of sounds. When the key or keys go down, the foot allows the pedal to rise to clear the previous sound and then lowers to catch the new sound. A seamless effect results.

4. With one finger, play the C major pentascale and connect one tone to the next with the pedal. The designation for pedal directs movement of the foot.

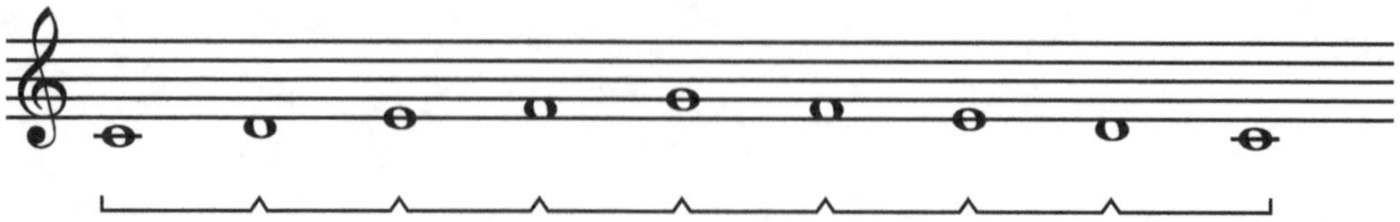

5. The key to proper pedal technique is to observe pedal markings and to *listen* — with emphasis on the word listen. All pedals are unique so your ear must be the final judge.

a.

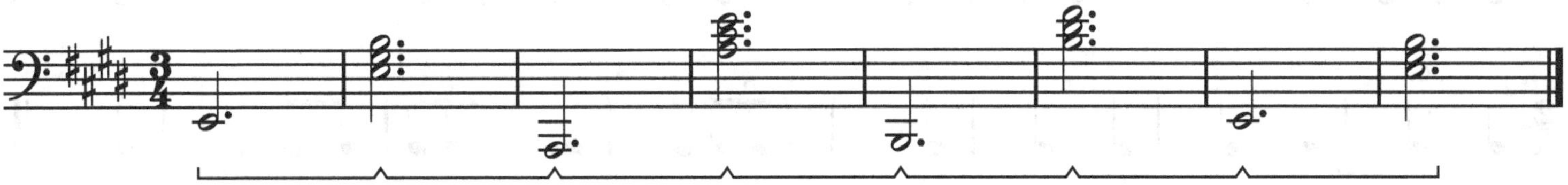

b.

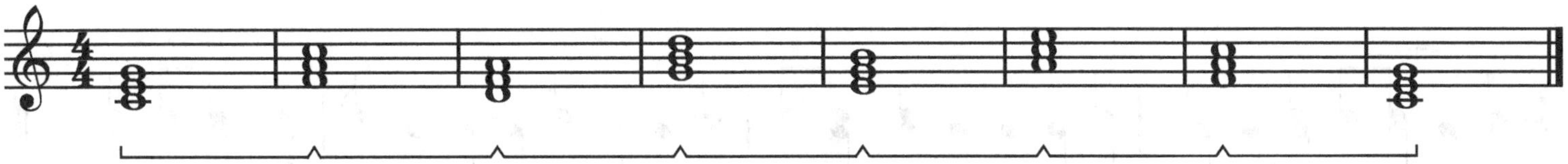

c.

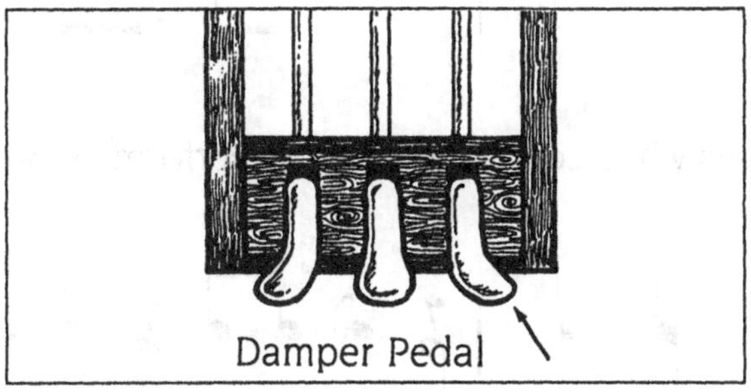

Go to the PDM Web site for video.

READING

1. *Rhythmic reading.* Tap the pattern while counting the beat.

a.

b.

c.

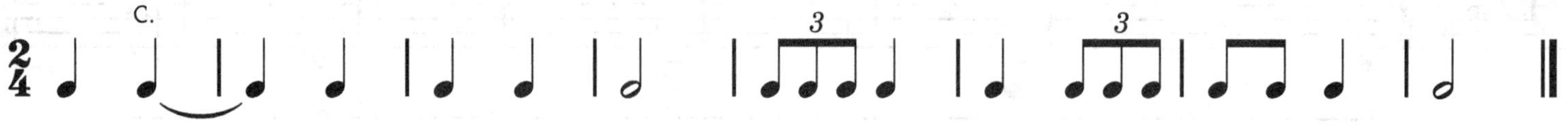

2. Tap the following rhythms as two-part ensembles.

a.

b.

c.

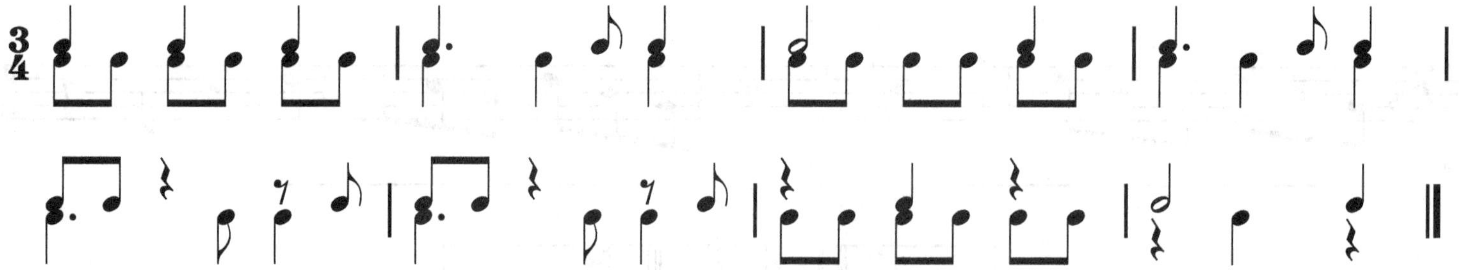

3. Tap the following rhythms while counting the beat. Perform as two-handed solos.

a.

b.

c.

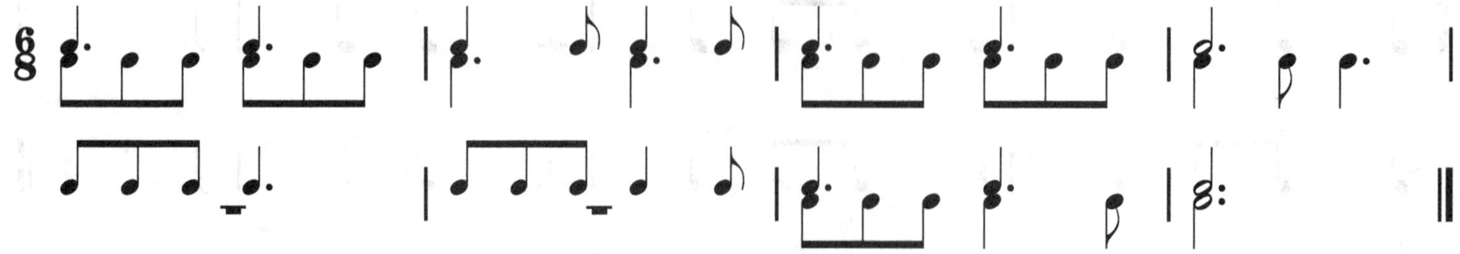

4. In the $\frac{4}{4}$ rhythm chart, use the following physical motions for given note values:

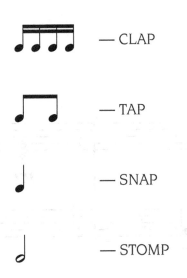

 — CLAP

 — TAP

 — SNAP

 — STOMP

Count aloud as you perform only the quarter notes.

Count aloud as you perform only the eighth notes.

Count aloud as you perform only the sixteenth notes.

Count aloud as you perform only the half notes.

Form a rhythm ensemble by assigning certain note values to certain students. When you perform together, you will hear all the rhythms given.

Go to the PDM Web site for more examples.

5. Sight read the following examples using root position triads. Before playing, notice:

- hand shifts
- range of linear material
- key signature
- rhythmic "considerations"

a.

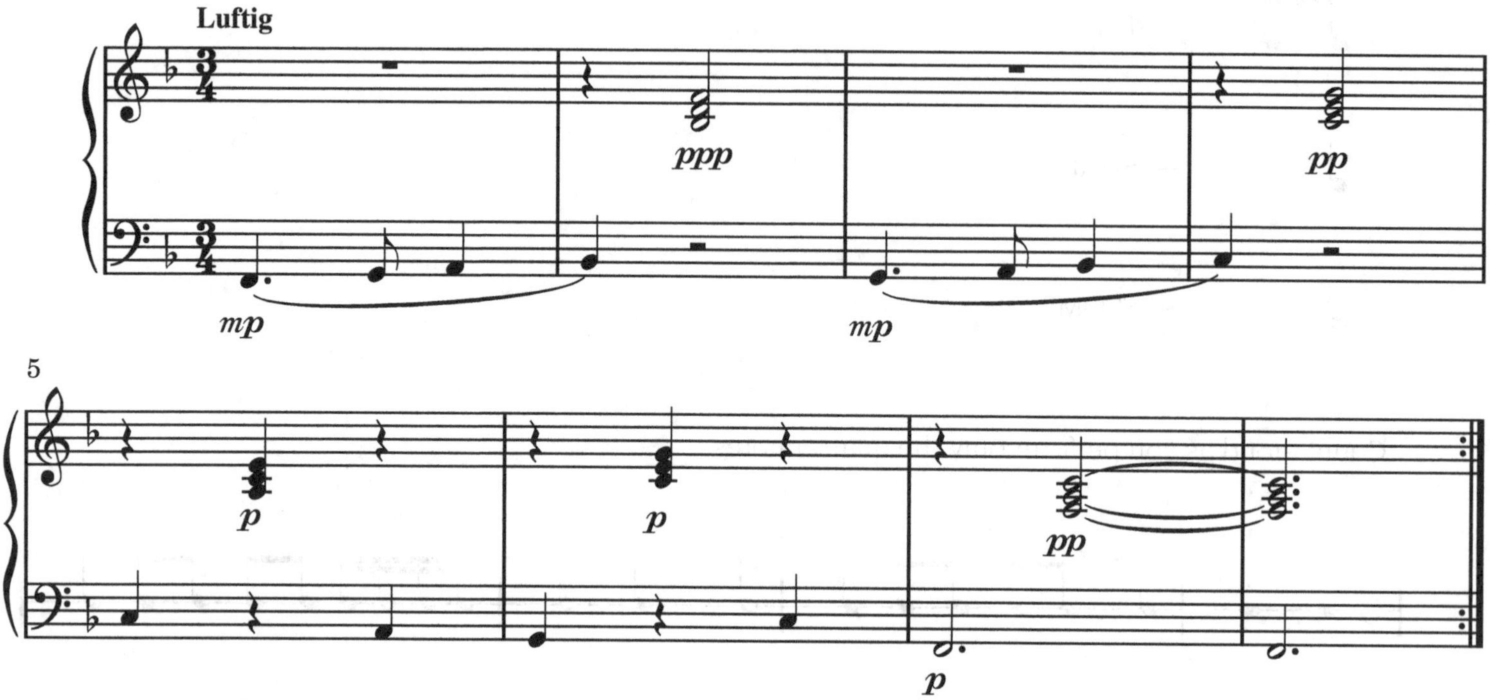

b.

c.

Go to the PDM Web site for more examples.

6. How many hand-position shifts are in A *Little Joke*?

A Little Joke

from 24 *Pieces for Children*

DMITRI KABALEVSKY, Op. 39, No. 6
(1904–1987)

KEYBOARD THEORY

1. Play triads in the left hand built on each tone of the C major pentascale. Determine the quality of each triad (major or minor) and assign a Roman numeral to it.

2. Play triads in the left hand built on each tone of the following major pentascales: C, D, E, F, G, A.

Play triads in the right hand built on each tone of the following major pentascales: C, D, E, F, G, A.

3. Play triads hands together in the keys of C, D, E, F, G, and A major. There should be no pause between key changes.

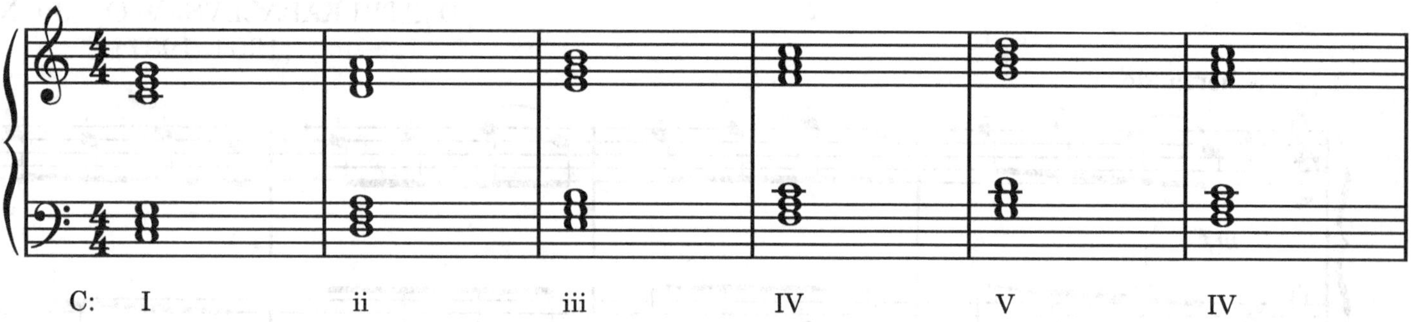

Go to the Web site.

4. Play the same pentascale triads rhythmically in $\frac{6}{8}$, two measures to a triad — one measure broken, hand-to-hand, followed by one measure blocked, hand-to-hand.

5. Play the pentascale triads I and V in the major keys indicated. Follow the example.

Play in C, D, E, F, G, and A major.

6. Play the pentascale triads I and IV in the major keys indicated. Follow the example.

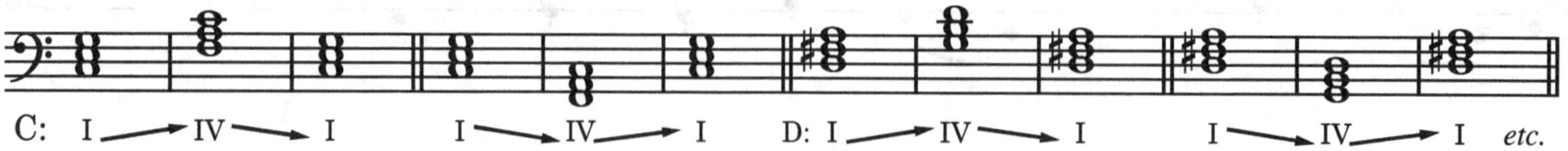

Play in C, D, E, F, G, and A major.

7. As a class, create an exercise that uses the I, IV, and V triads. Play in C, D, E, F, G, and A majors.

HARMONIZATION

1. Refer to the melodies on pages 49–50. Harmonize with triads instead of single tones.

2. When deciding harmonies to be used, consider the chord tones in the melody. Realize that for any single tones there are three triadic possibilities and that for two chord tones within one measure there are two possibilities.

a. The following is one possible realization.

b. This is another possibility.

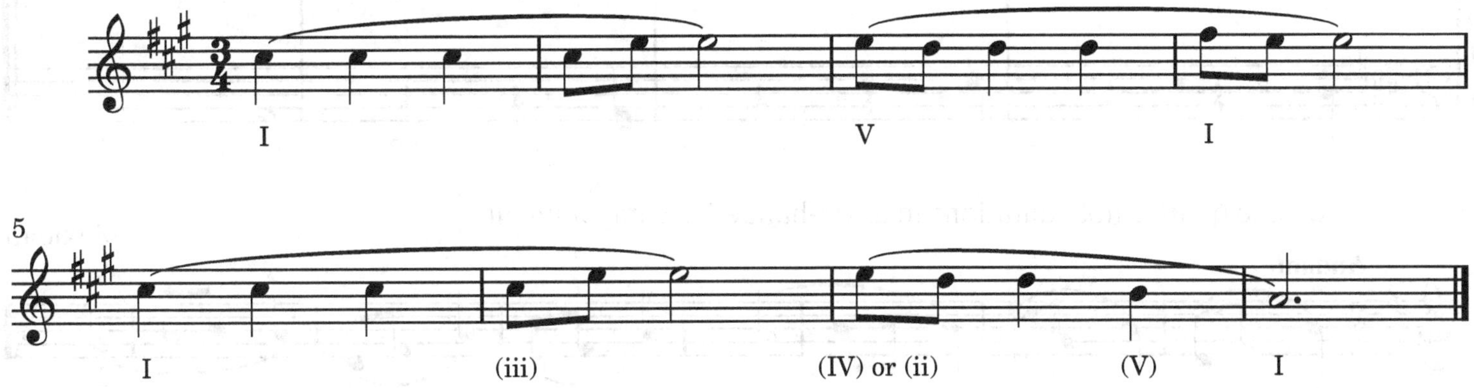

Try a two-handed accompaniment style for example b. Notice the "root-chord-chord" pattern.

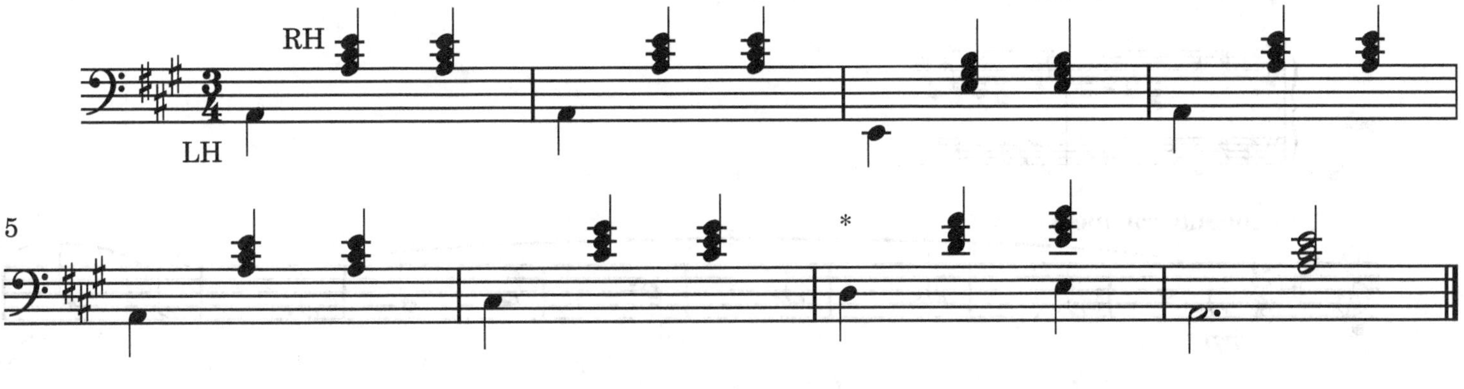

*Notice that the accompaniment pattern must change when the harmonic rhythm changes.

3. Choose from I, ii, iii, IV, and/or V to harmonize the following melodies with some form of two-handed accompaniment pattern. A suggested accompaniment style has been furnished for item a. Listen very carefully for a proper balance between melody and accompaniment. One of you may need to "adjust!"

a.

b. Use quarter-note durations in a two-handed accompaniment.

Mexican

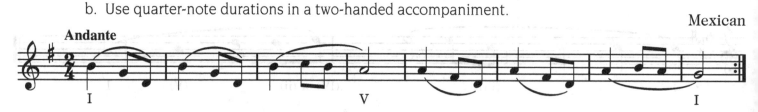

c. Keep the same pattern of broken triads for each harmony.

d. Use eighth-note durations in a two-handed broken chord style.

American

4. The following are *challenge* melodies. Choose between two different accompaniment styles:

- RH melody and LH triads
- no melody; two-handed "root-chord"

a.

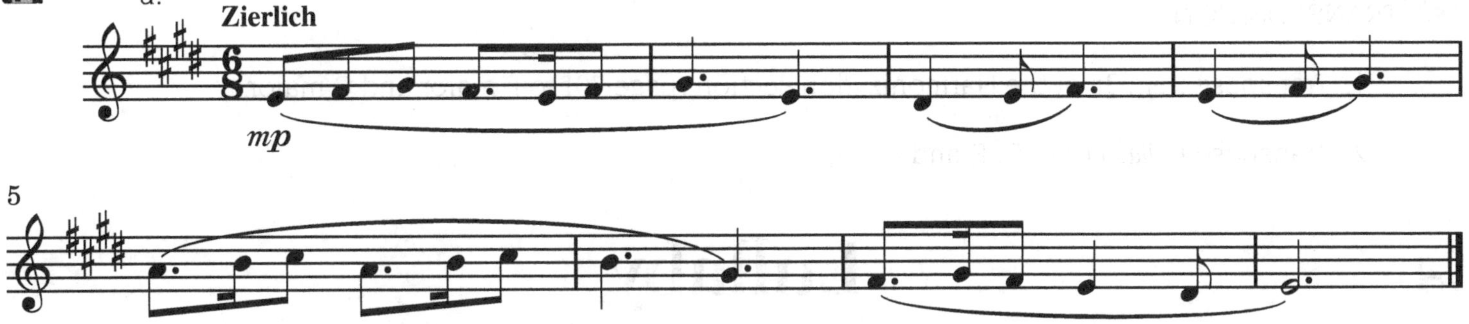

b.

Canadian

c.

Go to the PDM Web site for suggestions in choosing harmonies.

5. Return once more to the melodies on pages 49–50. Harmonize with a two-handed accompaniment while singing the melody.

TRANSPOSITION

1. Transpose item 3a of the Harmonization section (page 70) to F major and G major.

2. Transpose *Lullaby* to C, D, F, and A major.

Lullaby

LYNN FREEMAN OLSON

3. The following examples are to be transposed the interval of a tritone. To do so one note at a time is a difficult, if not impossible, task. Follow the steps listed to ensure success.
   - Do not play in written key
   - Determine melodic range
   - Observe melodic contour
   - Analyze harmonic content
   - Notice hand shifts
   - Determine beginning fingering

   a. Transpose to the key of C major.

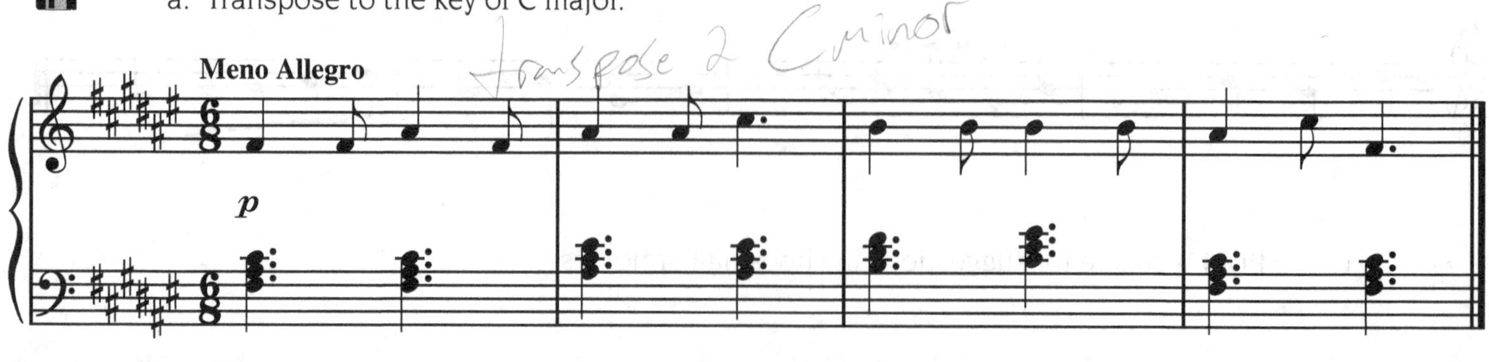

b. Transpose *up* to the key of A major.

c. Transpose *up* to the key of G major.

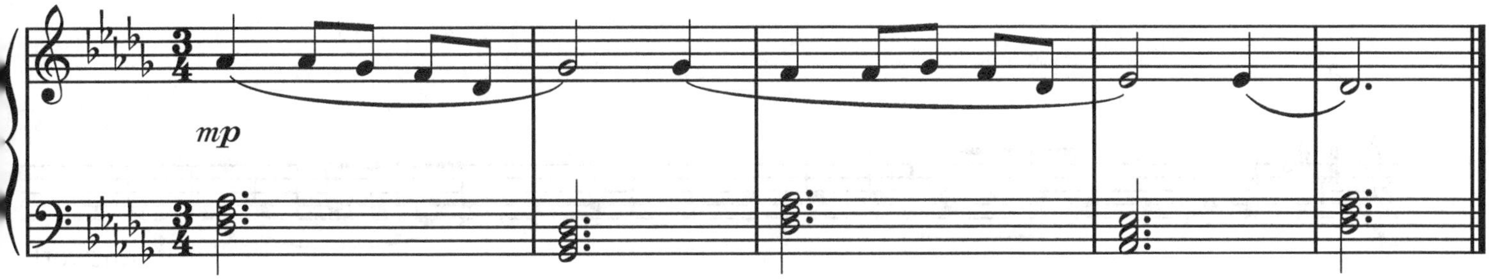

Go to the PDM Web site for additional examples.

IMPROVISATION

1. Play through each example:

Weak:

Stronger:

Is the second example stronger because of pitch, or because of rhythm, or because of a combination of the two?

2. Provide an "answer" for each of the following "questions." Play the question first and follow it with your answer. A steady tempo and a discerning eye toward the key signature are essential.

a.

answer!

b.

answer!

c.

answer!

d.

answer!

3. Work with a classmate on headsets. As a team determine a key and meter and play "Q & A" improvisations. Use four-bar phrases and trade parts so each of you creates a question and an answer.

Go to the PDM Web site for additional examples.

(The balance of this page has been left blank intentionally.)

ENSEMBLE

1. Play *Country Dance* six times, moving to the next part down each time (Part 6 moves to Part 1).

- first time, ***p***
- second time, ***mp***
- third time, ***mf***
- fourth time, ***f***
- fifth time, ***p***
- sixth time, ***pp***

Country Dance

LYNN FREEMAN OLSON

2. Play the Primo part (page 77) as your teacher or a classmate plays the Secondo.

Pop Goes the Weasel

Secondo

Folk Song
Arr. Marion Verhaalen

Pop Goes the Weasel

Primo

Folk Song
Arr. Marion Verhaalen

COMPOSITION

Go to the PDM Web site for representative student composition.

1. Compose a piece in the style of *Scherzo* (see page 60).

SUBSEQUENT REPERTOIRE

1. Look carefully for all ties before playing. While counting aloud, subdivide to ensure rhythmic accuracy through ties and dotted quarter notes. Notice the sign for pedal.

Go to the PDM Web site for a counting tutorial.

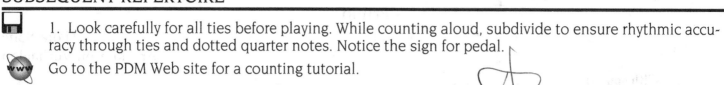

After the Rain

LYNN FREEMAN OLSON

Easily, but moving

2. Take a moment to pencil in right-hand fingerings for bars 2, 3, 4 and 6, 7, 8 as well as 13–16 and 21–24.

Allegro in G

ALEXANDER REINAGLE
(1756–1809)

3. Why would it be a good idea to circle measures 6, 22, and 34? Do you have a solution for the possible problem in each of those measures?

Pomp

VINCENT PERSICHETTI
(1915–1987)

Allegro con brio (𝅗𝅥. = 76)

21
sfz
26
sfz
sfz
sfz
con forza
31
36
sfz
sfz
ff
42
sffz

Extended Use of Intervals, Pentascales, and Triads/ Dominant Seventh

EXEMPLARY REPERTOIRE **Connections** Lynn Freeman Olson

INQUIRY

1. Scan *Connections*. Observe:

    - use of root position triads
    - use of broken chords
    - articulation
    - clef changes
    - form
    - Why the title *Connections*?

Go to the PDM Web site for the answer.

PERFORMANCE

1. As a class, discuss a sequence of practice steps that you feel will ensure success with this piece. List the steps in the space provided below.

    -
    -
    -
    -
    -

(This page has been left blank to avoid a difficult page turn.)

Connections

LYNN FREEMAN OLSON

Charged, but not forceful

18
mf
mp
cresc.
23
mf
dim.
27
mp
cresc.
31
mf
dim.
molto cresc.
35
LH
ff

TOPICS TO EXPLORE AND DISCUSS

- Robert Vandall
- Carl Czerny

SKILLS AND ACTIVITIES

TECHNIQUE

1. Triplet subdivision of the basic pulse will aid in steady rhythm.

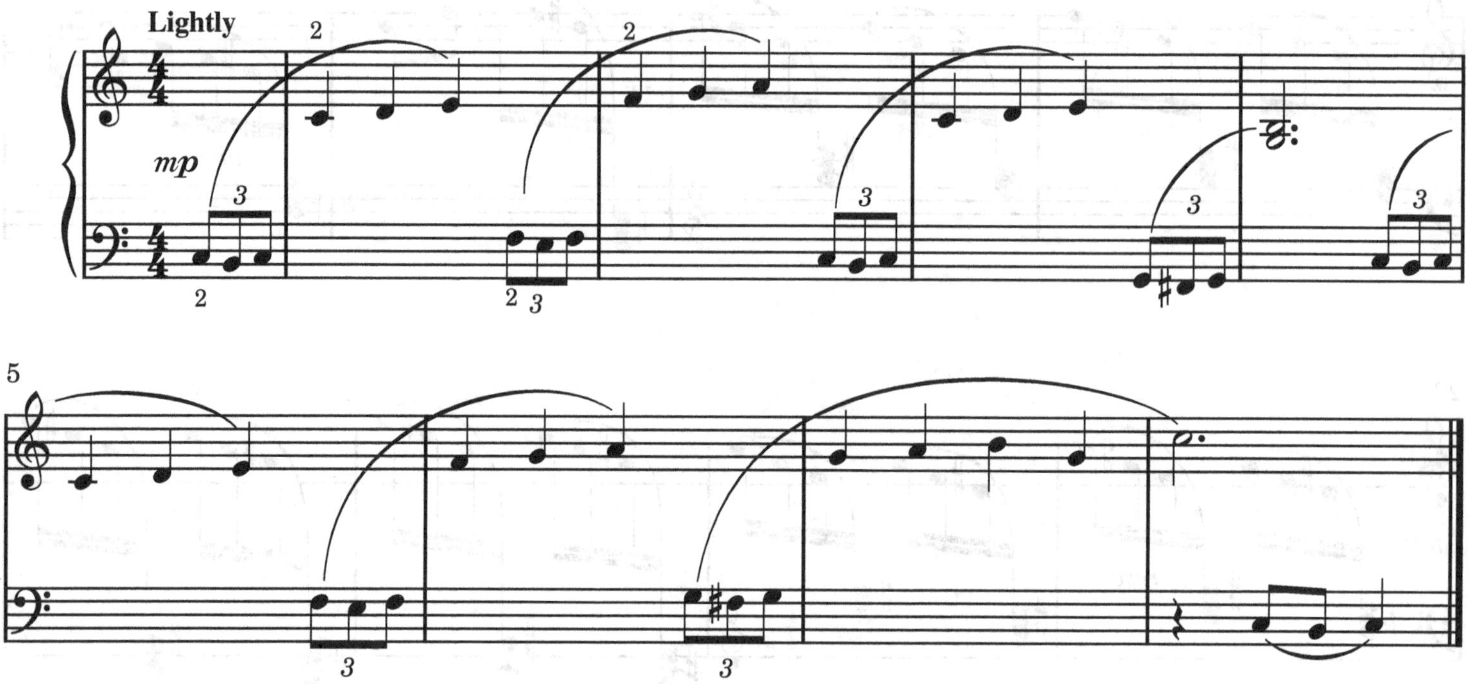

Go to the PDM Web site for further work with this example.

2. Play with careful attention to finger crossings.

a.

b.

3. Play with particular attention to extensions. In both examples the thumb should extend outward to accommodate the increased range.

a.

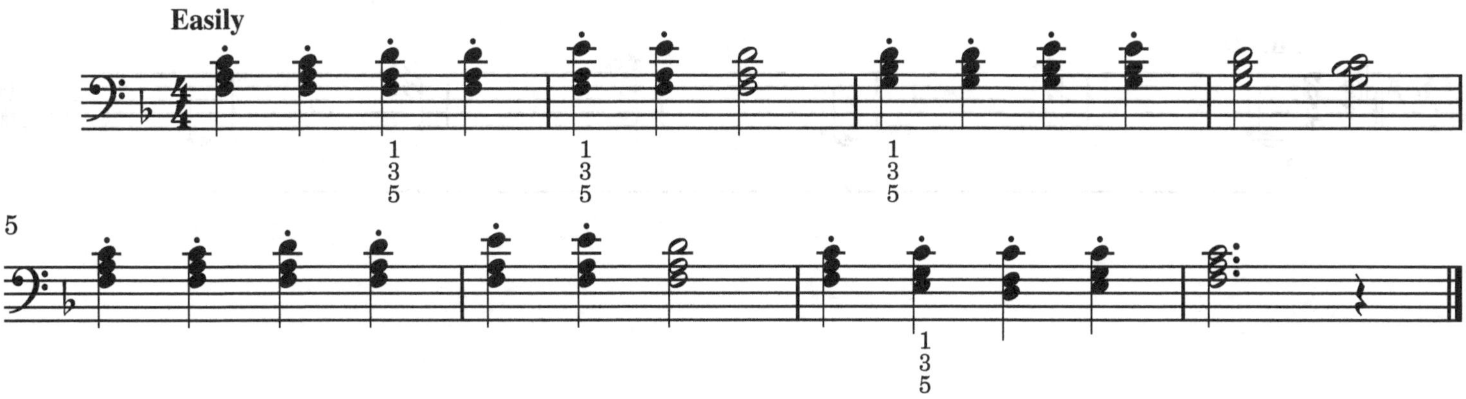

b.

4. The Bartók example uses a combination of staccato and legato articulation. What is the technical challenge in measures 6 and 7?

BÉLA BARTÓK
(1881–1945)

READING

1. Read with careful attention to pedal indications.

a.

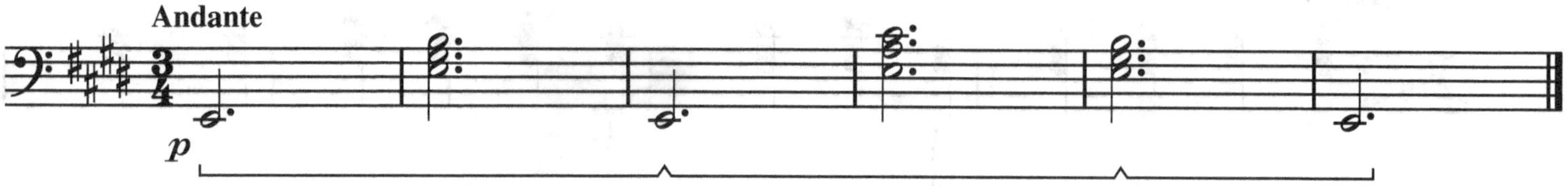

b.

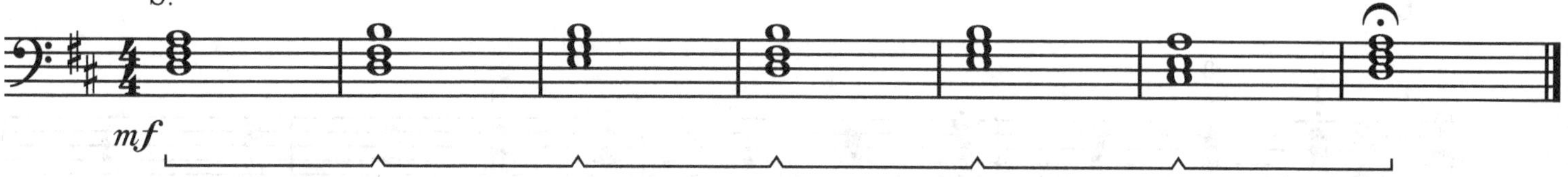

c.

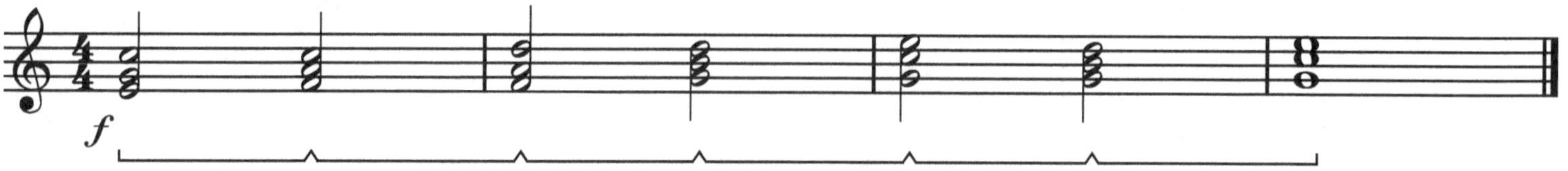

d.

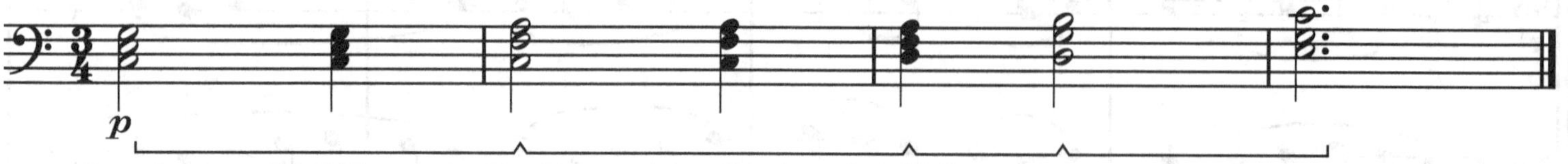

e. Activating the damper pedal makes it possible to shift to the new shape earlier.

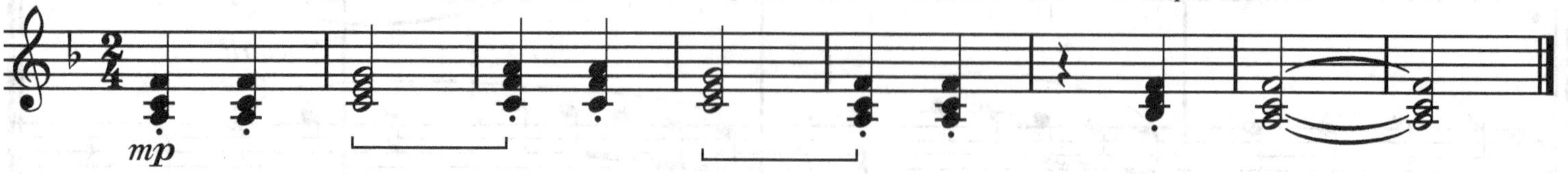

2. Play items 1. a.–e. again and conduct as you play.

3. Each example has been written in two different ways. Which arrangement do you find easier to play?

a.

* b.

c.

* d.

*(In these examples, the tones of the triads have been rearranged for convenience of playing.)

Go to the PDM Web site for additional examples.

4. Read through, blocking both hands; then play as written.

Dance

(Original in C)

CARL CZERNY, Op. 838, No. 11
(1791–1857)

Go to the PDM Web site for further reading examples including random chord shapes.

KEYBOARD THEORY

1. The root position triads in this progression move by 4ths.

In the left hand, double the roots of the triads and play the progression with hands together. Let the left hand also move in 4ths. Play in all white-key majors as you say the names of the pitches in each root position triad.

You will have smoother motion using the *closest position* of the triads.

To achieve the closest position, you will often move to an inversion (rearrangement) of the triad. In the preceding progression, the IV and V triads are inverted.

Using this closest-position progression, add left-hand roots. Try both the "dominant above" and "dominant below" left-hand positions. Again, play in all white-key majors. It is an excellent exercise to continue saying the names of the pitches in root position even though you are playing some of them as inversions.

2. A dominant 7th chord (V7) is the dominant triad plus a minor 7th above the root.

C Major

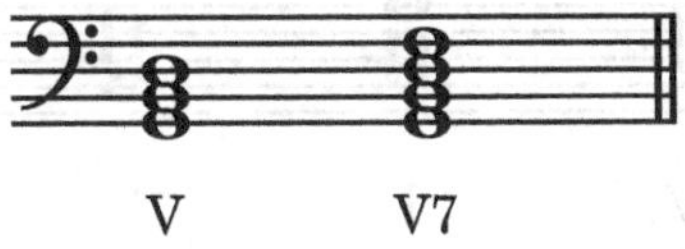

In accompaniments, the 3rd is often not included in the left-hand V7 chord.

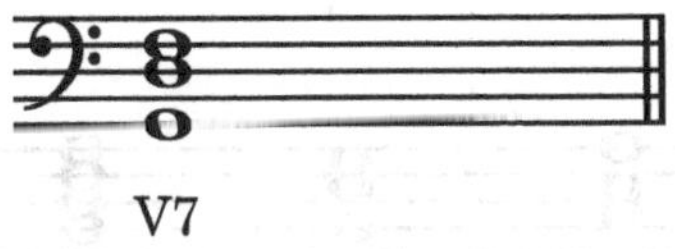

For each major key shown, play a left-hand V7 chord omitting the 3rd. Supply the omitted 3rd an octave higher in the right hand.

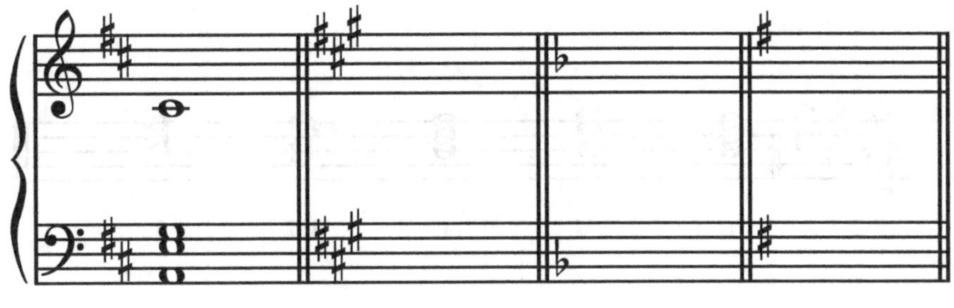

3. Study these common left-hand harmonic intervals found when playing V7 to I cadences.

Play these intervals in the following keys: G major, A major, F major, and E major.

4. In item 1 you found smoother motion from harmony to harmony by using *closest position* voicing. The progressions below use the same voicing. It is still a good idea to verbally *spell* each chord in root position **before** you *play* the closest position. Think:

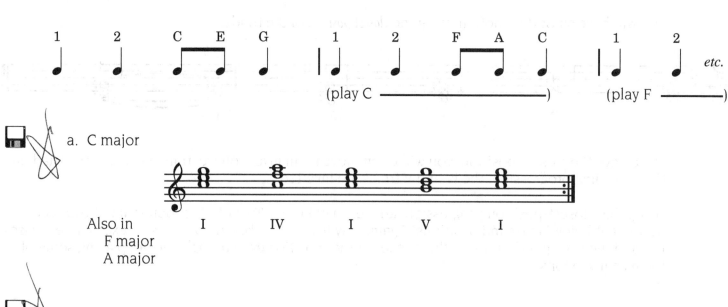

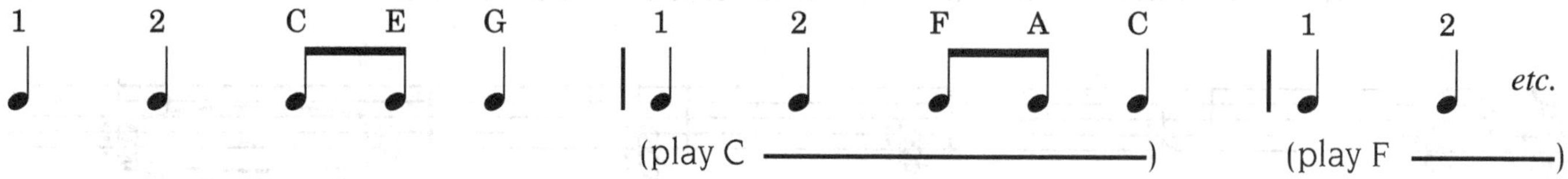

a. C major

I IV I V I

Also in
F major
A major

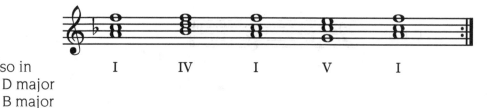

b. F major

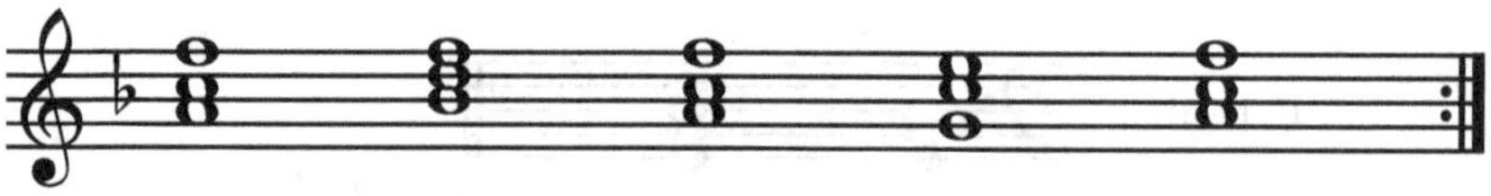

I IV I V I

Also in
D major
B major

c. E major

I IV I V7 I

Also in
G major
C major

d. B major

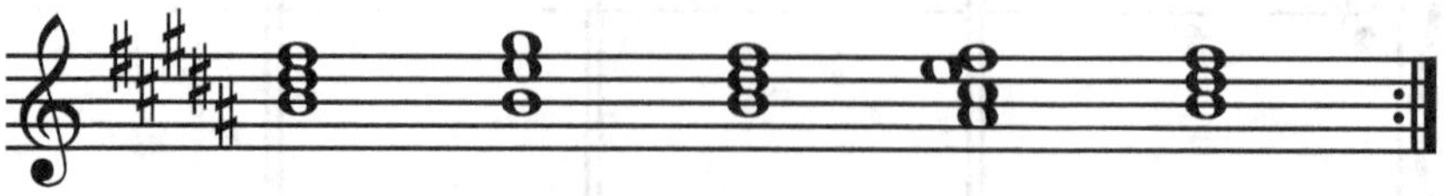

I IV I V7 I

Also in
A major
G major

5. Using the following progressions, verbally spell each chord in the root position but play the closest position. Remember, spell the chord *before* you play it!

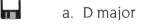

a. D major

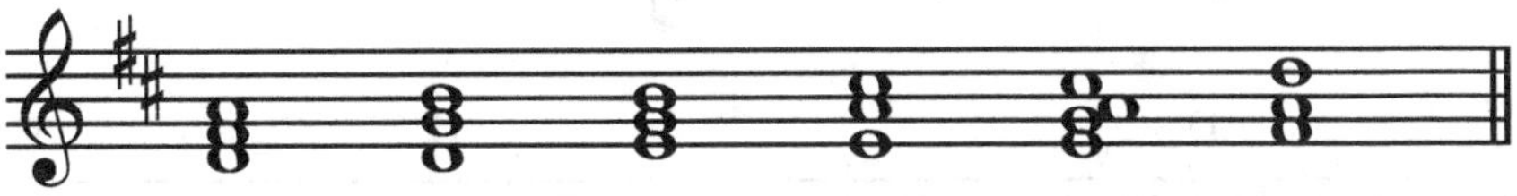

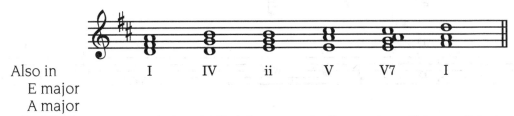

Also in E major, A major

I IV ii V V7 I

b. F major

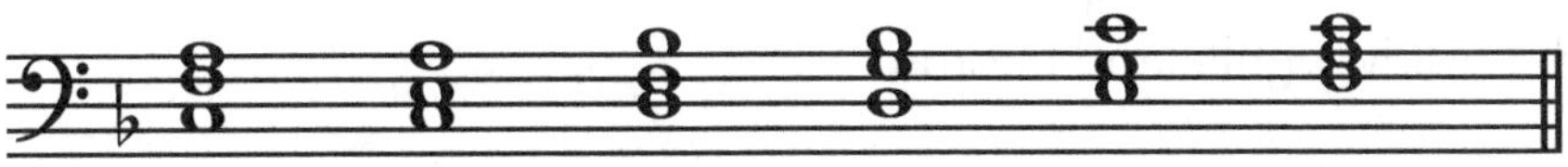

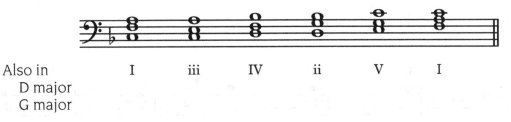

Also in D major, G major

I iii IV ii V I

c. C major

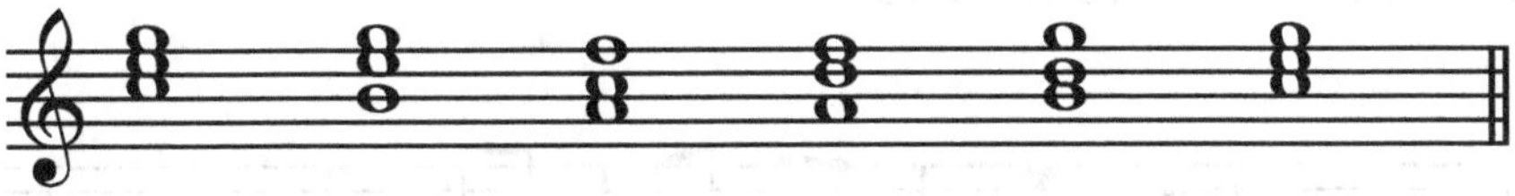

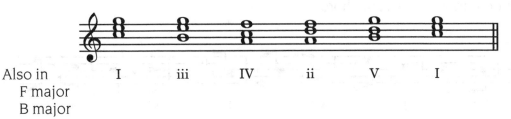

Also in F major, B major

I iii IV ii V I

d. A major

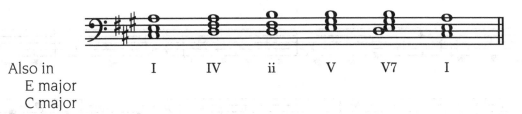

Also in E major, C major

I IV ii V V7 I

Go to the PDM Web site for further drill in closest-position progressions.

HARMONIZATION

1. Chords also may be designated by letter name instead of Roman numeral. Harmonize the following, moving to the closest chord possible each time.

   a. Play RH melody and LH chords.

American

Boisterously

b.

Traditional

Slowly

c. Left-hand melody, right-hand chords

English

Easily

d. Two-handed (root-chord, root-chord)

French

Allegro

e. Accompany with a two-handed "root-chord" style. The RH chords should be in closest position.

American

With spirit

f. Left-hand closest position chords with right-hand melody

British

Brightly

Go to the PDM Web site for alternate styles.

2. Complete the following melodies in the style indicated.

a.

American

b.

South American

TRANSPOSITION

1. Return to the challenge harmonization examples on page 71 and transpose each to two different major keys.

2. Return to *Lullaby* on page 72. Play again in transposed keys, this time using a broken-chord accompaniment.

I ii

Go to the PDM Web site.

3. The following examples are to be transposed the interval of a tritone. As in Chapter 3, use the following steps:

- Determine melodic range
- Observe melodic contour
- Analyze harmonic content
- Notice common tones
- Determine beginning fingering
- Do not play in written key

a. Play the last four bars in G major.

b. Transpose *up* to A major.

c. Transpose *down* to F major.

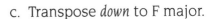

Go to the PDM Web site.

4. Efficient transposition includes an awareness of fragments, phrases, and sections that are repetitious. Scan *Vivace* for repetitions; then play in the keys of F major and G major. Do not play in the original key.

Vivace

CORNELIUS GURLITT, Op. 117, No. 8
(1829–1901)

IMPROVISATION

1. Play the following triad progression hands together. Use the keys of D major, F major, and A major. Use closest position voicing.

4/4 I | IV | ii | V | iii | ii | V | I :||

2. Improvise a right-hand melody consisting of *thirds of triads only*. Since the pitch content gives you very little chance for creativity, the interest must come from your use of rhythm and rests. You may always end your improvisation on tonic.

   Play the following example in the key of D major as another student plays the progression:

   Now try your own in the keys of F major and A major.

3. Notice the vast difference just one more pitch option can make to your improvisation when you are given a choice between *roots and thirds of chords only*. Compare this example to the previous.

   Now try one of your own with just roots and thirds.

4. Once again, add a chord tone to your choices and you now have available all three tones of the triad. Compare this last example to the previous two.

5. Partner with a classmate on headsets and take turns creating improvised melodies consisting of *triad tones only*. Use the recorded backgrounds for "stylistic inspiration!"

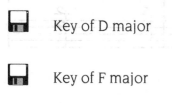

Key of D major

Key of F major

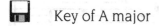

Key of A major

Go to the PDM Web site.

(This page has been left blank to avoid a difficult page turn.)

ENSEMBLE

1. Have fun!

"Dixie" for Two

DANIEL D. EMMETT
Arr. C. Michael Ehrhardt

10
1
2
mf
f
15
8va
1
2

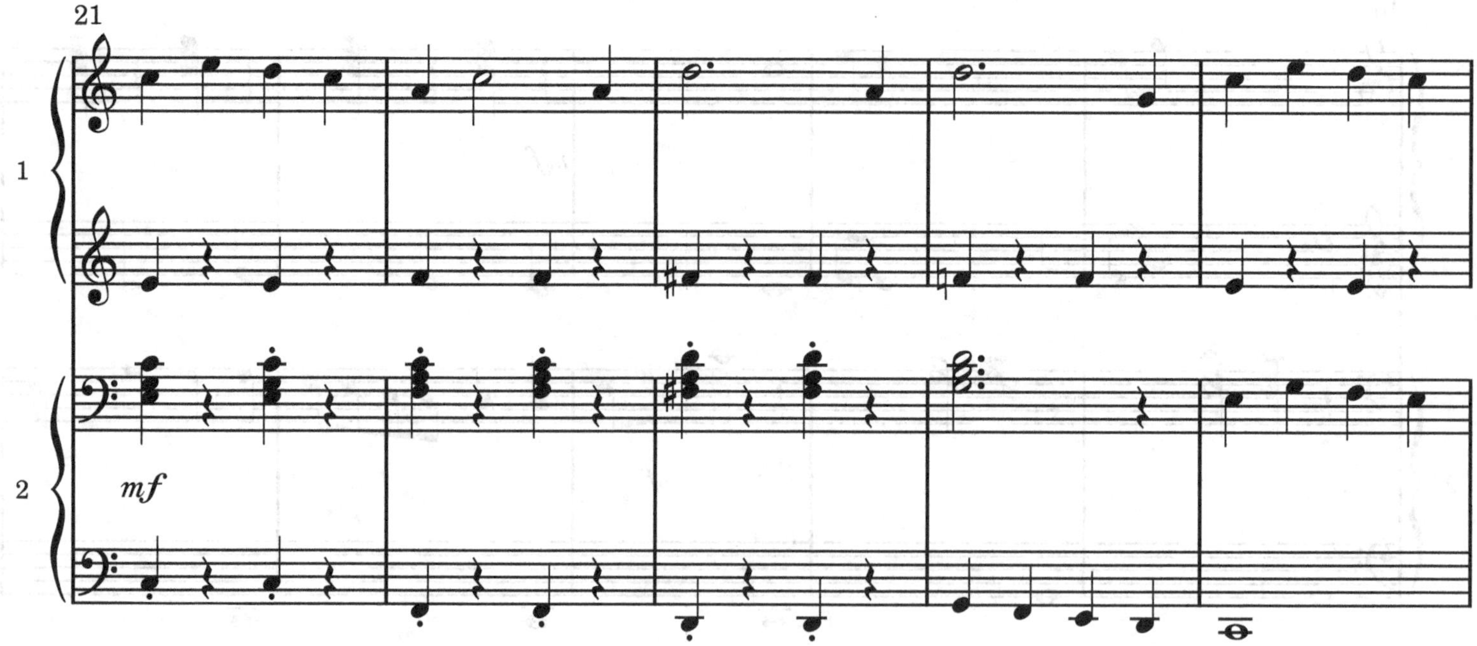
21
1
2
mf

26
1
2

31
8va
1
2
36
(8va)
accelerando
ff
1
2
accelerando
ff

2. Part 1 is to be improvised as a countermelody based on chord tones.

Under the Bamboo Tree

COLE AND JOHNSON
Arr. Lynn Freeman Olson

Happily
Part 1
Part 2
Part 3
Part 4
Part 5
mf
f
mp
simile
If you lak - a me lak I lak - a you, And we lak - a both the
Spoken: Oo-bah, oo-bah, Wow Wow
6
same, I lak - a say, this ver - y day, I lak - a change your name; 'Cause

11
1
2
I love - a you and love-a you true, And if you - a love-a me, One live as two,
3
4
5
simile
16
two live as one, Under the bam-boo tree.
f
Spoken: Wow Wow Wow

COMPOSITION

Compose a piece using ABA form with the B section in the dominant. The composition should be 24 measures in length.

- A section: Both hands are in the same pentascale position (any register), using parallel and/or contrary motion in a two-part texture.
- B section: Right hand plays melody against left-hand ostinato.

Go to the PDM web site for representative students compositions.

SUBSEQUENT REPERTOIRE

1. Use crisp staccato throughout. Discuss the form of *Triadique*. What is the major difference in the return of the A section?

Triadique

LYNN FREEMAN OLSON

2. Pay close attention to pedal markings, but don't forget to listen to the effect of your foot!

3

Adagio

ROBERT D. VANDALL

3. What is "different" in measures 9–12?

Summer Mood

from *Pop! Goes the Piano, Book I*

LYNN FREEMAN OLSON

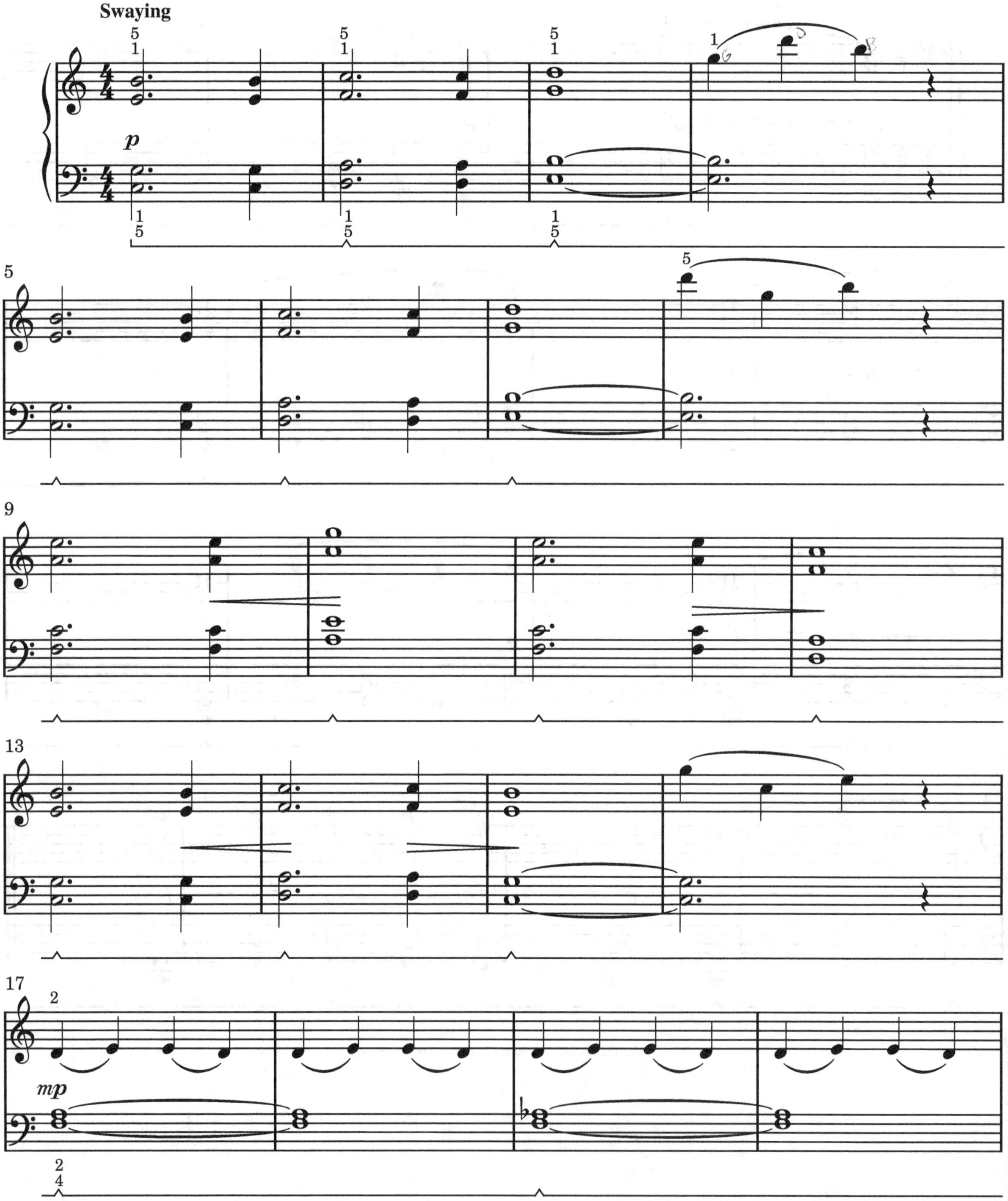

21
dim.
p
p
26
31
36
41
pp
p
pp

Chord Shapes/Pentascales with Black-Key Groups

EXEMPLARY REPERTOIRE **Arioso** Daniel Gottlob Türk

INQUIRY

1. Scan *Arioso*. Observe:
   - two-note slurs
   - use of sequence
   - hand shifts
   - rests
   - ornamentation

PERFORMANCE

1. Review the execution of the two-note slur. It is a "single" motion or gesture.

2. Spend time with hands-separate practice to solidify fingering shifts. Pencil in your score the shifts that must occur.

3. Discuss as a class the proper performance of a trill in the time period 1756–1813.

4. Isolate measures 6, 7, 8 and 14, 15, 16 for hands-together practice before attempting the full score.

Arioso

DANIEL GOTTLOB TÜRK
(1756–1813)

Go to the PDM Web site for fingering tutorial.

TOPICS TO EXPLORE AND DISCUSS

- Daniel Gottlob Türk
- Glenda Austin
- Dennis Alexander
- Chorale style/Keyboard style

SKILLS AND ACTIVITIES

TECHNIQUE

1. Play the following shapes.

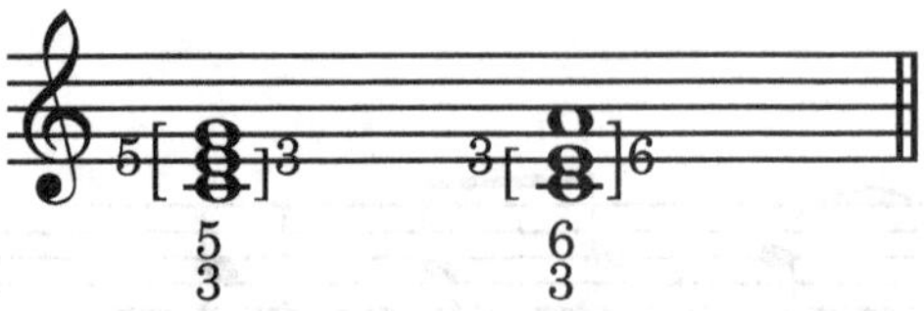

On white keys only, play a sequence of $^{5}_{3}$ to $^{6}_{3}$ shapes.

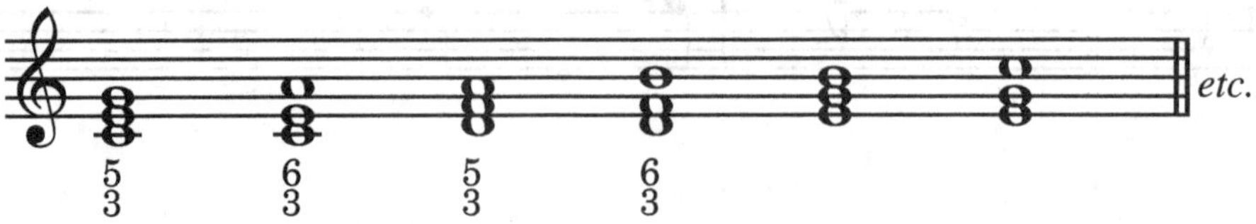

Play the same sequence with the left hand one octave lower.

Repeat the $^{5}_{3}$ to $^{6}_{3}$ sequence with each hand, this time sharping each F. Repeat, sharping each F and C. Repeat the sequence using major keys up through and including three sharps and three flats.

Key of G

Key of F

Key of D

Key of B♭

Go to the PDM Web site.

2. Using a pointer finger, play and name a major pentascale on each of the following black keys.

D♭/C♯ G♭/F♯

Play the two and three black-key groups, hands together, blocked.

RH	2 3	2 3 4
LH	3 2	4 3 2

Play again, and this time use thumbs as pivots to move from one black-key group to the other (thumbs on F).

Using the same principle, block the pentascale. Play the pentascale again as single tones, hands together.

Follow the same steps with G♭/F♯ and C♭/B (in B pentascale, left hand begins on finger 4, right hand on finger 1).

3. Play the following black-key-group pentascale drills, hands separately.

a.

b.

c.

d.

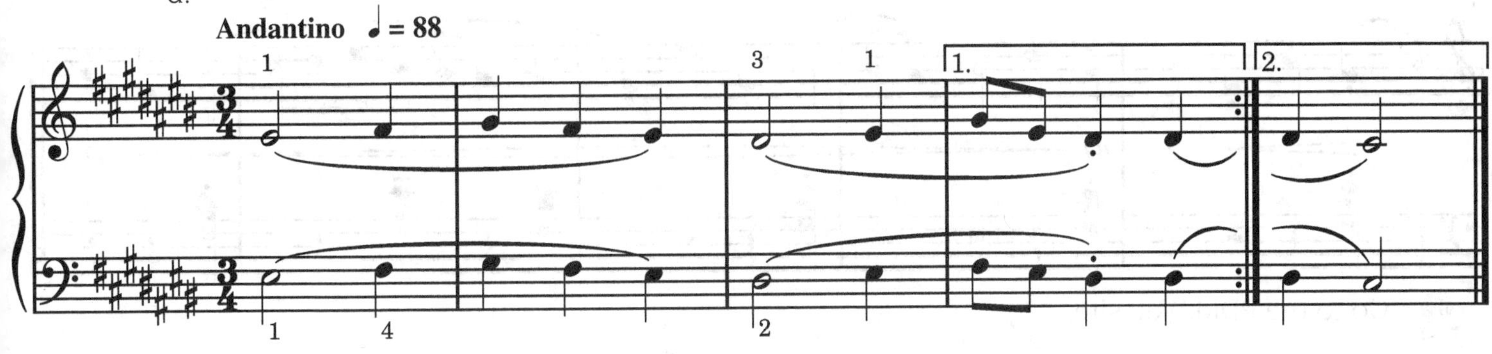

READING

1. Play these closest-position examples. Follow these steps with each item:
   - Notice key signature
   - Determine melodic range
   - Observe melodic contour
   - Quickly analyze LH closest-position chords
   - Notice common tones
   - Determine beginning fingering

a.

b.

c. Challenge example—determine fingering first!

Go to the PDM Web site.

2. Play these black-key-group pieces.

a.

b.

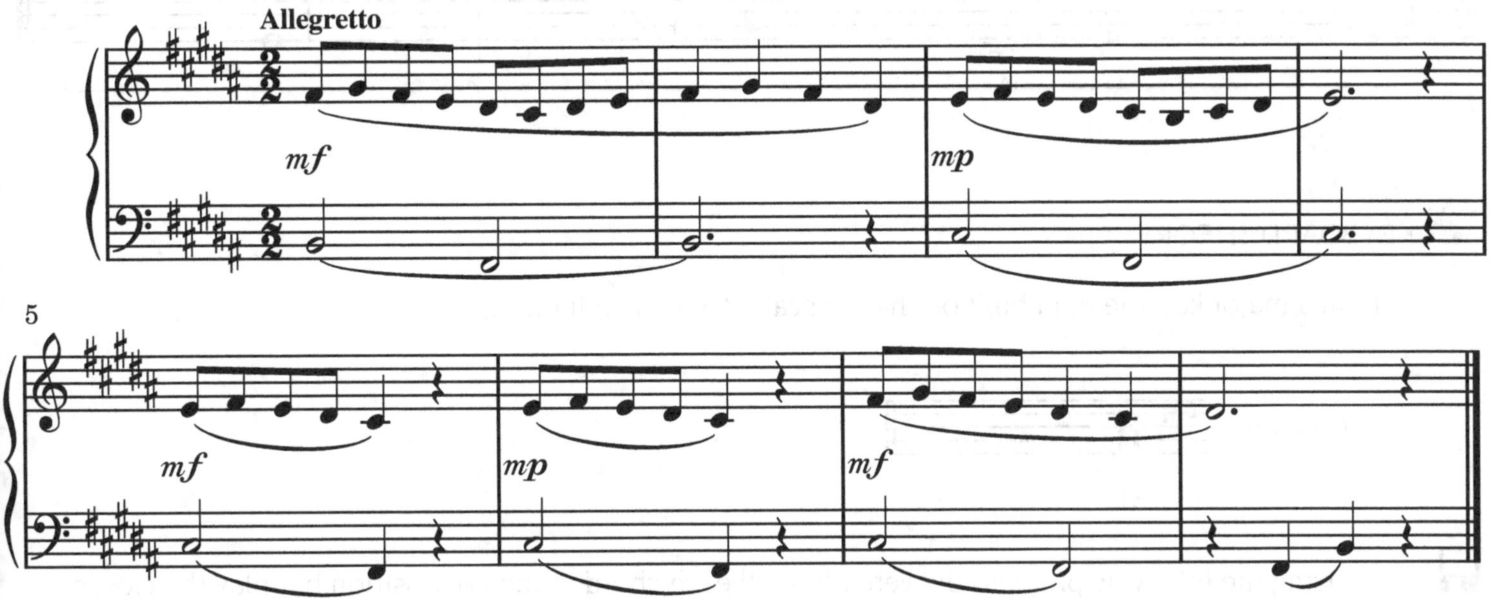

c.

3. Play through with right-hand blocked chords before playing as written.

Prelude

MARTHA HILLEY

KEYBOARD THEORY

1. In a major key, the triad built on the 6th scale degree is minor.

C major 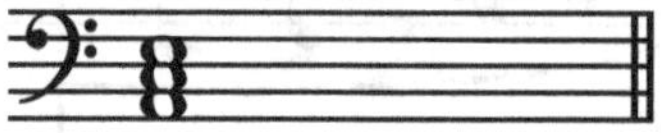

vi

Using the following progression, verbally spell each chord in the *root* position but play the closest position.

C major 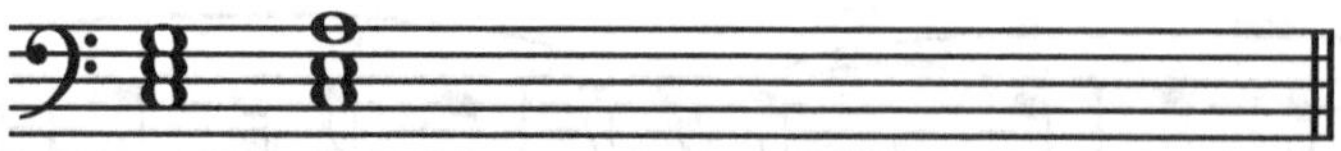

I vi IV ii V V7 I

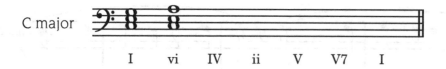

Also spell and play this progression in

D major

G major

A major

2. The most basic harmonic progression in music is that of dominant to tonic (V–I). In most instances, other progressions are elaborations of, and approaches to, this basic progression.

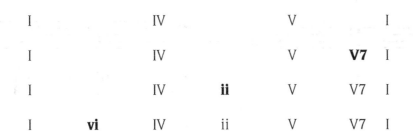

I		IV		V		I
I		IV		V	**V7**	I
I		IV	**ii**	V	V7	I
I	**vi**	IV	ii	V	V7	I

Go to the PDM Web site for more drill on this progression.

There is a secret life among chords. The vi has an affinity for IV; the ii is the stranger that comes in and ultimately strengthens the V–I relationship.

In V versus V7, there is more tension owing to the *tritone* provided by the 7th.

3. In playing four-part harmony, one may use *chorale style* or *keyboard style.*

Chorale style

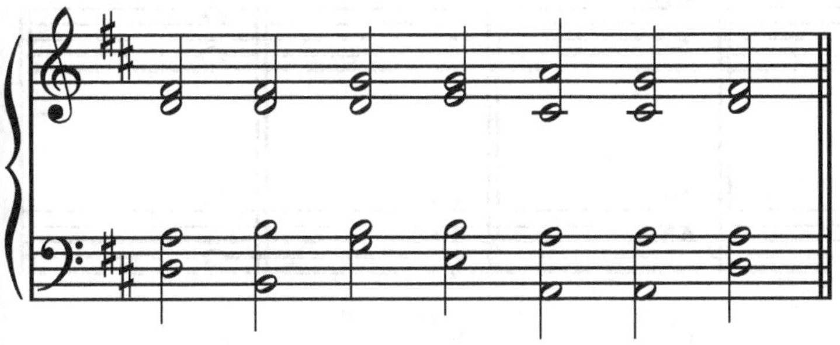

I vi IV ii V V7 I

Keyboard style

I vi IV ii V V7 I

As a general rule to follow, if the dominant 7th contains all four tones, the tonic will not contain a 5th. The reverse is generally true: If the 5th is omitted from the dominant 7th, the tonic resolution will contain all tones of the triad. Both instances allow for proper resolution of the augmented 4th/diminished 5th of the V7.

4. Play through the two examples below. Notice the different starting shape of the right hand. Pay particular attention to the resolution of the tritone in the dominant seventh chord.

*The tritone (F–B) must resolve to E–C, omitting the 5th of the I chord. Notice the soprano and alto voices double on C5.

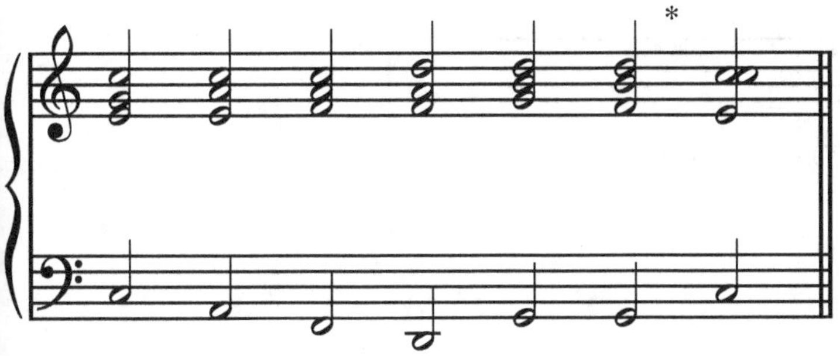

I vi IV ii V V7 I

I vi IV ii V V7 I

5. Inverted chords are nothing more than root position rearranged. Their shapes are most clearly seen through figured-bass designations.

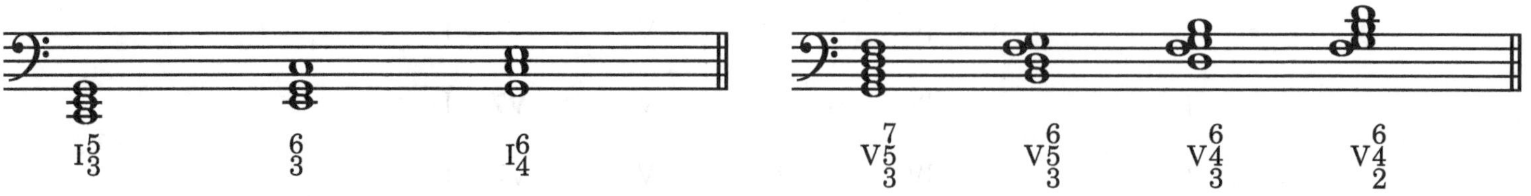

They are usually abbreviated as follows:

I   I6 I^6_4 V7 V^6_5 V^4_3 V^4_2 (V2)

6. All figured-bass designations are built on the *lowest sounding tone* regardless of the octave placement of the other tones.

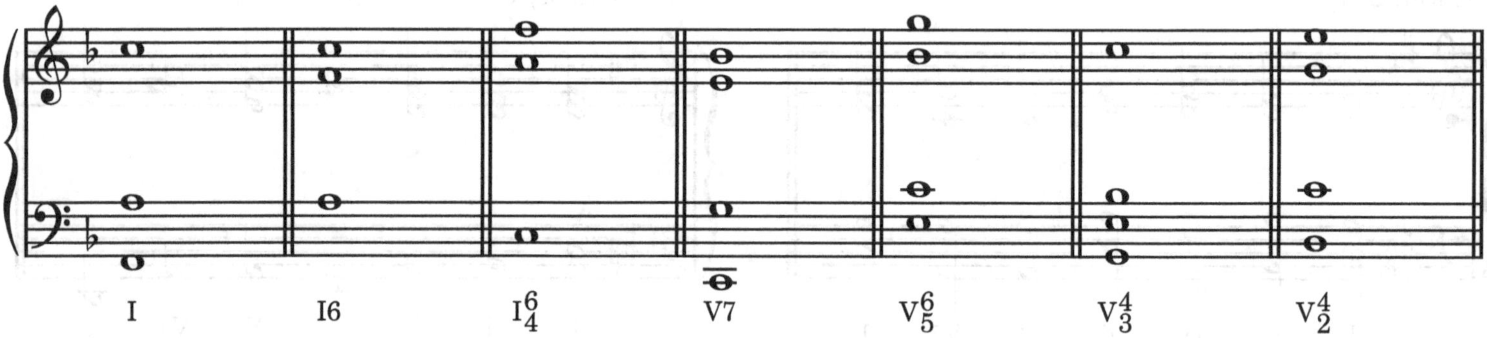

7. Chord inversions also may be designated by letter names (guitar symbols).

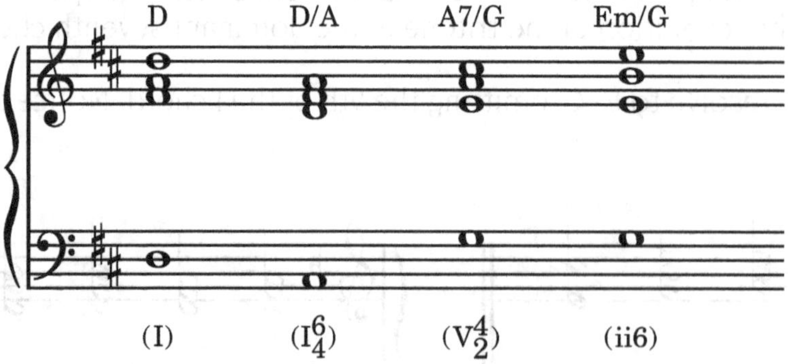

HARMONIZATION

1. Choose from I, V, V7, IV, ii, vi, and iii when harmonizing the following. Accompanying styles have been suggested for most examples.

a. Swiss

b. Closest-position chords; notice the octave placement for the accompaniment.

STEPHEN C. FOSTER
(1826–1864)

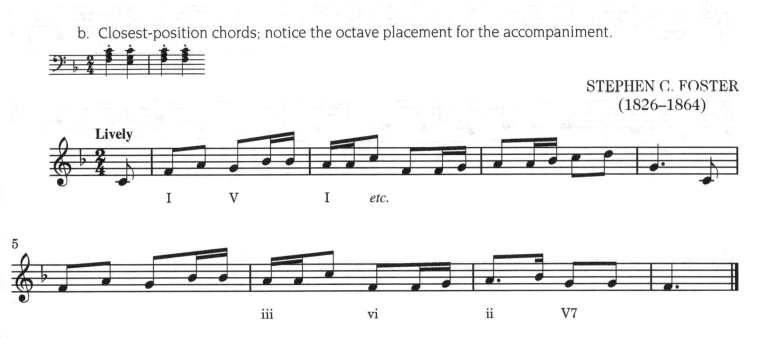

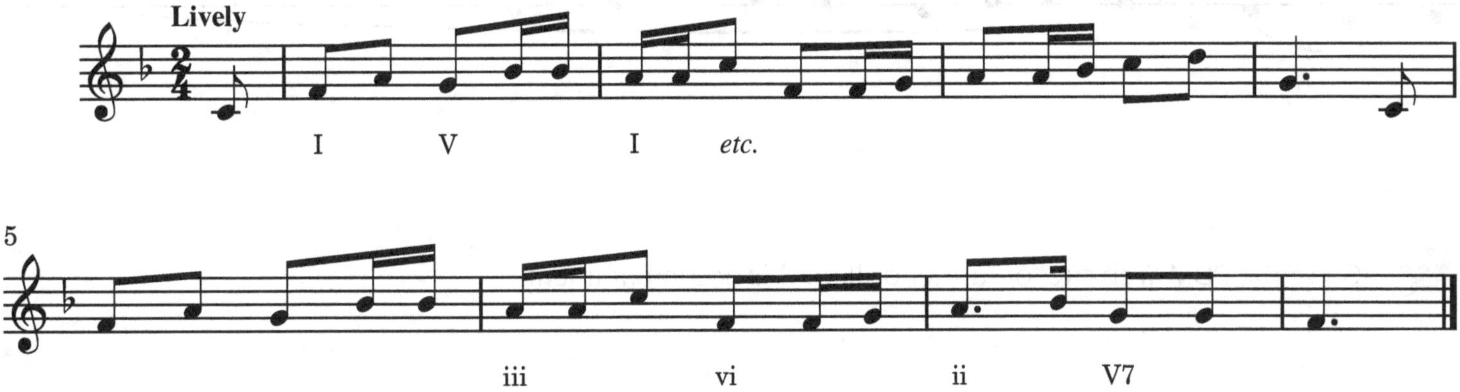

c. Broken chord

d. Two-handed accompaniment

Traditional

Go to the PDM Web site for further drill on this accompaniment.

e. Closest-position chords

f. Two-handed accompaniment

g. Two-handed broken chord

h. Left-hand broken chord

American

Go to the PDM Web site for a tutorial.

i. Use a two-handed accompaniment for *We Wish You a Merry Christmas*.

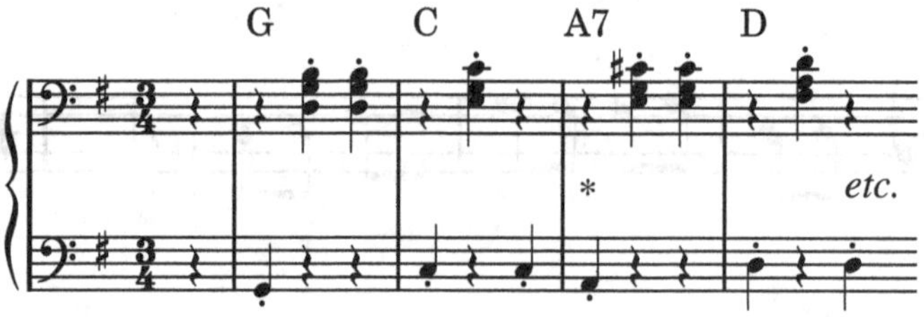

TRANSPOSITION

1. The following examples are to be transposed the interval of a tritone. As before, use the following steps:
   - Determine melodic range
   - Observe melodic contour
   - Analyze the harmonic content
   - Notice common tones
   - Determine beginning fingering
   - Do not play in the original key!

a. Transpose *up* to B♭ major.

b. Transpose *down* to D major.

c. Transpose *up* to G major.

d. Transpose *down* to C major.

RYAN FOGG

e. Transpose *down* to F major.

JACOB HINES

f. Transpose *up* to A major.

ADAM CLARK

Go to the PDM Web site for more examples.

IMPROVISATION

1. Use the following progression to create a right hand *chord-tones-only* melody. Choose from the keys of B-flat or E major. If necessary, refer to the steps in Chapter 4 (p. 98).

4/4 I | vi | IV | I | IV | ii | V | I ||

2. An example of such an improvisation in the key of E major might be:

3. Not a bad melody as melodies go—however, there are ways to add more interest to your improvisation. Go back to your improvised melody and add some *lower neighbor tones*. Be sure to follow good music practice—sequence, repetition, etc. My melody in item 2 might now look like:

4. Now add a simple "root tone" bass line in your left hand. Voila!!! You will notice mine has a slight rhythmic interest added to the roots:

Go to the PDM Web site.

ENSEMBLE

1.

Deck the Halls

Traditional
Arr. Susan Ogilvy

9
1
2
3
4
5
6
14

(This page has been left blank to eliminate a difficult page turn.)

2. If performed on two separate instruments, be careful of overuse of pedal. If played on one instrument, secondo pedals for both parts.

Silent Night

Secondo

FRANZ GRUBER
Arr. Dennis Alexander

Andante moderato

17
21
mp
rit.
(2nd time only)
a tempo
26
31
rit.
8va

Silent Night

Primo

FRANZ GRUBER
Arr. Dennis Alexander

Andante moderato

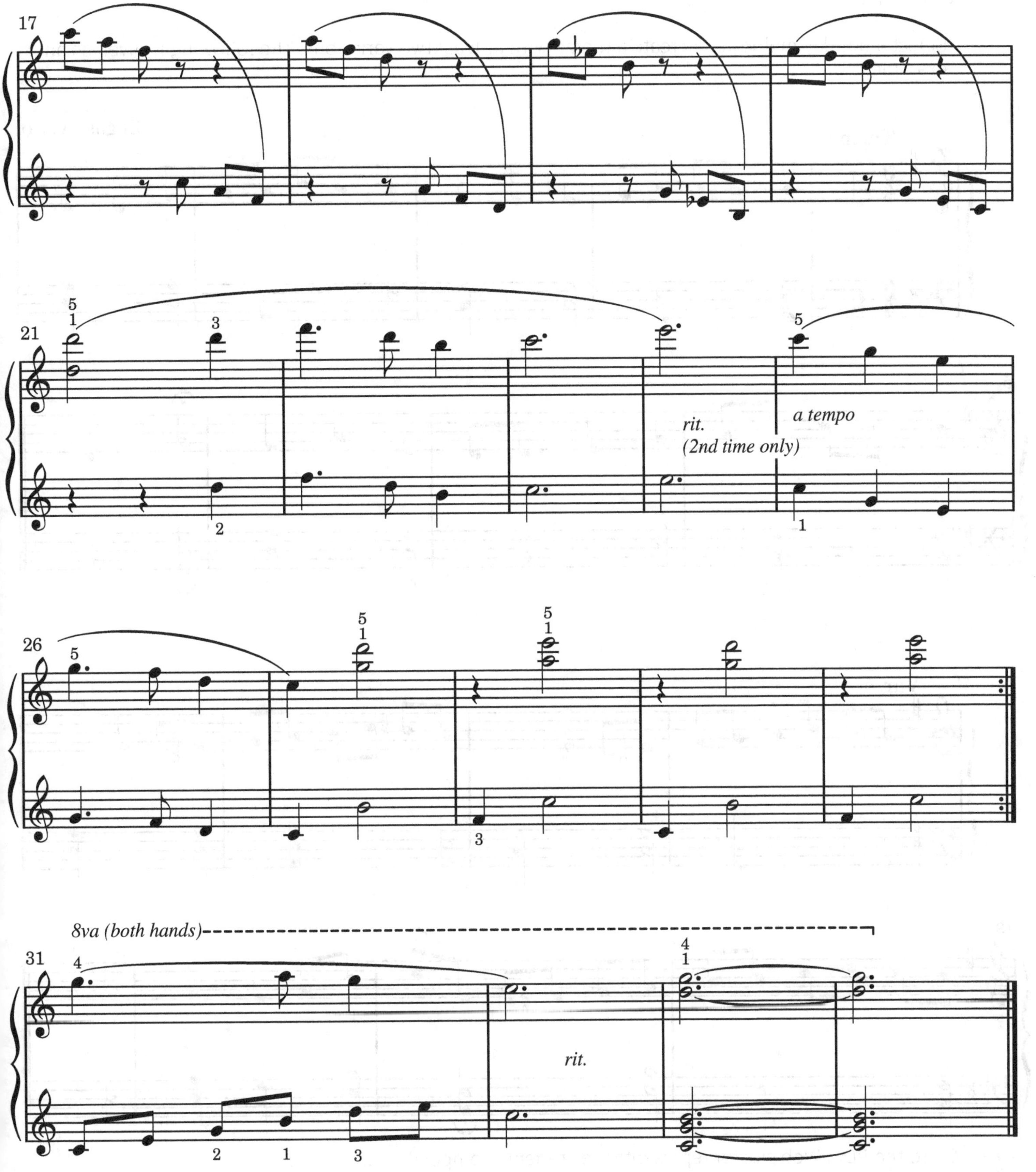
17
21
rit.
(2nd time only)
a tempo
26
8va (both hands)
31
rit.

COMPOSITION

Select a holiday melody and create a theme with at least two variations. The following is given as an example.

Theme **English Carol**

9 **Var. 1**

Go to the PDM Web site for representative students compositions. *etc.*

1. This Israeli holiday song is in a minor key. Take the time to analyze the harmonic content.

Heiveinu Shalom Alaychem

(We Bring You Peace)

Arr. Allan Small

Maoz Tzur

(Rock of Ages)

Traditional Hanukkah Melody
Arranged by Caroline Baxter

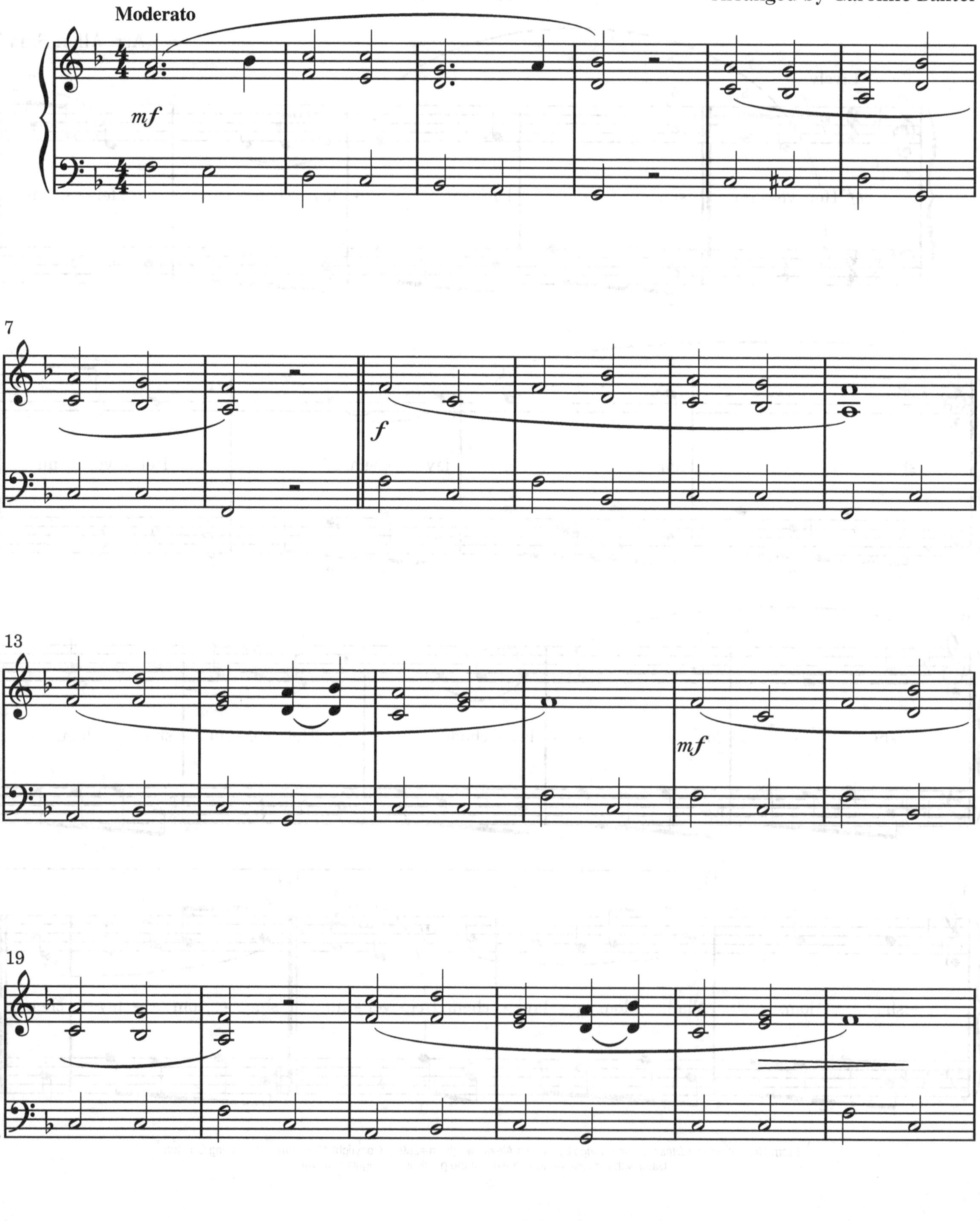

25
mp
31
mf
37
pp
43
decresc.
ppp

3.

The First Noël

The first Noël the angel did say,
Was to certain poor shepherds in fields as they lay;
In fields where they lay keeping their sheep
On a cold winter's night that was so deep.
Noël, Noël, Noël, Noël
Born is the King of Israel.

Arr. Glenda Austin

13
17
21
cresc.
deliberate
f
Lunga
25
a tempo
rit.
mf
a tempo
30
morendo
pp

Scalar Sequences/Modal Patterns/Black-Key-Group Major Scales

EXEMPLARY REPERTOIRE **Prelude, Op. 37, No. 5** Giuseppe Concone

INQUIRY

1. Scan *Prelude*. Observe:

    - scalar sequences
    - clef changes
    - open chord structure: root position and inversion (analysis)
    - chromatic scale

PERFORMANCE

1. Play the following sequence on a flat surface.

♭3 2 ♭3 5 4 ♭3 2 1

2. Play the following sequence on a flat surface.

♭3 2 ♭3 5 4 ♭3 2 1 → 4 ♮3 4 5 4 ♭3 2 1 → ♭3

Repeat several times until position shift is secure.

3. Play the first four measures from the score, repeating the right-hand scalar pattern.

4. A common fingering for the chromatic scale is:

   - white to black—1 to 3
   - white to white—1 to 2

   Play the three-octave chromatic scale from the score.

5. Play all bass tones and chords in rhythm. (Teacher fills in scalar passages.)

6. Look away from the score and "talk it through."

7. Take a deep breath and play as written.

Prelude

GIUSEPPE CONCONE, Op. 37, No. 5
(1801–1861)

TOPICS TO EXPLORE AND DISCUSS

- Giuseppe Concone
- Robert Starer
- Zoltán Kodály

SKILLS AND ACTIVITIES

TECHNIQUE

1. Chromatic exercises

   - Using the principles of chromatic scale fingering stated on page 142, determine a right-hand fingering for the following example.

   - Play with right hand.
   - Determine a left-hand fingering for the same example and play the left hand one octave lower.
   - Play with hands together, paying particular attention to fingerings for natural half steps.

2. Play the following as written with the nondominant hand.

3. Play again. This time fill in the rests by playing C's (when you end a pattern on C) or G's (when you end on G) with the other hand.

4. Swing the exercise by playing the eighth notes in a long-short pattern  and syncopating the fill-in tones.

5. In Chapter 5, you used the black-key-group fingering principle. This principle forms the basis of fingering for the following major scales.

D♭/C♯ G♭/F♯ C♭/B

- Block the D♭ major scale with hands together, two octaves up and down.
  2 blacks–thumbs–3 blacks–thumbs, etc.
- Play the D♭ major scale as individual tones. Keep fingers close to the keys, covering positions as shifts occur.
- Transfer the same principle to the other black-key-group scales and play.

Go to the PDM Web site for additional chromatic scale and black-key-group examples.

READING

1. Plan a fingering before playing.

2. Place fingerings in the score where shifts occur.

3. Think about melodic "turn-arounds" before you play.

Go to the PDM Web site for additional black-key-group reading.

4. What is the tonal center? Observe the key signature. On what mode is this based?

Tune for a Warm Day

LYNN FREEMAN OLSON

5. Would this be considered use of alternating meter or variable meter? Perform at an "up" tempo.

Evens and Odds

ROBERT STARER
(1924–2001)

6. On what tonality is *Medieval Garden* based?

Medieval Garden

SALLY ETTER

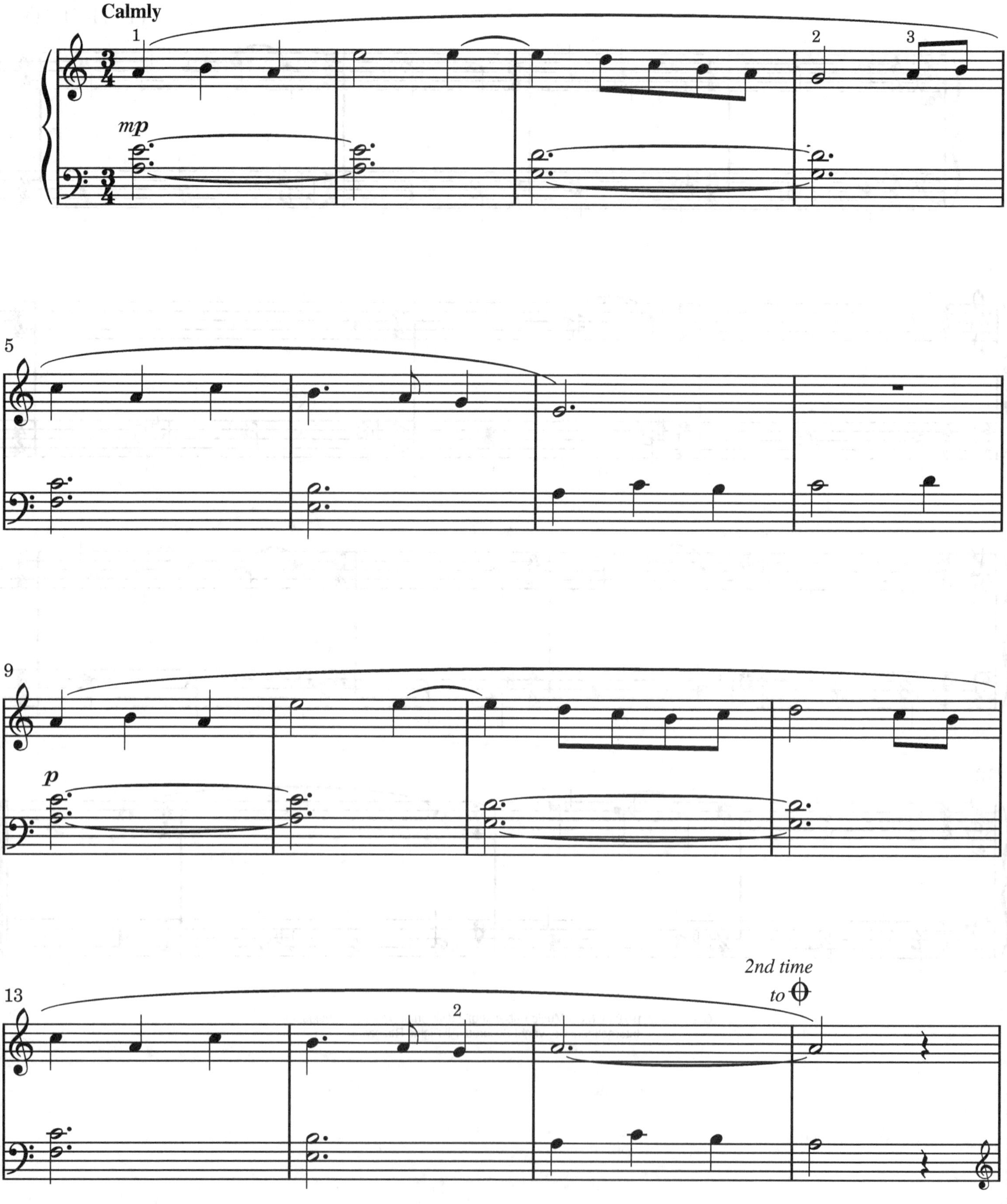

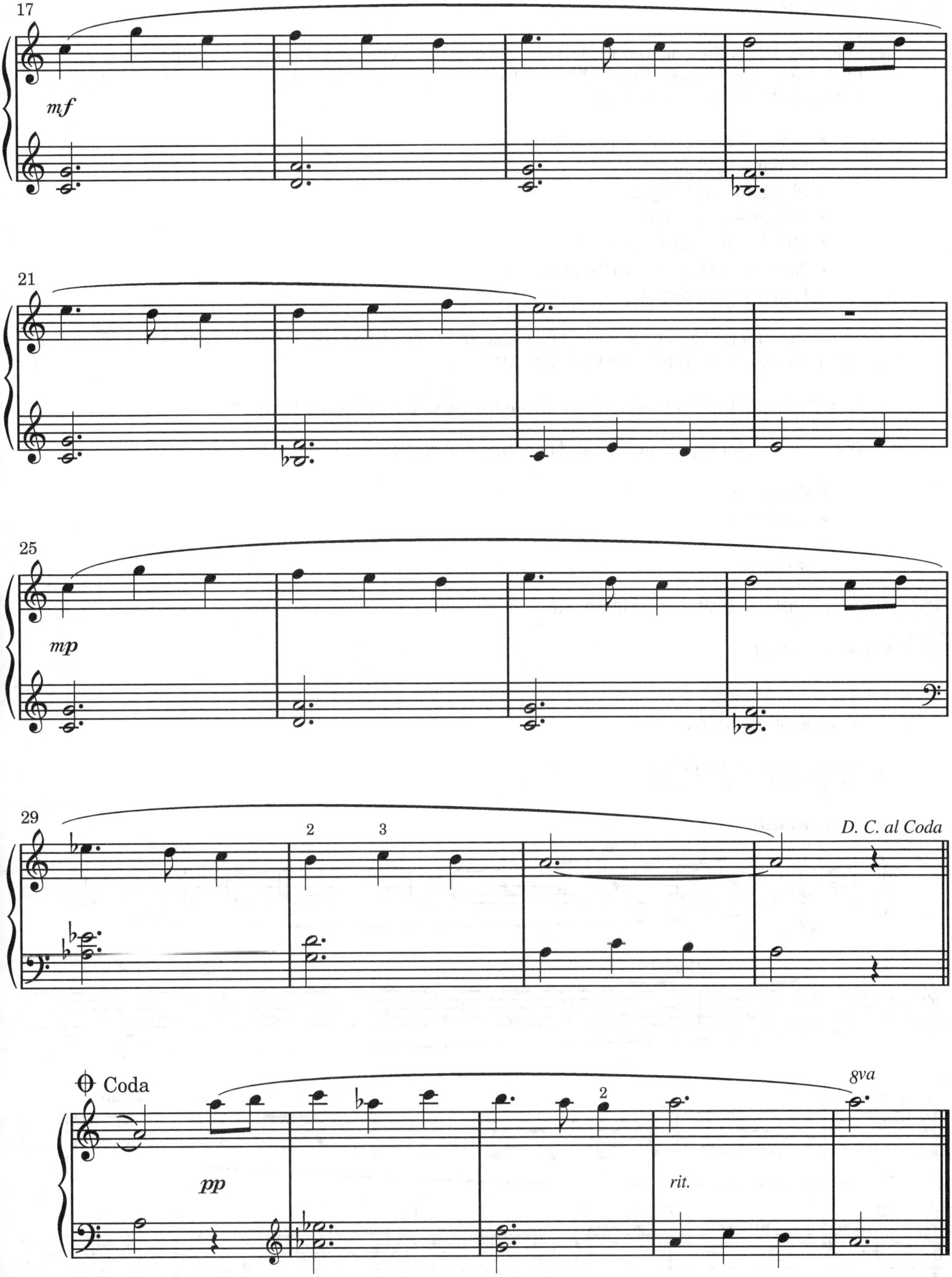
17
mf
21
25
mp
29
2
3
D. C. al Coda
Coda
pp
2
rit.
8va

KEYBOARD THEORY

1. Think the key of D♭ major and play a scale beginning on the 2nd degree and ending on the 2nd degree an octave higher. This is the E♭ *Dorian* mode. We can build seven different modes starting on the seven tones of a major scale:

   - Ionian—1st degree (major scale)
   - Dorian—2nd degree
   - Phrygian—3rd degree
   - Lydian—4th degree
   - Mixolydian—5th degree
   - Aeolian—6th degree (natural minor)
   - Locrian—7th degree

   Think the B major key signature and play a scale beginning on the 2nd scale degree and ending on C♯ an octave above. This is the C♯ Dorian mode.

   Experiment with other modal scales. Always think of the major key signature.

2. Determine major key signatures and fingering before playing:

   - C♯ Ionian
   - C Locrian
   - A♭ Dorian
   - E Lydian

Go to the PDM Web site for additional drill on modes.

HARMONIZATION

1.

   a. Closest-position chords

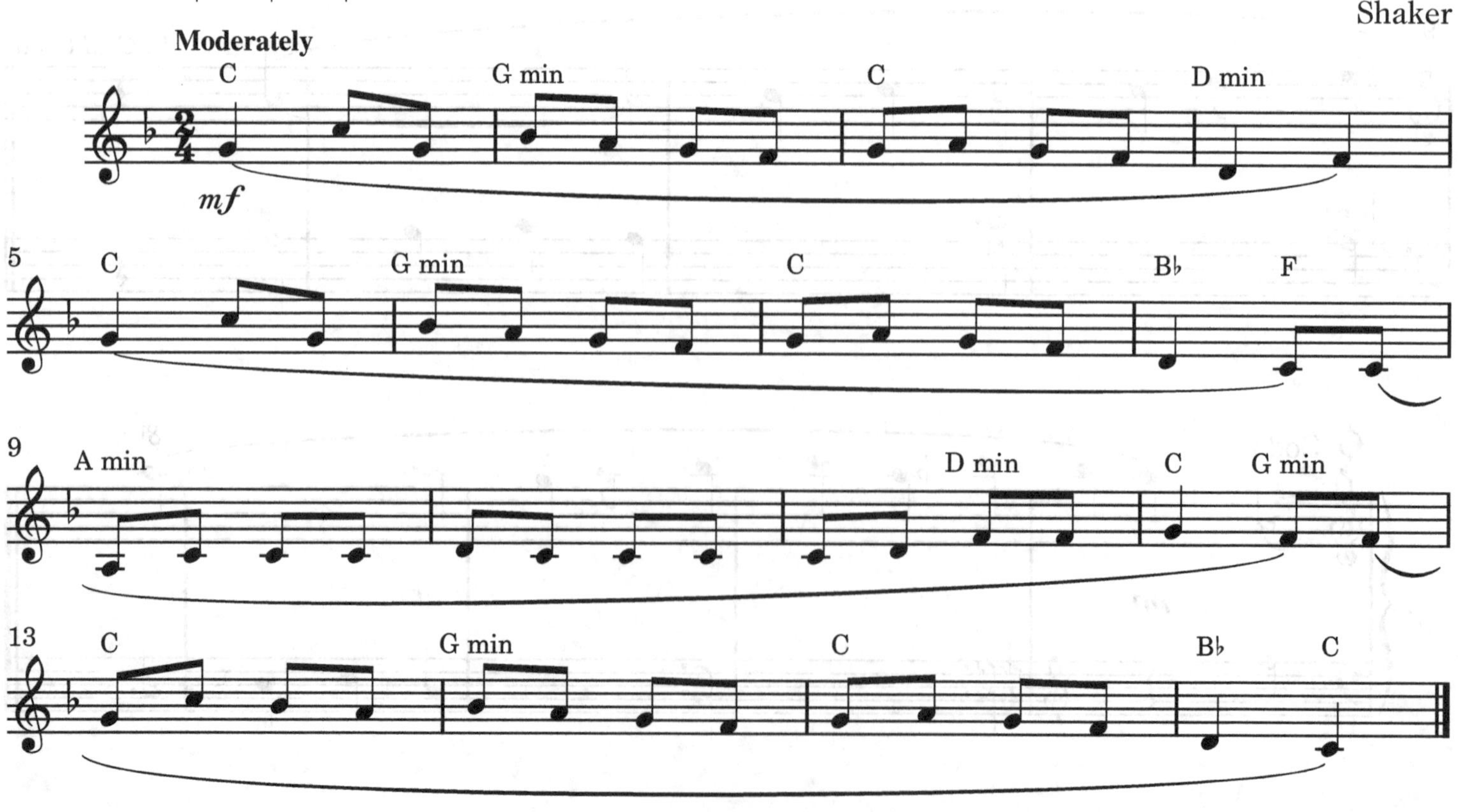

b. Closest-position chords — the syncopated melody is a bit of a challenge.

DANIEL D. EMMETT
(1815–1904)

c. Modified keyboard style (challenge)

Traditional

d. What is the modality? If the tonal center remained as is but the modality changed to Mixolydian, what key signature would you use?

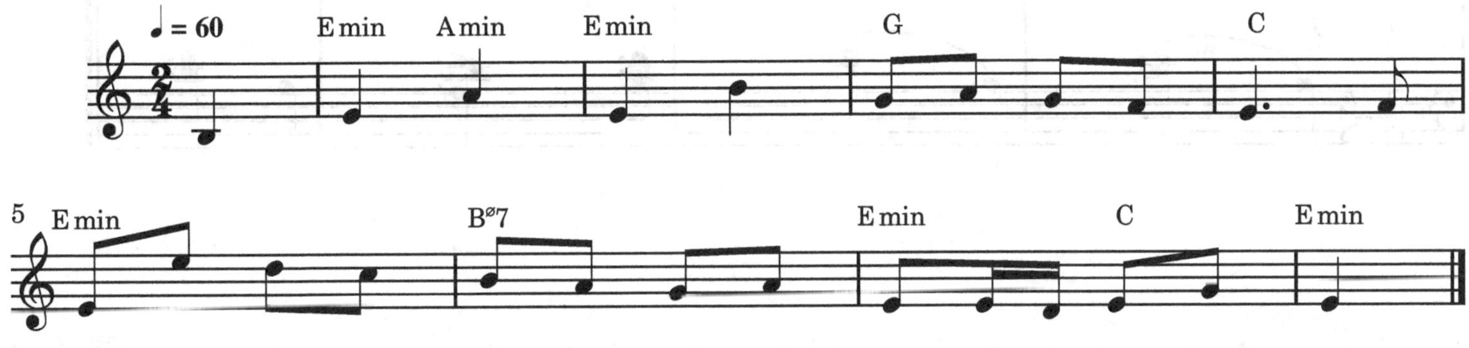

e. Two-handed style.

Vivacetto **French**

Go to the PDM Web site for "original" modal harmonization examples.

TRANSPOSITION

1. The following examples are to be transposed the interval of a tritone. As before, use the following steps:
   - Determine melodic range
   - Observe melodic contour
   - Analyze the harmonic content
   - Notice common tones
   - Determine beginning fingering
   - Do not play in original key!

   a. Transpose *down* to the key of E major.

Liscio

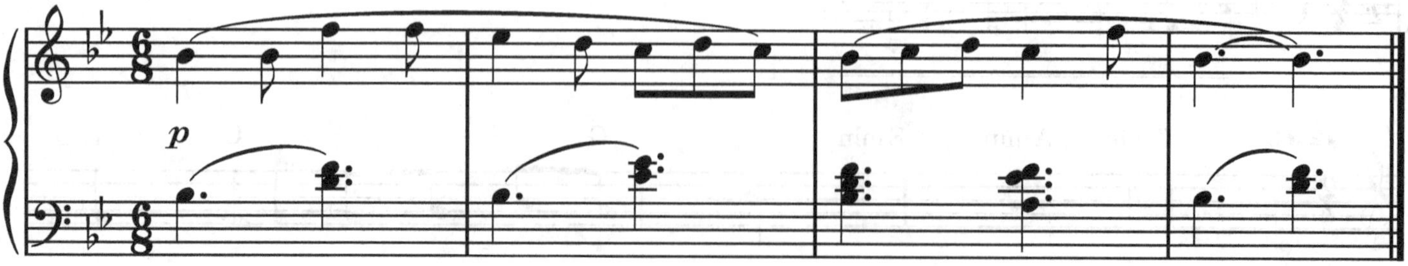

b. Transpose *up* to B♭ major.

c. Transpose *down* to C major.

Go to the PDM Web site for additional tritone transpositions.

2. Transpose *Plaint* so that

- tonic is G
- tonic is D

Do not change mode. What is the signature for each?

Transpose *Plaint* so that

- mode is Dorian
- mode is Lydian

Do not change the tonal center of E. What is the signature for each?

Plaint

LYNN FREEMAN OLSON

3. Transpose *The Chase* to E major and A major.

The Chase

from *First Lessons for the Piano*

CORNELIUS GURLITT, Op. 117, No. 15
(1820–1901)

IMPROVISATION

1. Determine the modal scale for each example and improvise melodically as your "paired partner" plays the ostinato accompaniment. Trade parts and repeat. Share your improvisation in a class performance.

   a. F♯ Dorian

   b. ______________

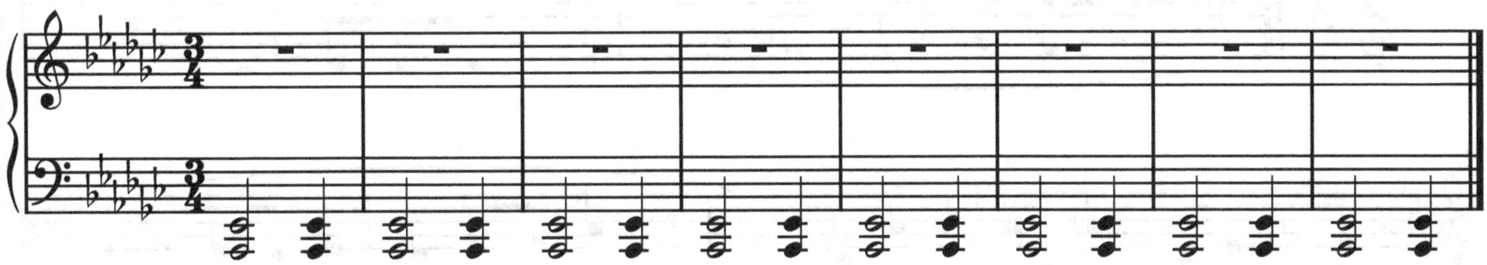

   c. ______________

Go to the PDM Web site for additional modal exercises.

2. Use the following progression to improvise a *chord-tones-only* melody. Choose from the keys of E♭ or A major.

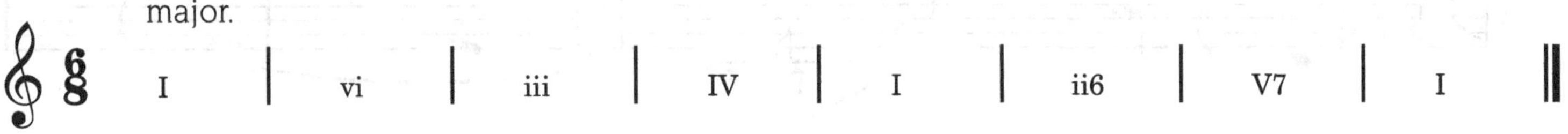

3. An example of such an improvisation might be:

4. Adding some *lower neighbor tones* could give me this:

5. Adding some *upper neighbor tones* could give me this:

6. Rounding it off with some *passing tones* could give me this:

7. Add some type of complementary bass and you've got it!

Go to the PDM Web site for additional improvisation exercises.

ENSEMBLE

1. Listen carefully to have exact coordination of the melodic material in each part. Always be aware of balance.

In the Meadows

ALEXANDER GRETCHANINOV, Op. 99, No. 1
(1864–1956)

2. Play with disk accompaniment.

Shuffle

SUSAN OGILVY

11
1
2
3
4
5
6
cresc.
cresc.
cresc.
cresc.
cresc.
cresc.
16
f
f
f
f
simile
f
f

Go to the PDM Web site for video performance.

(This page has been left blank to avoid a difficult page turn.)

Gondellied

Piano I

FELIX MENDELSSOHN
(1809–1847)
Arranged by Laura Spitzer

12
P.
S.
f
mp
p
18
poco riten.
a tempo
mp cresc.
p cresc.

(Piano I)

36
poco riten.
a tempo
p
P.
S.
cresc.
42
ritard.
pp
dim.

Gondellied

Piano II

FELIX MENDELSSOHN
(1809–1847)
Arranged by Laura Spitzer

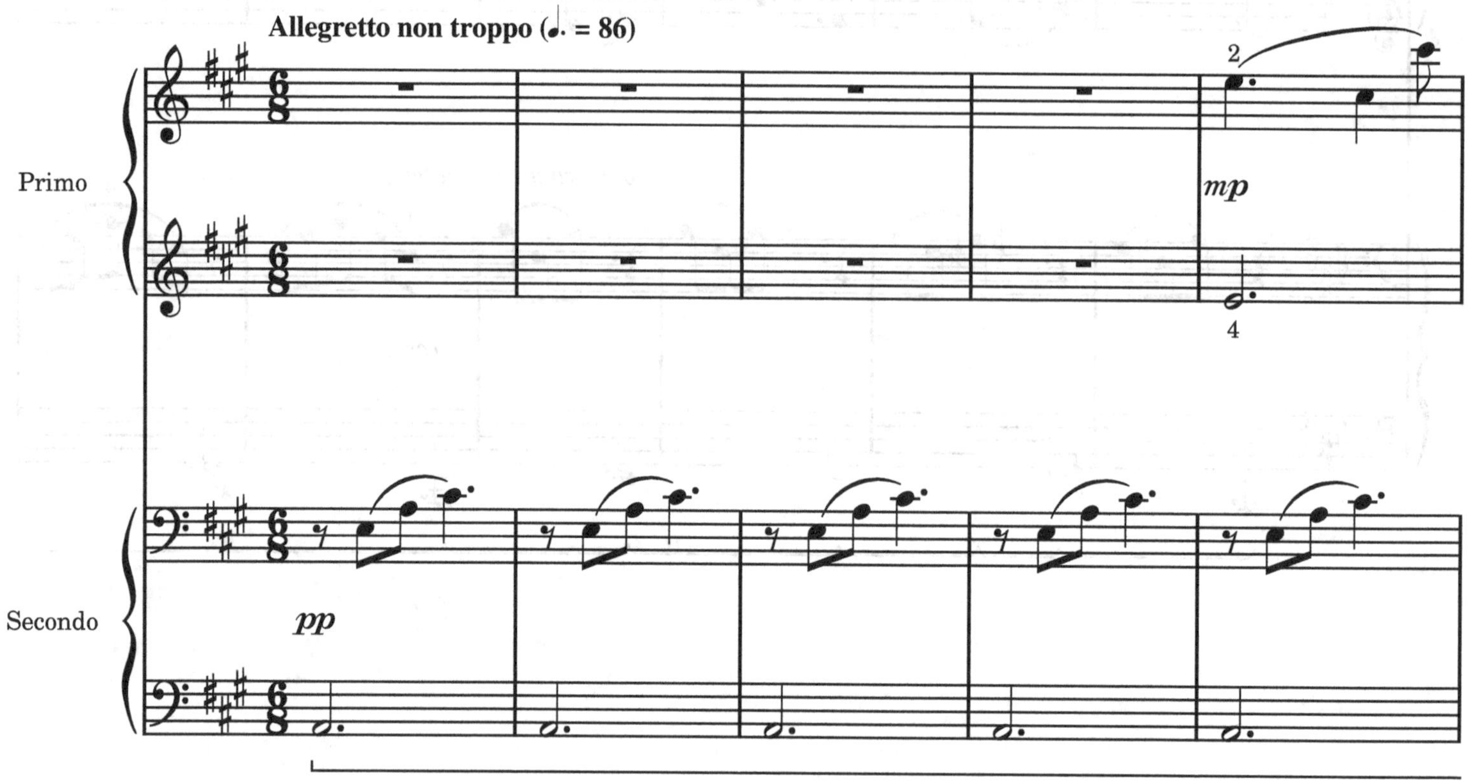

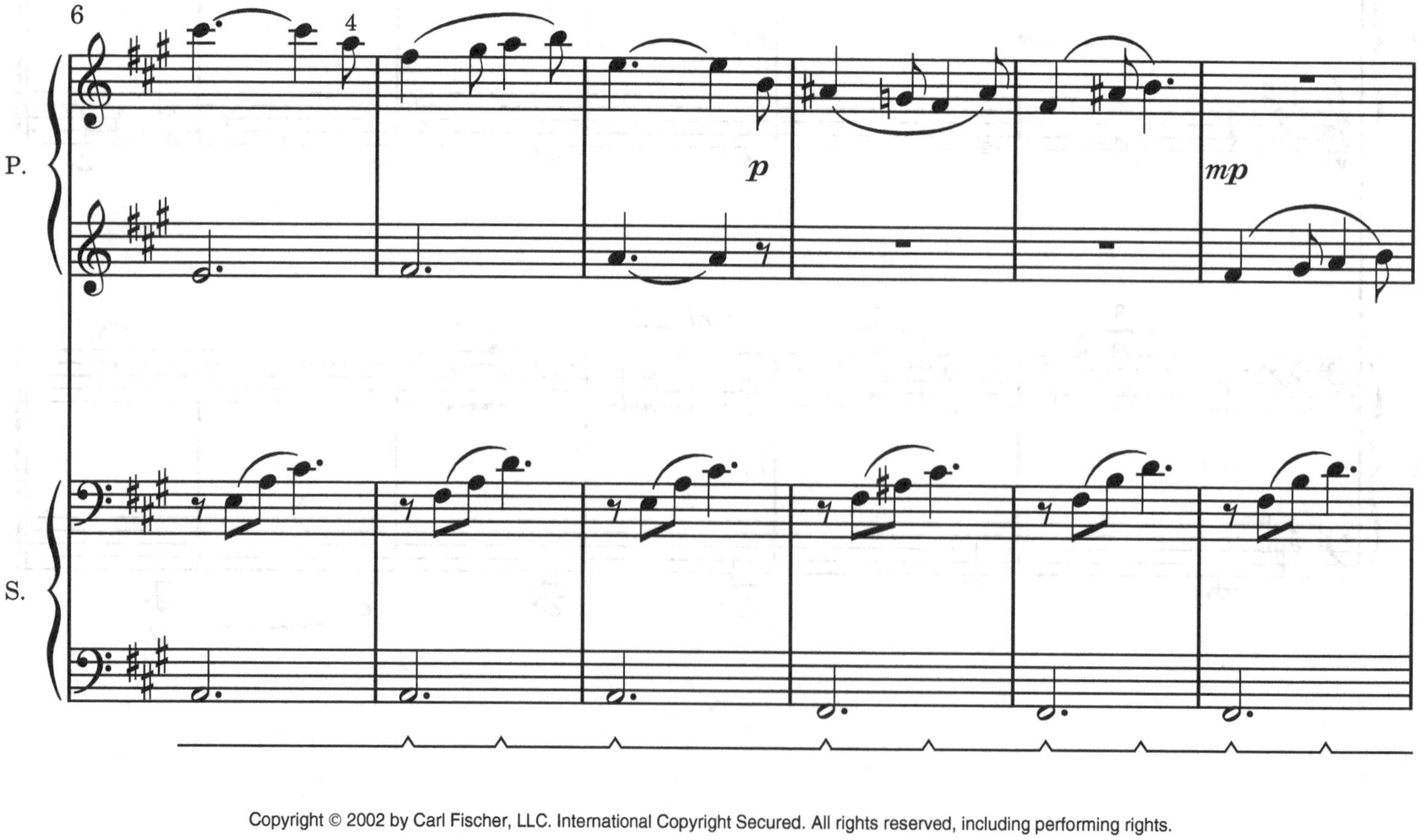

12
P.
mf
mf
S.
mp
p
18
poco riten.
a tempo
P.
mp
p cresc.
poco riten.
a tempo
S.
p cresc.

(Piano II)

36
P.
S.
poco riten.
a tempo
pp
p
cresc.
poco riten.
a tempo
cresc.
42
ritard.
dim.
pp
ritard.
pp

COMPOSITION

Create modal pieces to match the words of these two poems by Ogden Nash.

1. For "The Panther," use C Dorian.

The Panther
The panther is like a leopard,
Except it hasn't been peppered.
Should you behold a panther crouch
Prepare to say Ouch.
Better yet, if called by panther,
Don't anther.

2. For "The Pizza," use a combination of G Lydian and G Locrian.

The Pizza
Look at itsy-bitsy Mitzi!
See her figure slim and ritzy!
She eatsa
Pizza!
Greedy Mitzi!
She no longer itsy-bitsy!

Go to the PDM Web site to see examples of student compositions.

SUBSEQUENT REPERTOIRE

1. Eighth notes remain equal throughout. Is this an example of alternating or variable meter?

Gypsy Melody

ZOLTÁN KODÁLY
(1882–1967)

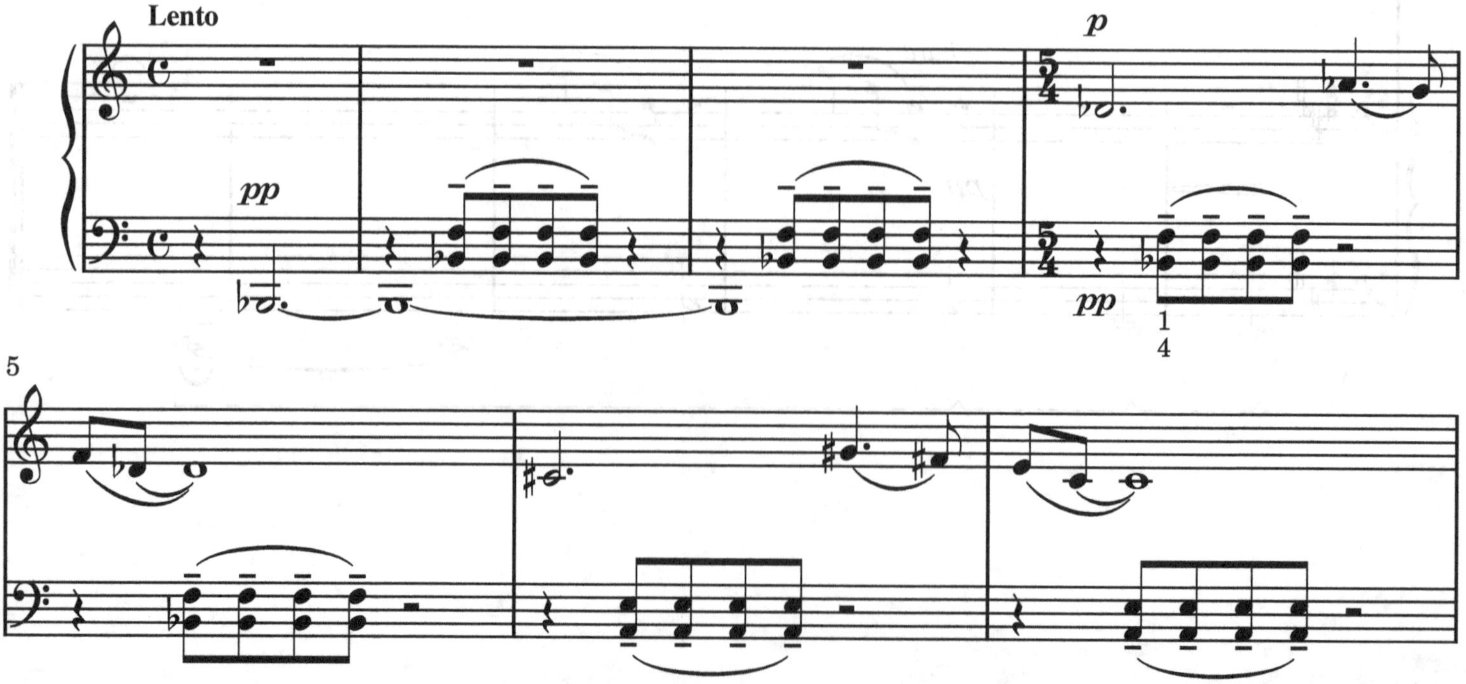

simile
accelerando
cresc.
allargando
Tempo I
più f
sf
dim.
ritard.

2. As a class, discuss the execution of these indicated articulations used throughout the Theme. Also, be aware of double-stemming in the Variation.

Theme and Variation

CORNELIUS GURLITT, Op. 228
(1829–1901)

3. Notice the quality of all triads. What is the meaning of "svegliato"?

Furtive Gestures

LYNN FREEMAN OLSON

White-Key Major Scale Fingerings/Blues Pentascale and the 12-Bar Blues

EXEMPLARY REPERTOIRE **Fuga** Ludwig van Beethoven

INQUIRY

1. Scan *Fuga*. Observe:

   - entrances of the fugue *subject*

     There are several terms that pertain to fugues. Discuss these with your classmates and teacher. The most relevant terms to this particular piece are:

     - subject
     - answer
     - episode
     - stretto
     - contrapuntal

2. Determine a workable fingering. Take the time to pencil in critical fingering shifts where they occur.

PERFORMANCE

1. Work on headsets with a partner. Compare your fingering and make any necessary adjustments. Take turns playing treble and bass clefs. Listen carefully for subject entrances (answers).

Fuga

LUDWIG VAN BEETHOVEN
(1770–1827)

TOPICS TO EXPLORE AND DISCUSS

- Beethoven and his contemporaries
- Origin of the blues/Scat syllables
- Bourrée
- 12-tone row

SKILLS AND ACTIVITIES

TECHNIQUE

1. The following is traditional C major scale fingering (two octaves).

RH	1	2	3	1	2	3	4	1	2	3	1	2	3	4	5
LH	5	4	3	2	1	3	2	1	4	3	2	1	3	2	1

Away from the keyboard on a flat surface, play the scale upward and downward. Say "3"s and "1"s when those fingers play together. Now play on the keyboard, slowly and steadily. This fingering also is used for D major, E major, G major, and A major.

2. Play the following scale exercise. What do you notice about the relationship of RH and LH fingerings?

Play also in the keys of D, E, G, and A major.

3. Review the black-key-group scales.

Go to the PDM Web site for additional drills of white-key major scales.

READING

1. Use traditional scale fingerings.

Moderato

CORNELIUS GURLITT, Op. 117, No. 12
(1829–1901)

2. Study the scalar sequences carefully before you play.

Moderately slow

3. Think about the fingering in measure 3.

4. First practice the scale of A major. Then play *The Chase*.

The Chase

KATHERINE K. BEARD

5. Determine a RH fingering before you play — the LH fingering should be obvious! Also, talk about a possible dynamic scheme and tempo indication.

Etude

LYNN FREEMAN OLSON

Go to the PDM Web site for additional scalar pattern pieces as well as rhythmic reading.

KEYBOARD THEORY

1. The note given is the leading tone in a major key. Play a *keyboard style* cadence pattern, V7–I, with the leading tone and its neighbor tonic in the soprano voice.

Example:

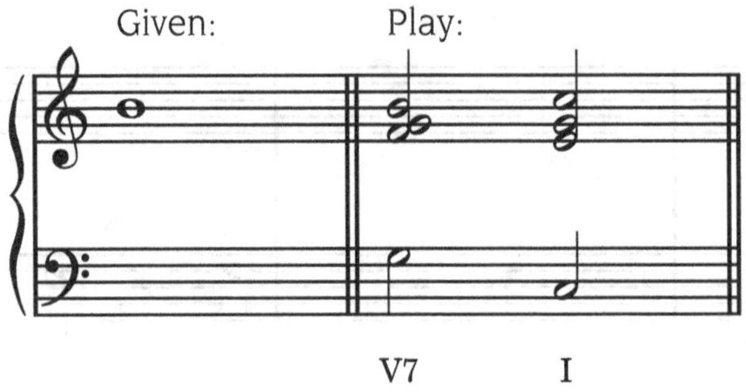

Play each given leading tone. Then, in the next measure, play the V7 to I *keyboard style* cadence as shown above.

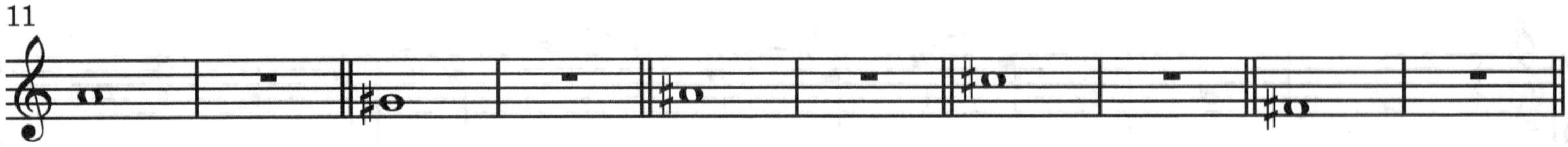

Go to the PDM Web site for tutorial.

2. In which major scales can the following melodic intervals function as written?

Play each scale and sing only the given interval in numerals.

3. The numerals here refer to scale degrees. Complete a major scale upward on the keyboard while singing the degree numbers. Finish with a tonic root-position triad.

Example:

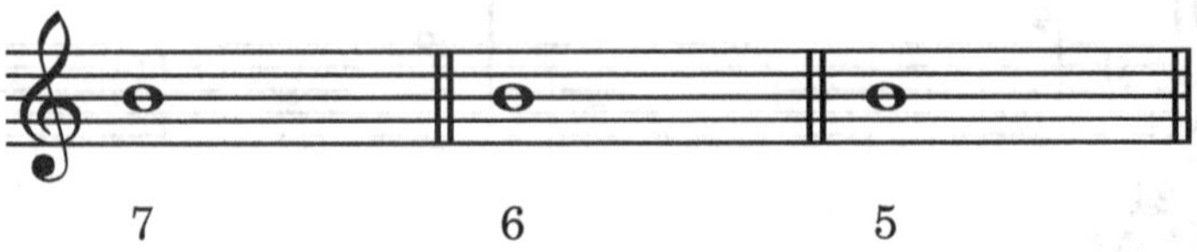

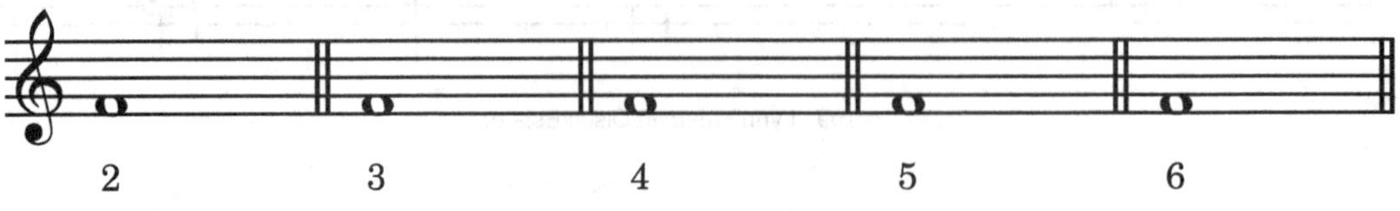

4. Play the following in three major keys using right hand only.

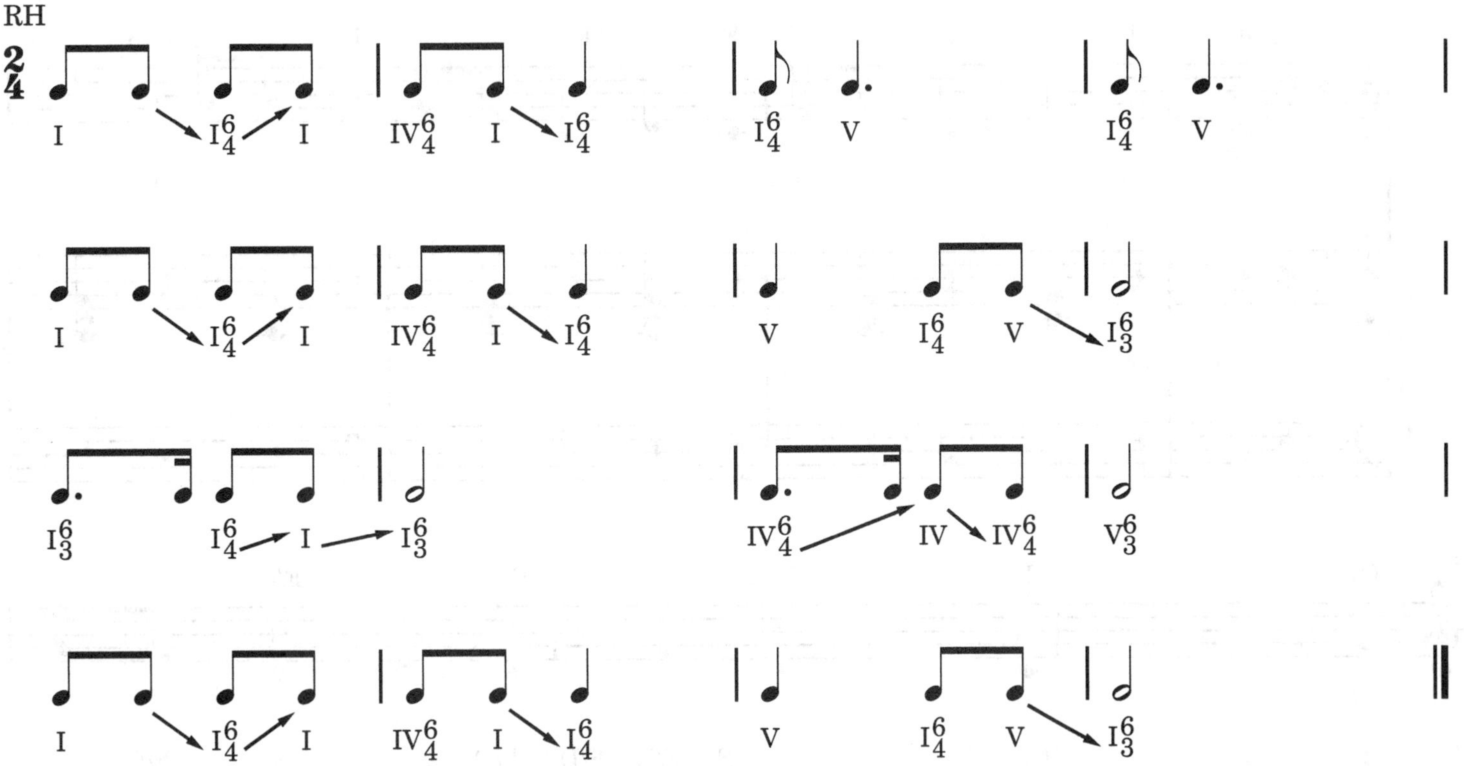

5. For each example, give the key signature and then play the modal scale (decide fingering).

- Phrygian on F
- Locrian on G
- Lydian on D♭
- Dorian on B
- Mixolydian on F♯
- Aeolian on E

HARMONIZATION

1. Complete in the indicated style.

   a. Left-hand broken chord

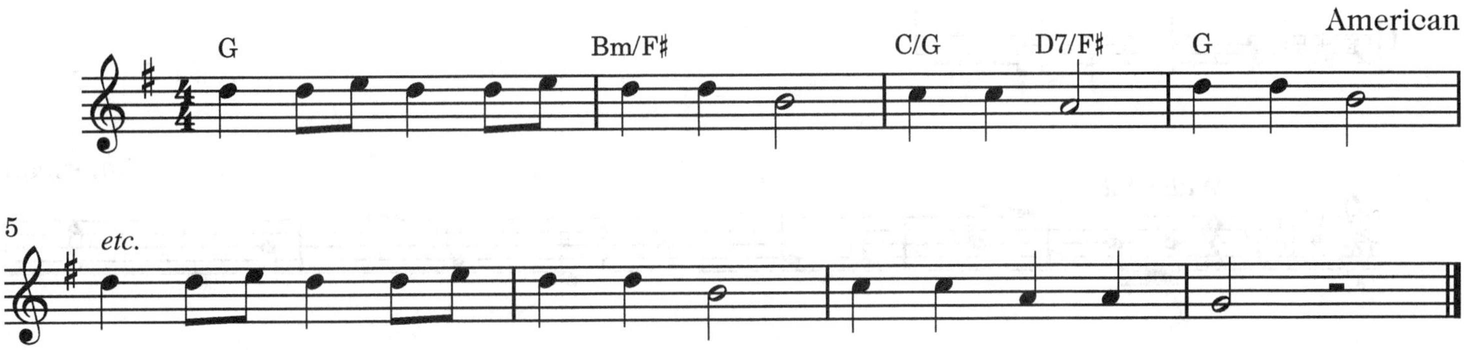

b. Play through first with melody and indicated bass.

American

c. Two-handed "root-chord" pattern

American

d. Two-handed style

American

Go to the PDM Web site for tutorial.

TRANSPOSITION

1. Transpose the Concone *Prelude in B♭* (page 139) to C major. Plan a fingering that will facilitate transposing the same prelude to B major.

2. The following exercises are to be transposed the interval of a tritone. *Follow the steps!*

a. Transpose *up* to G major.

b. Transpose *up* to A major.

c. Transpose *down* to C major.

d. Transpose *down* to D major.

Go to the PDM Web site for additional tritone transposition..

3. Transpose *Tune for a Warm Day* (page 142) to F Aeolian.

IMPROVISATION

1. The blues pentascale is 1, 4, and 5 of a major pentascale with a flat 3 and an added flat 5.

Key of C: C, E♭, F, G♭, G♮

In beginning blues improvisation, this pentascale provides a foolproof vehicle because the melodic tones fit the basic harmonies used.

Play:

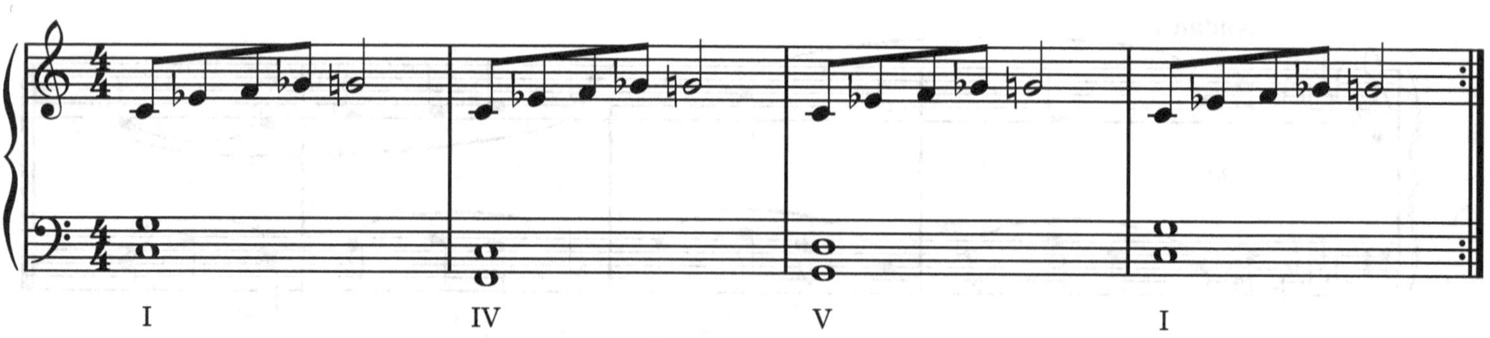

Traditional blues eighths are played with a swing, much the same as *notes inégales*, but with the emphasis on the second note in each pair. Play the preceding example with "swinging eighths."

2. *Scat syllables* offer a natural model for rhythmic ideas in blues improvisation. It makes no difference how inexperienced or technically advanced you are at the keyboard, you should start memorizing these nine rhythms immediately. By practicing scat every day, you will program these rhythms into your subconscious "bank" of rhythmic ideas. With subconscious control, you will find that you can create an infinite number of new rhythms that automatically suit your own musical moment. Next practice scatting and playing these ideas using the F blues pentascale.

3. The following is a possibility for the first four bars of a chorus of 12-bar blues. Notice the repetition in the first three bars. This is a use of "idea, repeat, repeat, and extend" (thank you, Ann Collins!) and will help to give your improvisation some cohesive integrity. The *form* of 12-bar blues is A A B. Listen to most blues tune lyrics and you will hear this form in the words. Give your improvisation the same form both tonally and rhythmically. Write in your choice of rhythms for the remaining eight bars and play a blues melody using the G blues pentascale.

doo BAH doo BAHP
doo BAH doo BAHP
doo BAH doo BAHP BAHP
BAH doo BAH doo BAHP

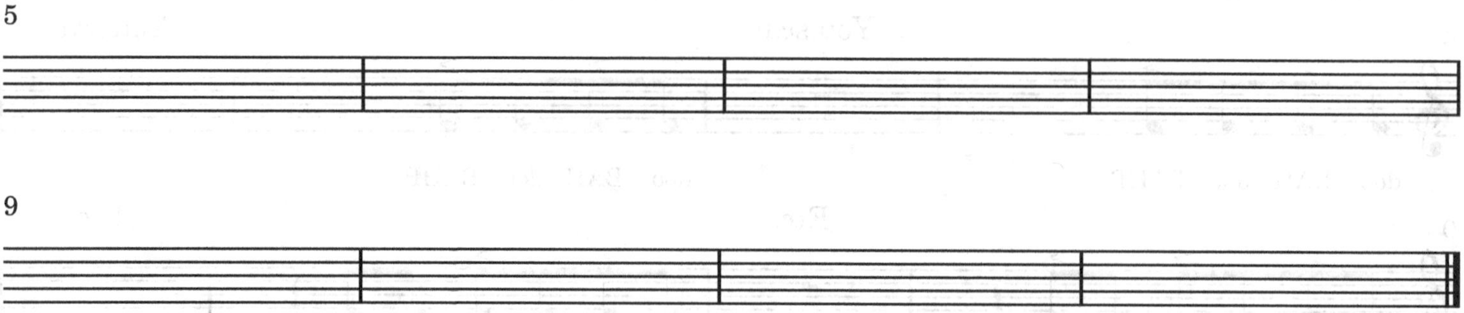
5
9

4. Repeat the pentascale scats, this time adding left-hand roots of triads. Follow this progression:

I	IV	I	I	
IV	IV	I	I	
V	IV	I	I	(V) used as a substitute for the final I when playing two choruses—called a "turn-around"

Go to the PDM Web site for blues backgrounds.

ENSEMBLE

1. Eighth notes are *not* in a swing style.

Solitude

CHRISTOPHER NORTON

Wistfully
Primo
Secondo
p
p

4
7
10
mf
mf

13
f
dim.
dim.
16
poco rit.
mp
mp

(This page has been left blank to eliminate a difficult page turn.)

2. As a challenge, play Parts 4 and 5 as one part.

Hello! Ma Baby

JOSEPH E. HOWARD
Arr. Olson/Ogilvy

9
1
2
3
4
5
6
f
f
13
mf
f
mf
f

17
1
2
3
4
5
6
21
p
mp
p
mp
p
mp

25
1
2
3
4
5
6
mf
cresc.
cresc.
cresc.
mf
29
mf
mf
mf
mf

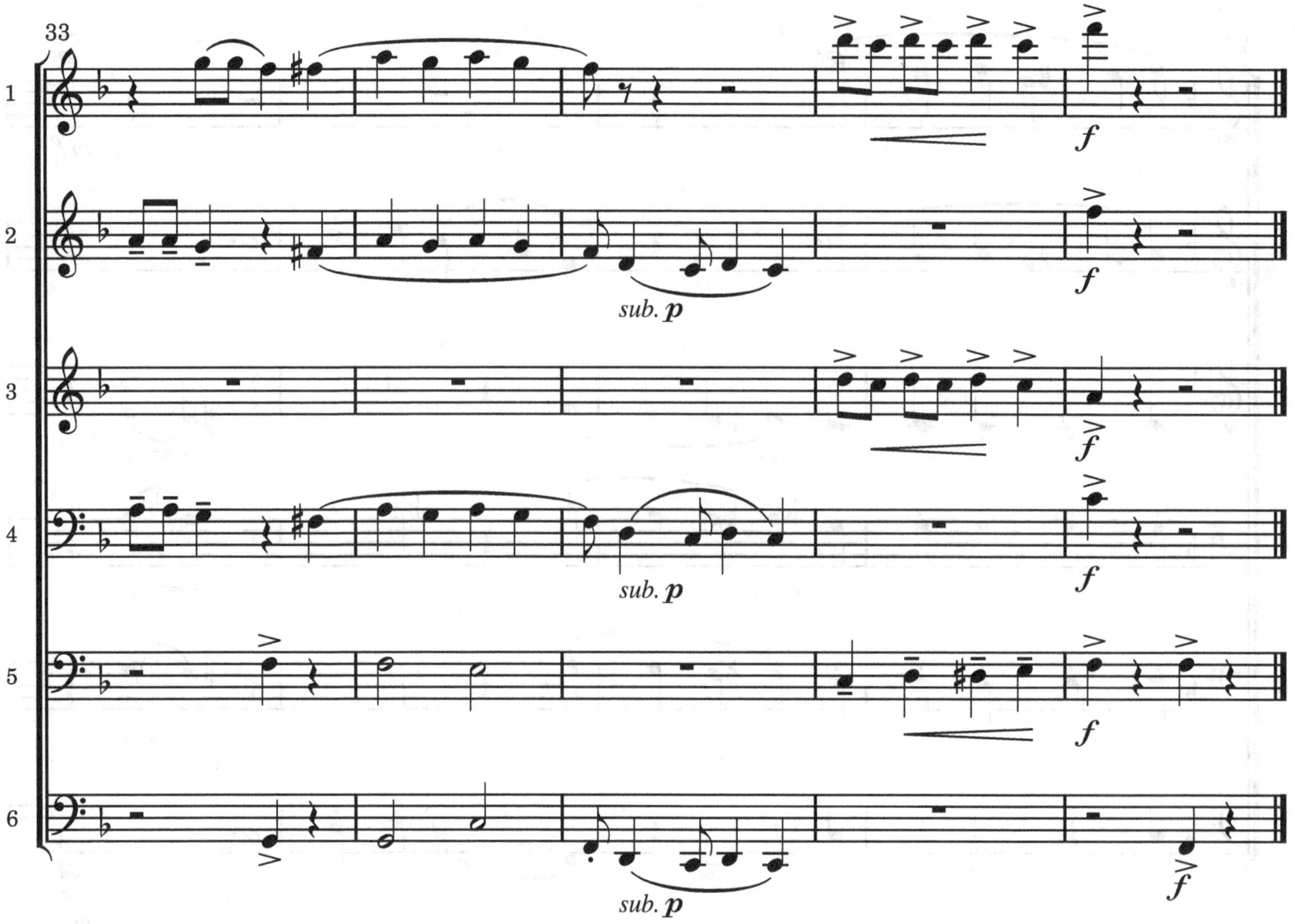

3. Play a total of four times so you get to play each of the parts. Be ready for the turn-arounds.

Bourrée

GEORGE FRIDERIC HANDEL
(1685–1759)
Arr. by Dawn Costello Miller

Go to the PDM Web site for a video performance.

Name ____________________
MUS 1620 Exam 2, Spring 2019 Practice

1. Write the requested chords. Be sure to write in the clef of your choice.

C#o7 Dmaj7 Bb7 Gm7 Dm7(b5) G#7 Bm(maj7) Dm7

2. Fill in the chord grids using techniques we've discussed in class.

7

			A
		A	
	A		
A			

o7

			F#
		F#	
	F#		
F#			

m7

			Db
		Db	
	Db		
Db			

3. Write the progression ii V7 I.
Chords can be in any inversion, in any key, but must use good voice leading.

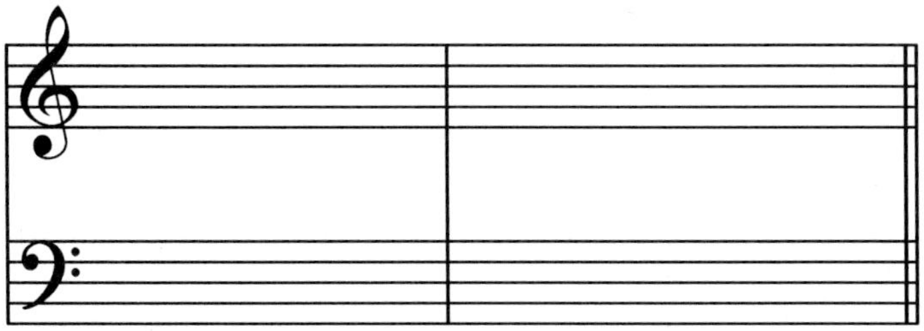

4. Provide a Roman numeral analysis for the following excerpt.
(Be careful with the half notes that sustain into the next chord!)

Dictation Quiz

A. Identify the 7th chords. Maj7, Dom 7, m7, °7, m(maj7)

1. ________
2. ________
3. ________
4. ________
5. ________
6. ________
7. ________
8. ________

B. Rhythmic Dictation

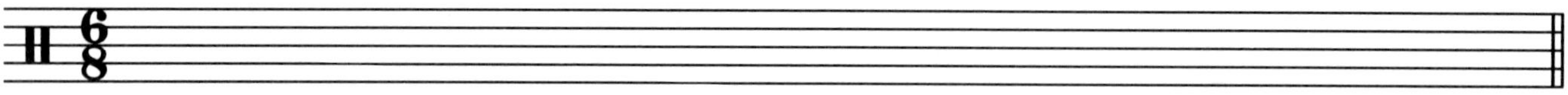

C. Melodic Dictation

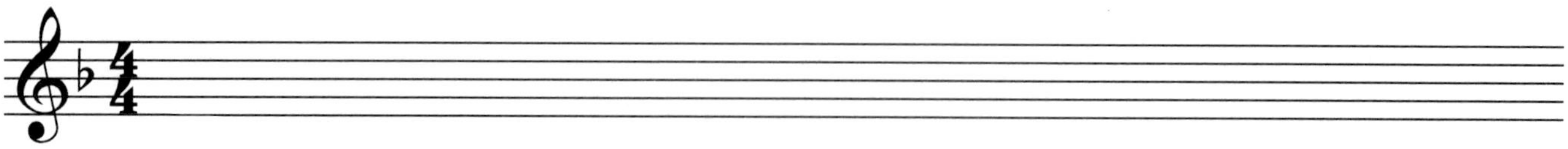

Play through *Dripping Faucet* by Alan Shulman. Compose a light "descriptive miniature."

Dripping Faucet

ALAN SHULMAN

Go to the PDM Web site to see examples of student compositions.

SUBSEQUENT REPERTOIRE

1. Where does a mode first occur? What is the form?

In Row and Mode

from *Shorties*

DAVID FEINBERG

Go to the PDM Web site to see further details about a 12-tone row.

2. Notice the right-hand range of *Musette* by Le Couppey. Block finger groups to provide smooth crossings. Determine a dynamic scheme.

Musette

FELIX LE COUPPEY
(1811–1887)

3. The entire piece is played with only one finger of either hand — a "one-finger, one-foot" prelude.

Finger Painting

LYNN FREEMAN OLSON

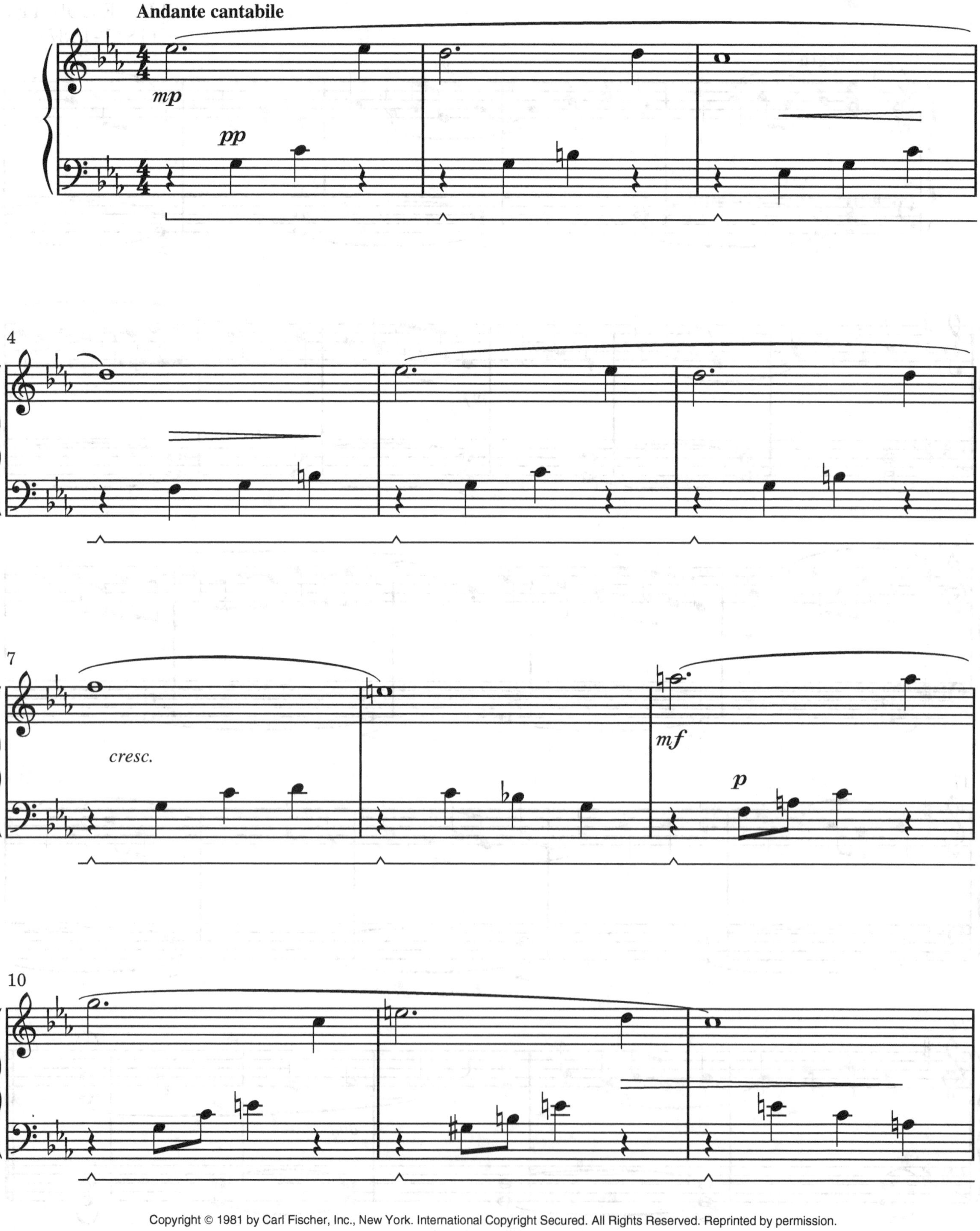

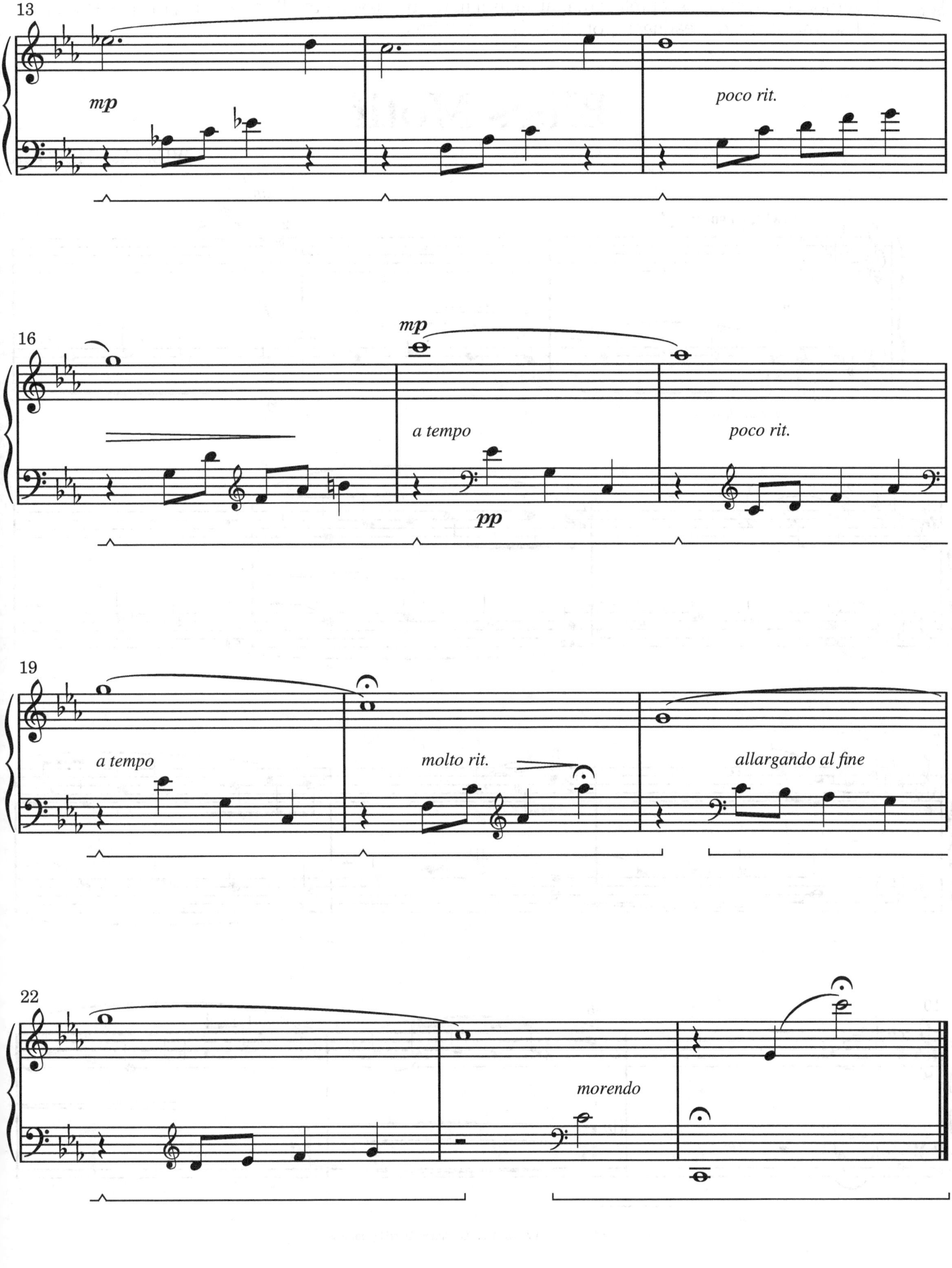
13
mp
poco rit.
16
mp
a tempo
pp
poco rit.
19
a tempo
molto rit.
allargando al fine
22
morendo

4. Although the composer prefers that all eighth notes be played literally as written, the player may take the liberty of treating any or all as ♩♪ (triplet) patterns.

Blues Motif

WILLIAM GILLOCK

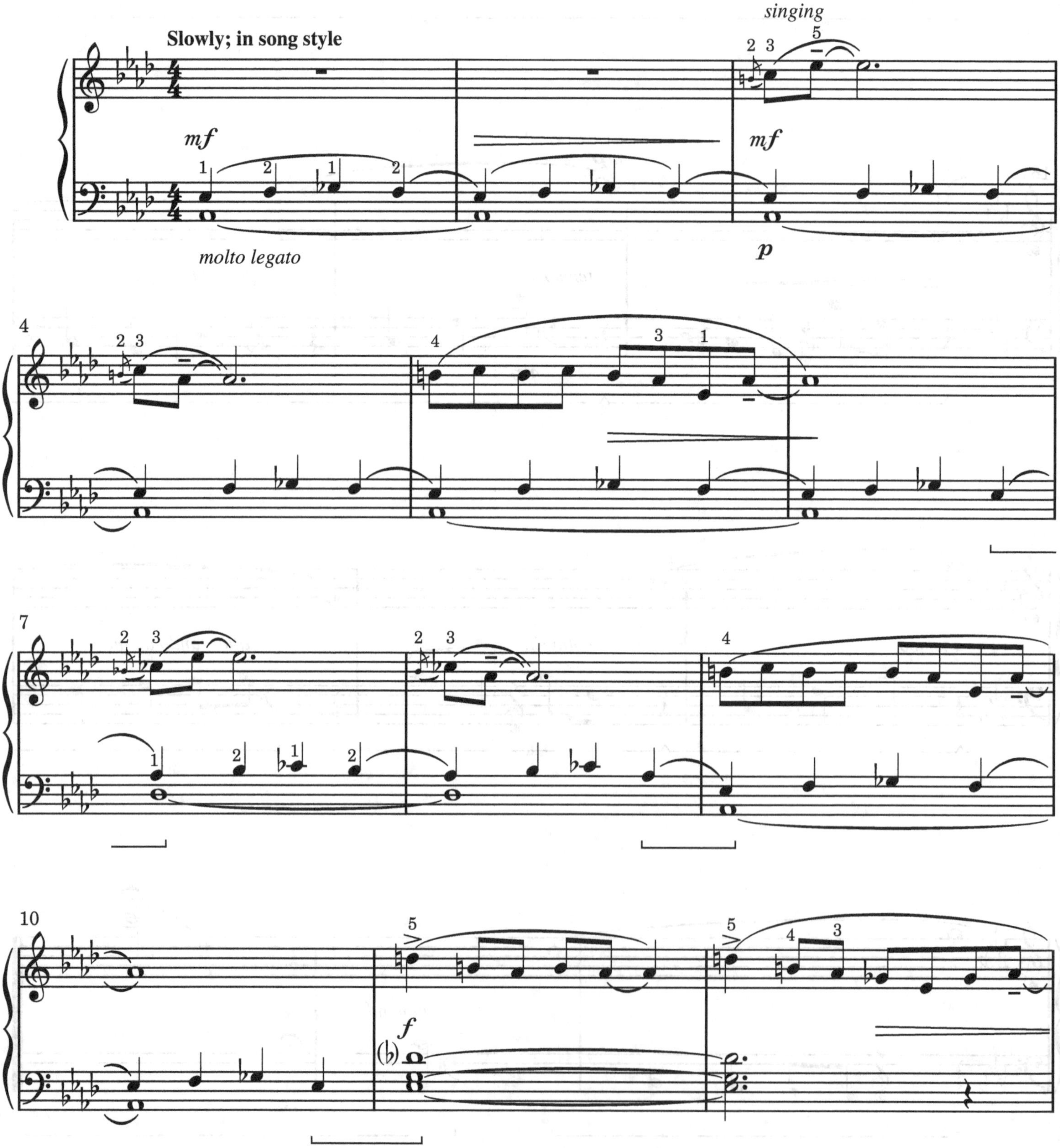

retarding
RH
LH

White-Key Minor Scale Fingerings/Diatonic Harmonies in Minor

EXEMPLARY REPERTOIRE **Little Invention in C Minor** Katherine Beard

INQUIRY

1. Scan *Little Invention in C Minor*. Observe:

   - all entrances of the main theme
   - use of stretto
   - change in harmonic structure
   - suggested finger shifts

PERFORMANCE

1. Play through once hands separately as you carefully identify all entrances of the main theme and note those in your score.

2. Isolate for practice measures that have expansion and contraction of the hand (i.e., 8–9, 11–12, etc.).

(This page has been left blank to avoid a difficult page turn.)

Little Invention in C Minor

KATHERINE BEARD

21
f
mf
25
mf
p
29
p
33
37
p

TOPICS TO EXPLORE AND DISCUSS

- Parallel minor versus relative minor
- Mazurka
- Passamezzo

SKILLS AND ACTIVITIES

TECHNIQUE

1. Indicated mordents begin on the beat.

2. Plan the fingering shifts before you begin.

Study in E

MARTHA HILLEY

3. Play the C major scale upward and stop on A. Now *flat* the A and continue with the same fingering combinations you used for the C major scale. Study the fingerings below and compare them to the fingering sequence on page 172. You already know this combination!

READING

1. Articulation, fingering, and a "sense of key" are critical for success.

a.

JACOB HINES

b.

c.

d.

RYAN FOGG

e.

ADAM CLARK

f.

JACOB HINES

2. What form of the minor is used?

BÉLA BARTÓK
(1881–1945)
Sz. 52

3. Discuss harmonies before playing.

Etude

LUDVIG SCHYTTE
(1848–1909)

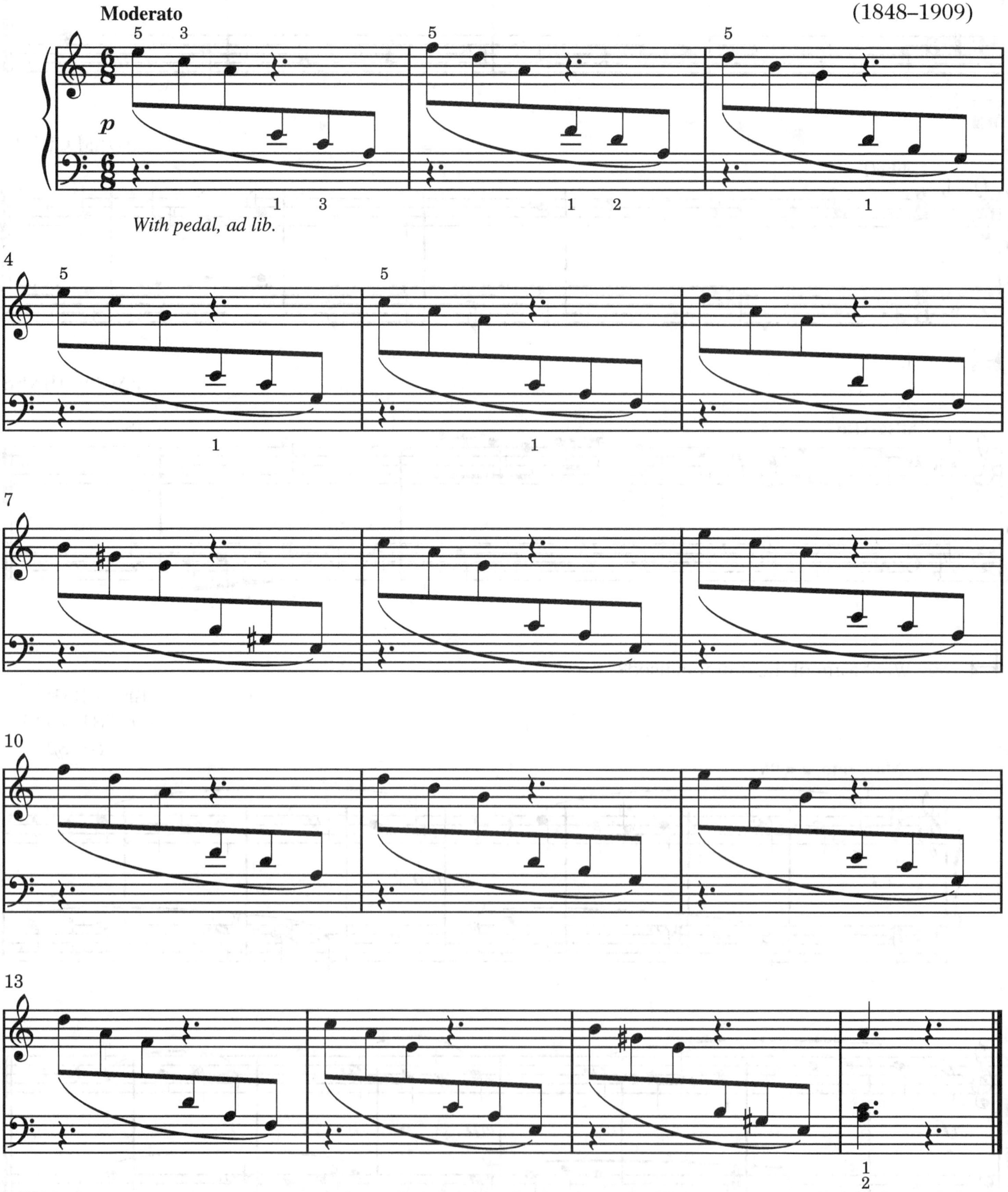

4. Determine the quality of scalar passages and the use of sequence before playing.

Etude in A Minor

CORNELIUS GURLITT
(1820–1901)

Allegretto

Go to the PDM Web site for additional minor key reading.

1. Play triads on each tone of the major scale as indicated.

Root on top:

Root on middle:

2. Play this triad sequence with the root on top. Play in all major keys except B♭ and E♭.

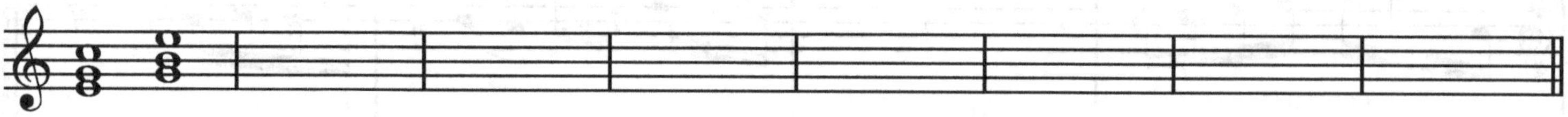

Play again, doubling the root in the bass.

Play the same triad sequence with the root in the middle. Repeat with a left-hand doubled root.

3. All minor scales are derived from their relative majors and use the same key signatures. The natural minor scale can be observed within the major scale pattern, beginning on the 6th scale degree.

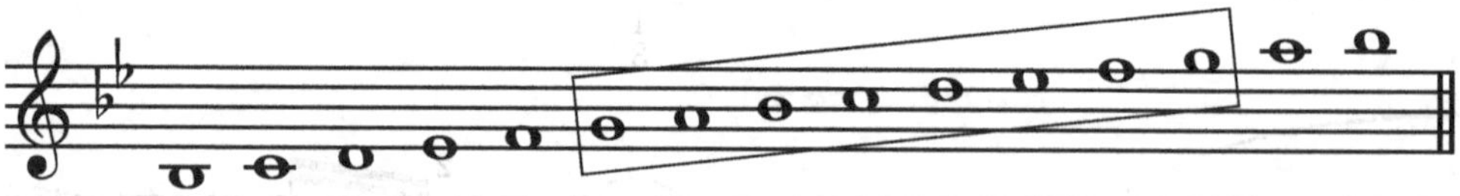

There are two commonly used altered forms of the natural minor scale. The *harmonic* form is the result of the major quality of the dominant 7th chord and therefore uses an accidental to produce a leading tone that is a half step below tonic.

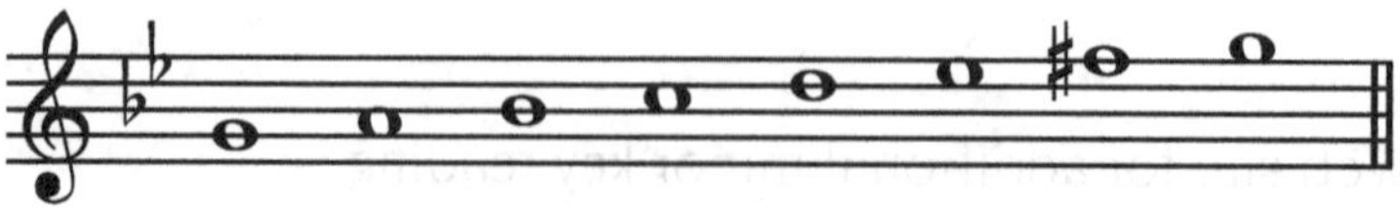

The *melodic* form uses an additional accidental in the ascending pattern to avoid the awkward augmented 2nd.

When descending, melodic returns to the natural form of the minor.

4. The following white-key minor scales use the same fingering as their parallel major scales. Refer to the fingerings used on page 172.

   - C natural, harmonic, and melodic minor
   - D natural, harmonic, and melodic minor
   - E natural, harmonic, and melodic minor
   - G natural, harmonic, and melodic minor
   - A natural, harmonic, and melodic minor

   Play these minor scales two octaves, up and down (natural, harmonic, melodic) with no break between keys.

5. *Diatonic triads in minor*. Play the following triads in D minor.

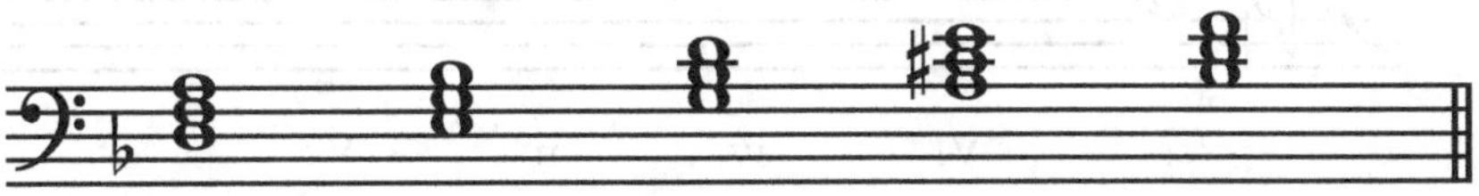

Using the following harmonic progression, verbally *spell* each chord in root position but *play* the closest position possible.

a. G minor

Also in
D minor
A minor

b. E minor

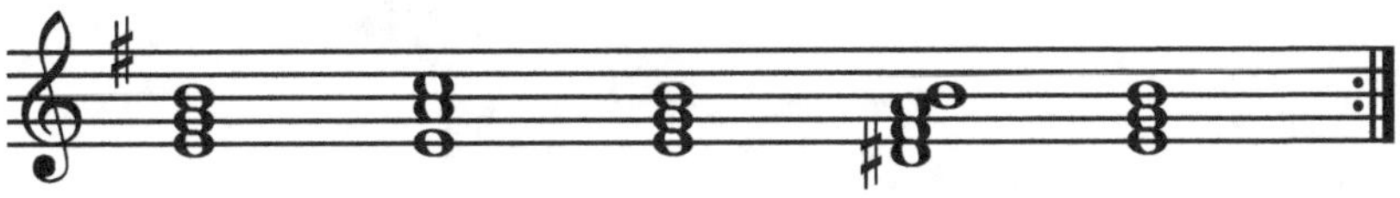

Also in
C minor
F minor

c. F♯ minor (Challenge)

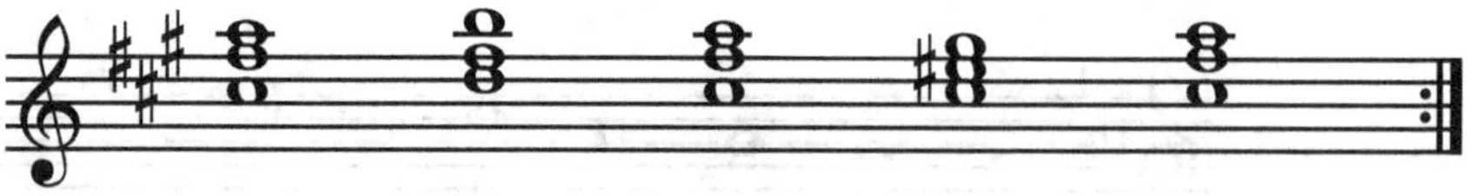

i iv i V i

Also in
B minor
C♯ minor

Go to the PDM Web site for additional drill on items 5a, 5b, and 5c.

6. Using the following progression, verbally spell each chord in root position but play the closest position.

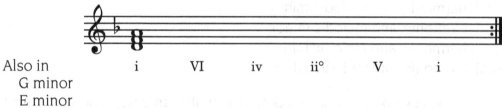

a. D minor

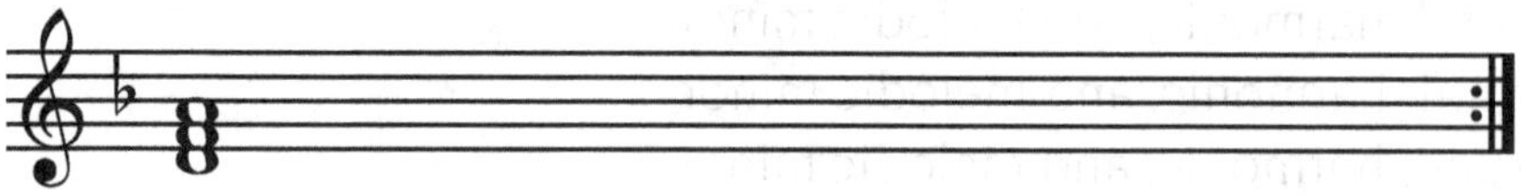

i VI iv ii° V i

Also in
G minor
E minor

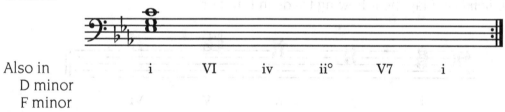

b. C minor

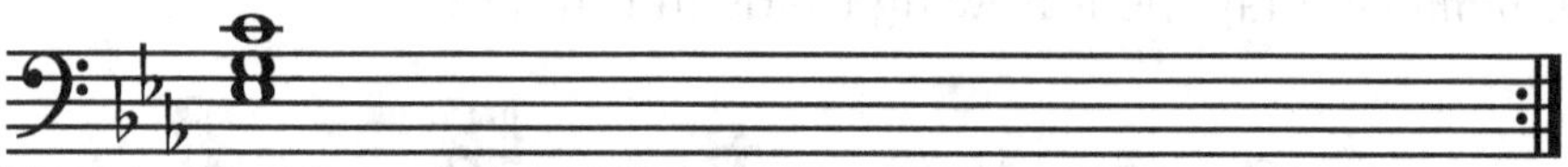

i VI iv ii° V7 i

Also in
D minor
F minor

c. C♯ minor (Challenge)

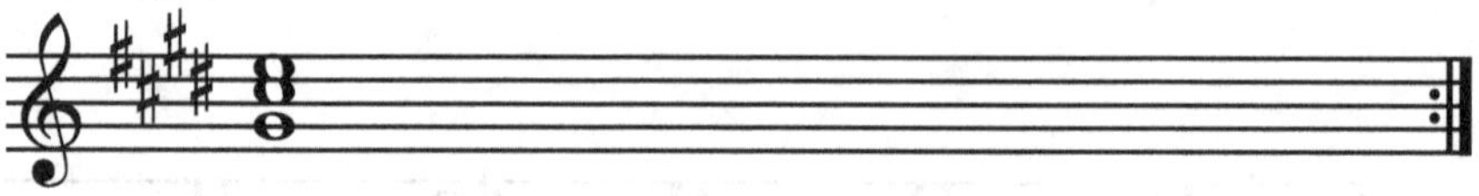

i iv ii° V i

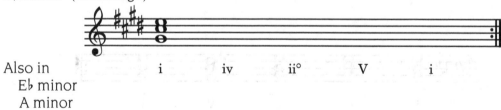

Also in
E♭ minor
A minor

HARMONIZATION

1. Harmonize the following with chords given. Suggested styles of accompanying are furnished.

   a. Broken chord

French

Go to the PDM Web site for further drill on item a.

   b. Two-handed

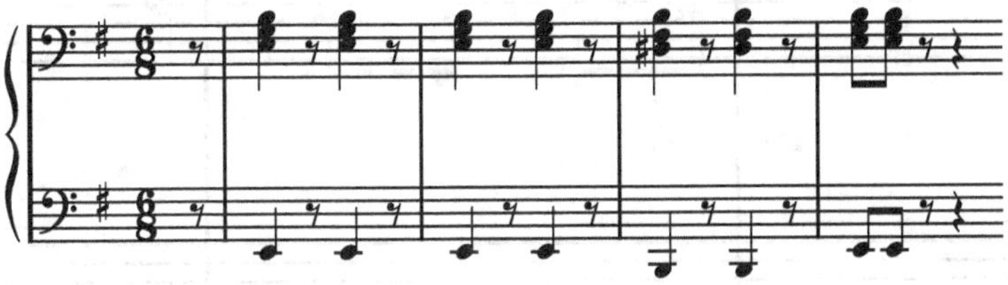

British

Go to the PDM Web site for further drill on item b.

   c. Choose an appropriate accompaniment style.

2. Complete the following:

   a. Left-hand broken chords

Great Lakes Chantey

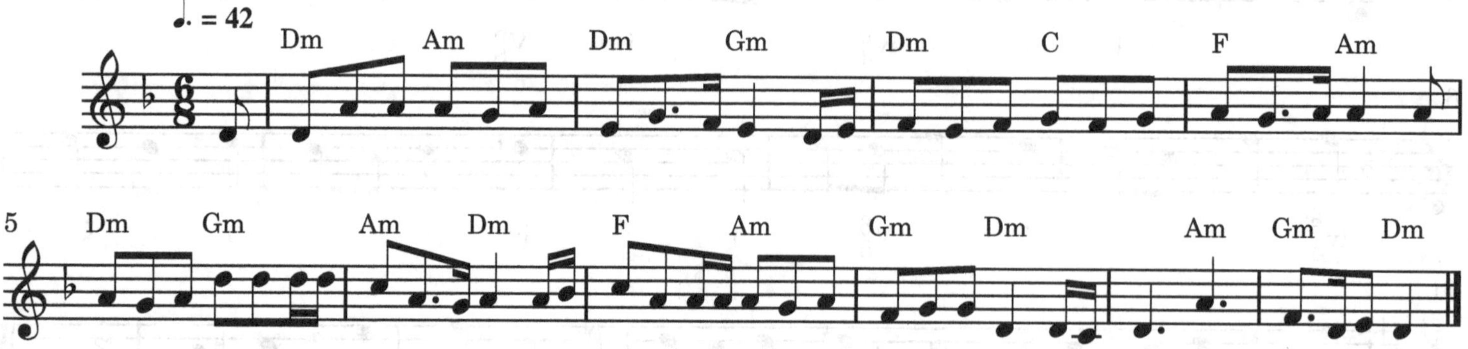

   b. Keyboard style—the melodic pitch must remain as the highest voice.

3. Play the following melodies by ear and determine appropriate harmonies for each.

   - *Johnny Has Gone for a Soldier*
   - *Joshua Fit Da Battle of Jericho*
   - *Sometimes I Feel Like a Motherless Child*
   - *Scarborough Fair*

Go to the PDM Web site for help in getting started with these melodies.

TRANSPOSITION

1. The following are to be transposed an interval of a tritone. *Follow the steps.*

a. Transpose *up* to B minor.

ADAM CLARK

b. Transpose *up* to G minor.

RYAN FOGG

c. Transpose *down* to D minor.

JACOB HINES

d. Transpose *down* to C minor.

KEVIN RICHMOND

e. Transpose *down* to E minor.

SANDRA RAMAWY

Go to the PDM Web site for additional tritone transposition.

2. Transpose *Etude* by Schytte (page 208) to B minor.

3. Transpose the following extension exercise to the keys of A♭ and C♯ major.

4. Transpose *Hopak* by Goedicke to the natural and harmonic forms of G minor.

Hopak

ALEXANDER GOEDICKE
(1877–1957)

5. Return to the Olson *Etude* (p. 175) and transpose it to D major.

IMPROVISATION

1. Play the following expansion of the blues pentascale in F.

2. The beginning 12-bar blues progression is based on three chords: I, IV, and V. To expand this harmonic basis, each triad may be given a dominant 7th quality.

F major

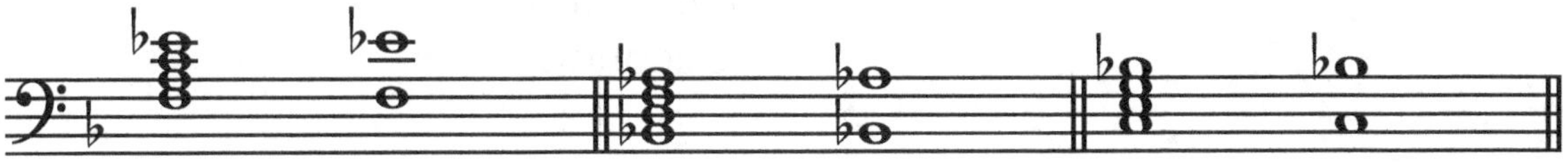

I (open) IV (open) V (open)

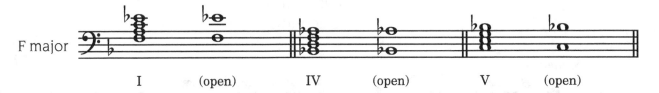

Play open 7ths that follow this blues progression in F

I	IV	I	I
IV	IV	I	I
V	IV	I	I

3. Choose a partner. One person will scat and play melody as the other plays 7ths. Use the key of F major.

4. For ease of movement around the keyboard, tritones substitute quite effectively for mid-range seventh chords. Compare these tritones to the full seventh chords used above.

F major

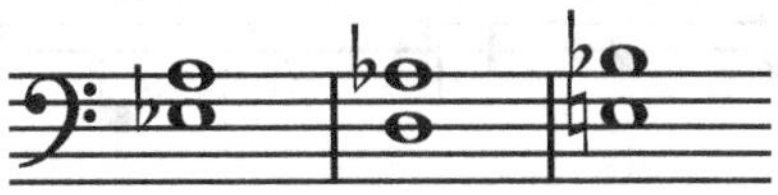

I IV V

5. Choose a partner. Play an "up-tempo" blues improvisation ensemble in F major.

   Part 1—one chorus of blues scale melody followed by one chorus of tritones

   Part 2—one chorus of tritones followed by one chorus of blues scale melody

   Note the Octave Placement of the Tritones!

Two choruses will have a V chord turn-around at the end of the first chorus.

Go to the PDM Web site for additional improvisation.

6. Return to *Etude* on page 208. As your teacher or a classmate plays the score as written, improvise a melody at least one octave above. Your improvisation should consist of chord tones, passing tones, neighbor tones, etc.

ENSEMBLE

1. Trade parts for the second 16 bars.

Minuet

(*Don Juan*)

Secondo

W. A. MOZART
(1756–1791)

Minuet

(*Don Juan*)

Primo

W. A. MOZART
(1756–1791)

2.

Mazurka

Secondo

JON GEORGE

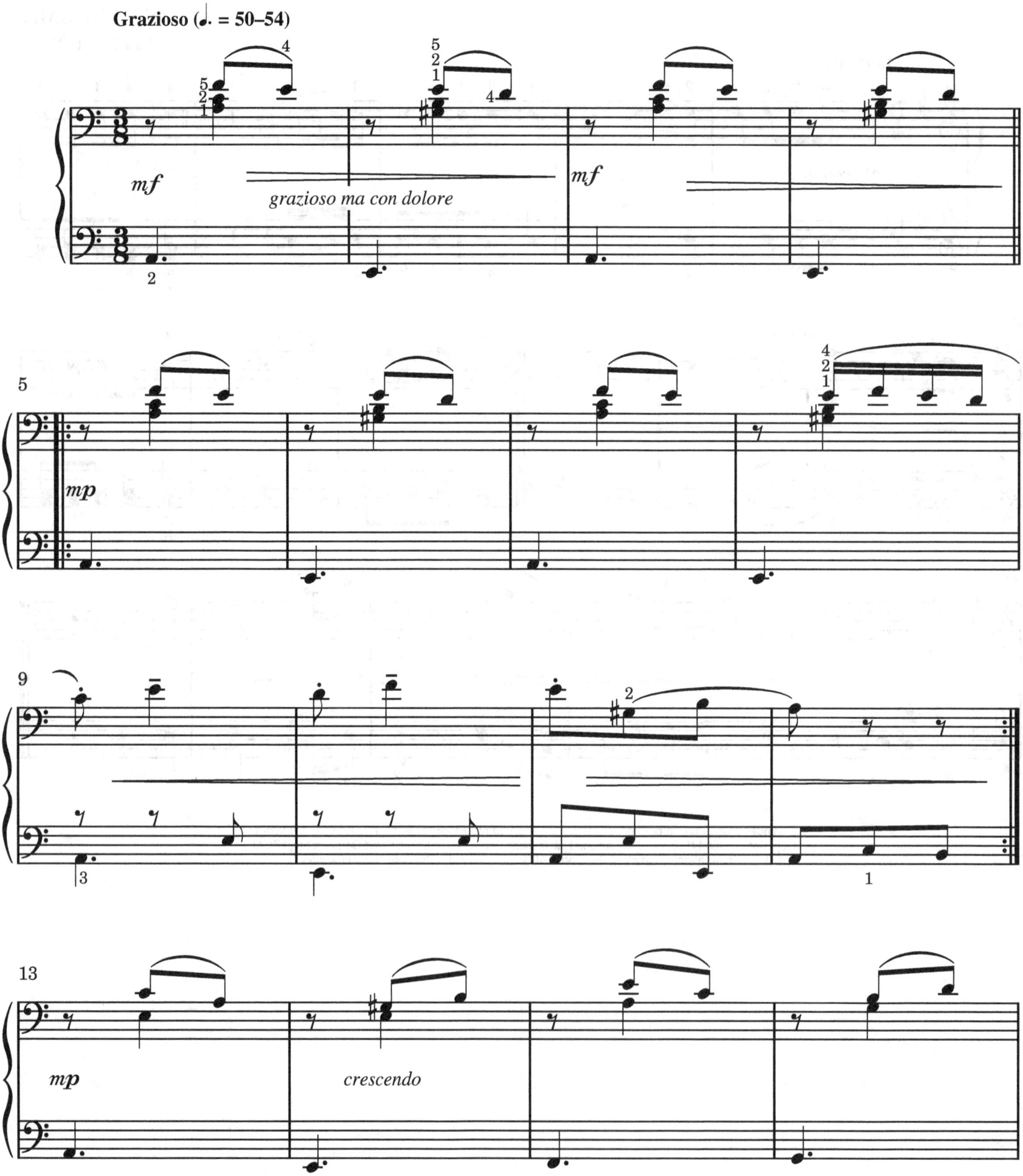

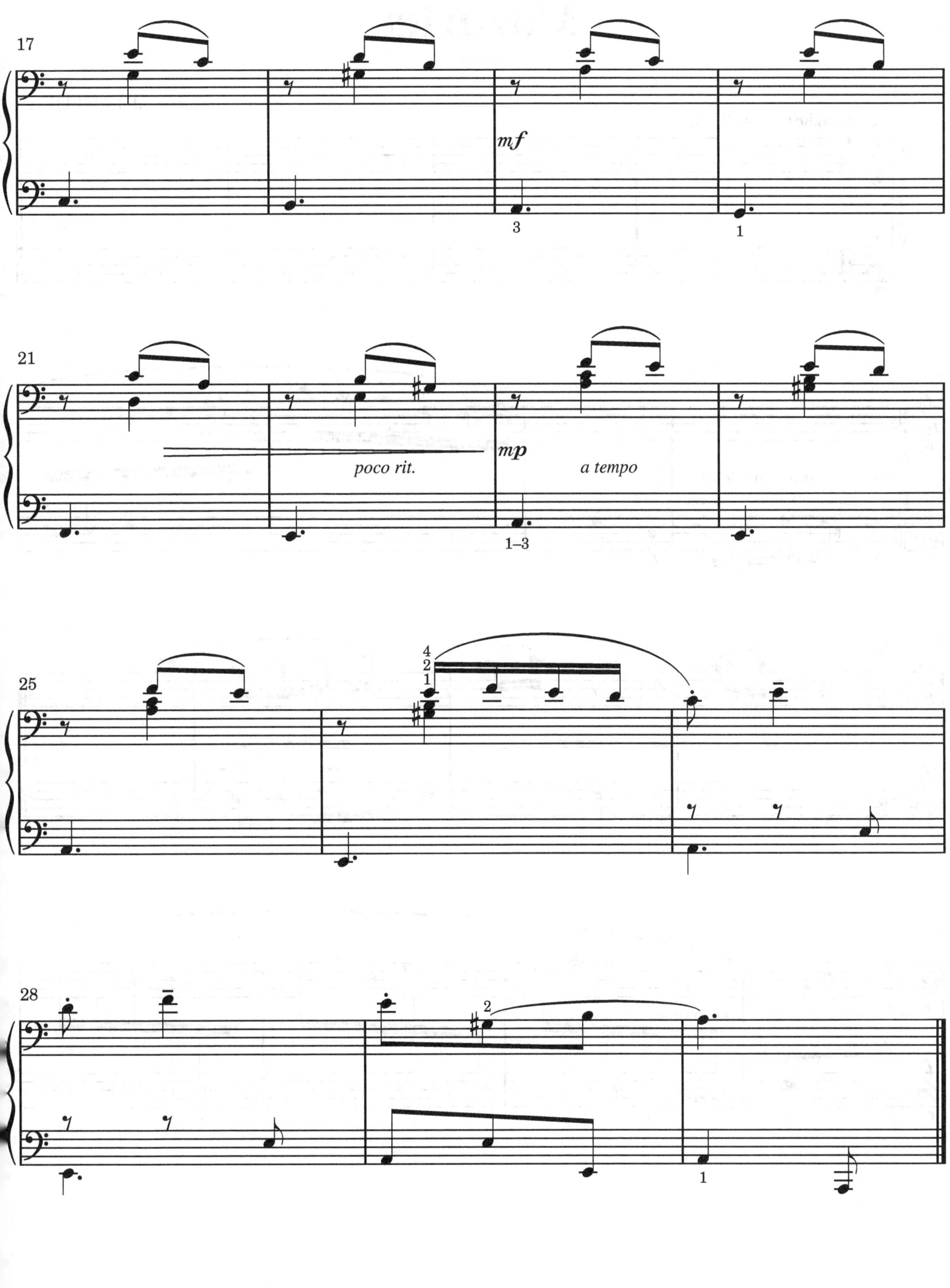
17
mf
21
poco rit.
mp
a tempo
25
28

Mazurka

Primo

JON GEORGE

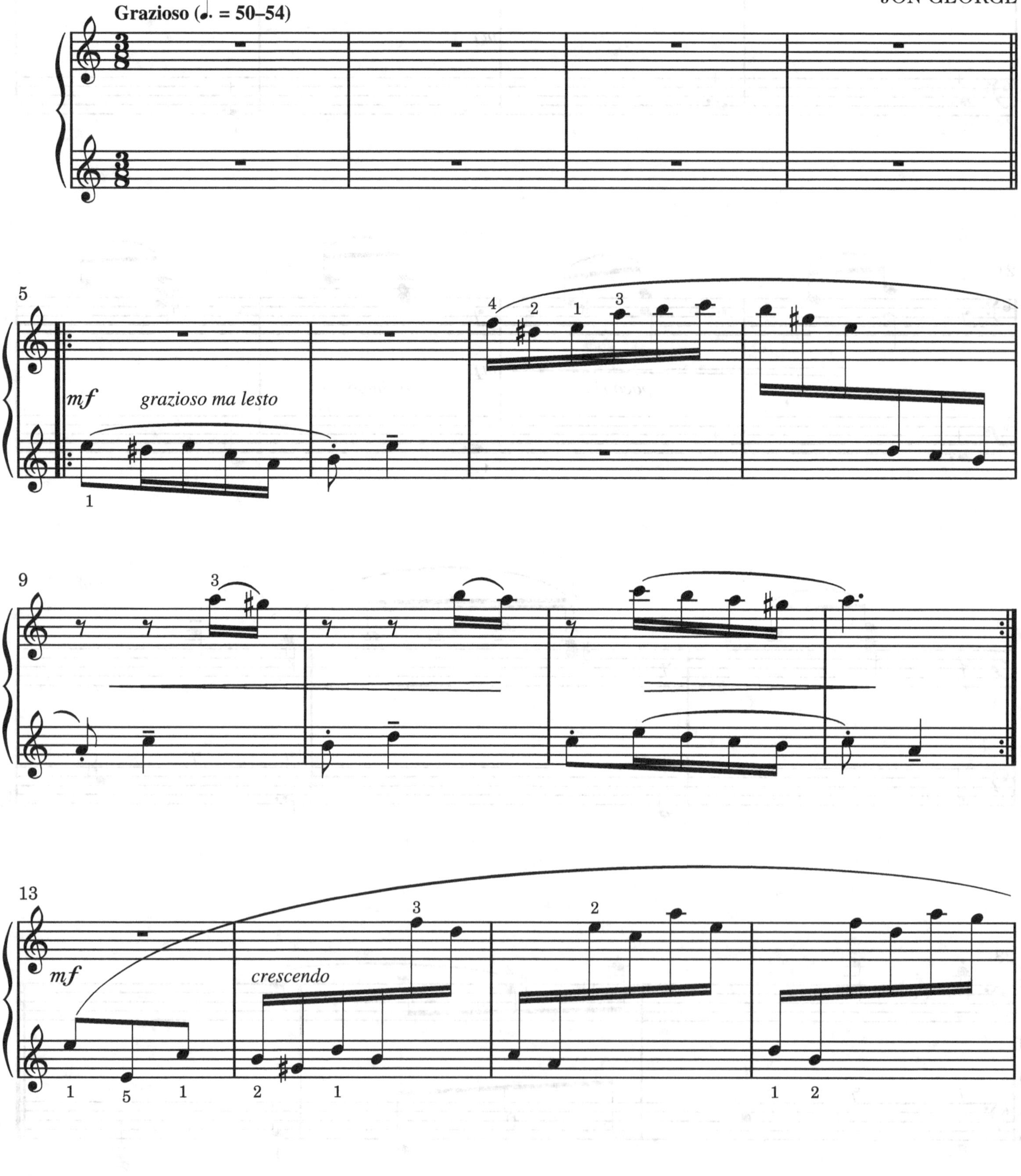

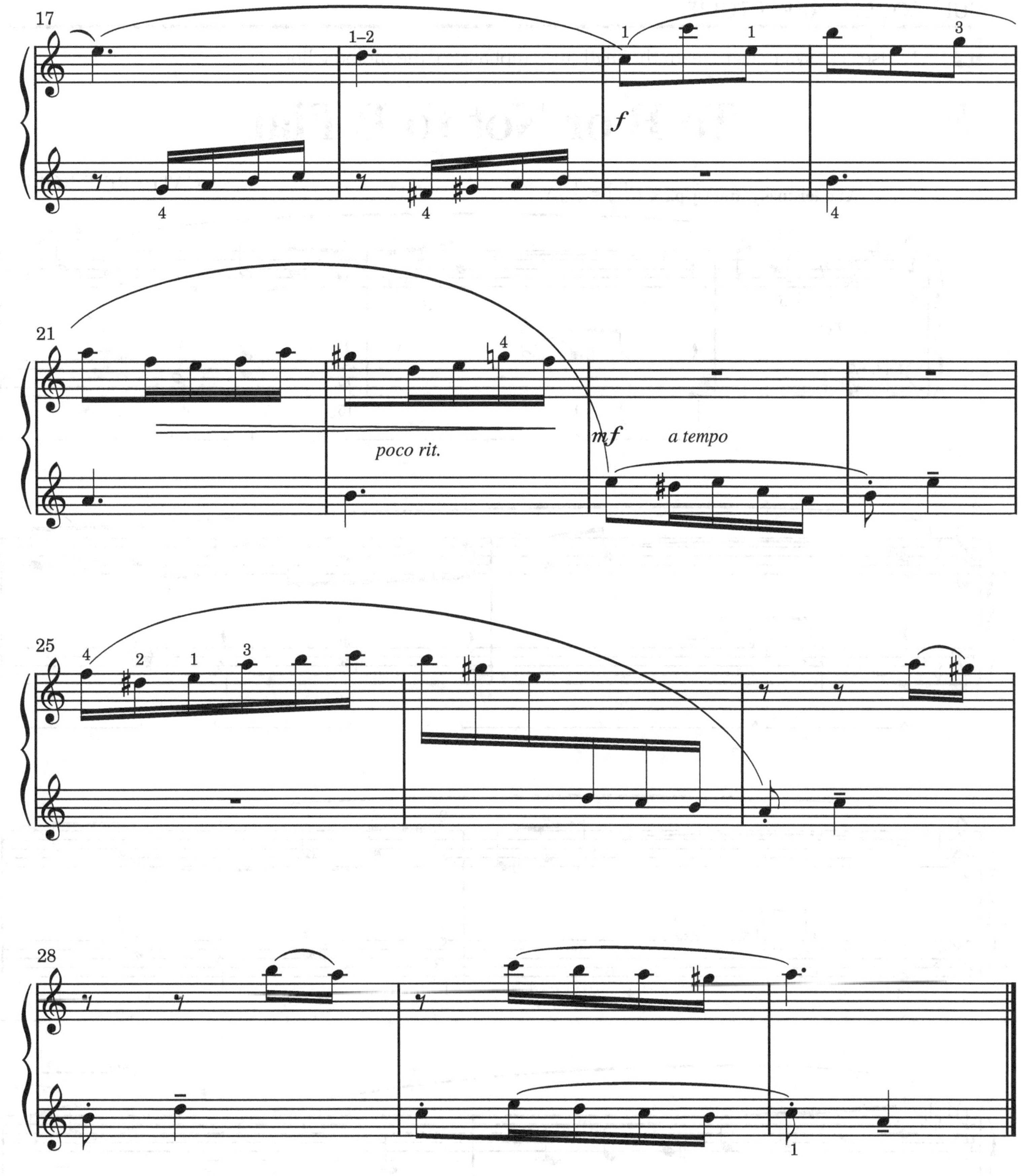

COMPOSITION

1. Compose a two-chorus blues solo in the key of F or G. The melody should come from the blues scale of the key and the accompaniment will consist of tritones in whatever rhythm you feel is appropriate. The MIDI disk will furnish a bass line and drums to complete the "Blues Trio." You may transpose the key of the disk and adjust the tempo as needed. Use the progression from page 217 with a dominant turn-around at the end of the first chorus.

Go to the PDM Web site for representative student compositions.

SUBSEQUENT REPERTOIRE

1. Use scat syllables to learn the rhythmic emphasis of the melodic line.

To B or Not to B Flat

CATHERINE ROLLIN

At a leisurely, bluesy pace

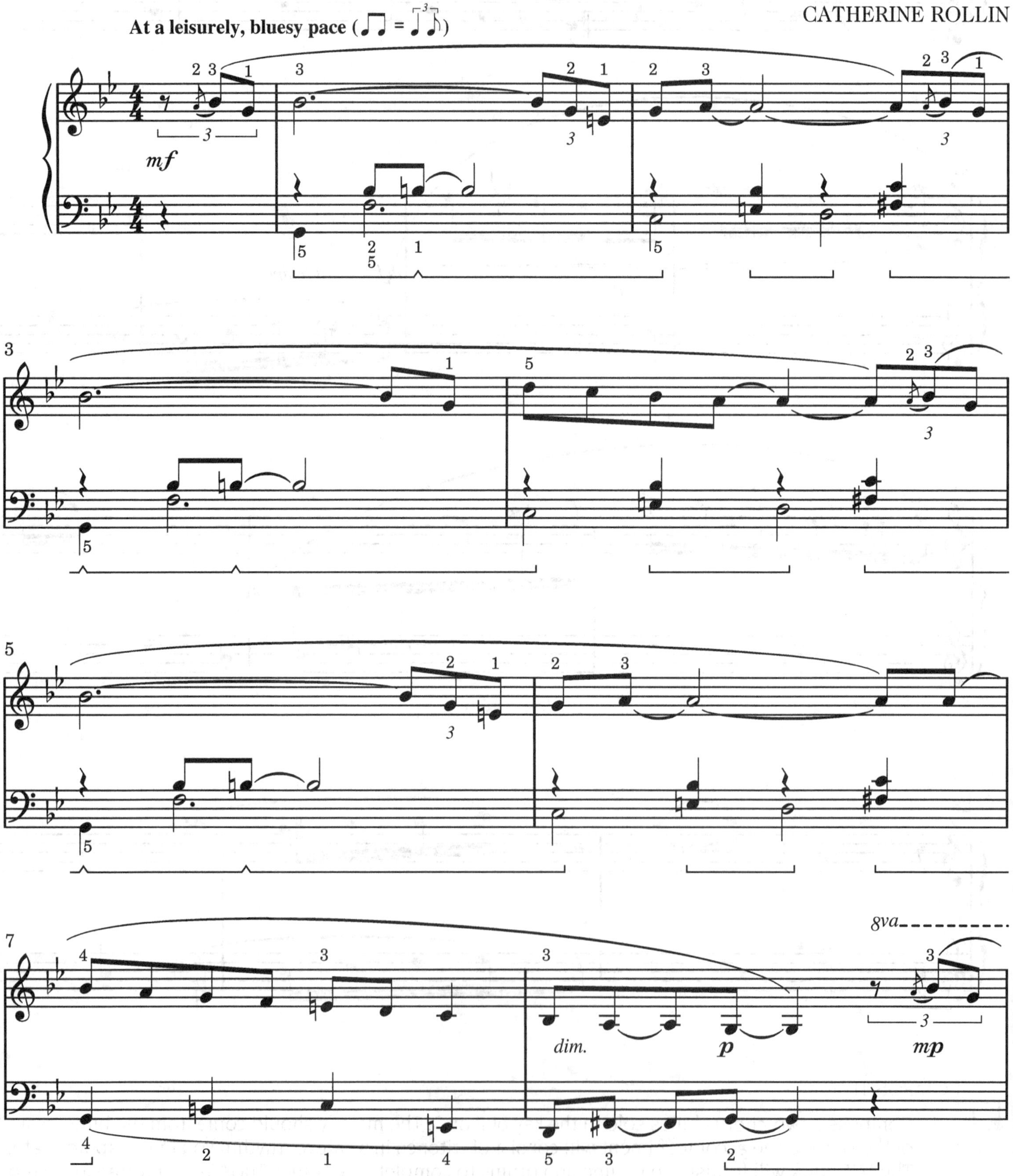

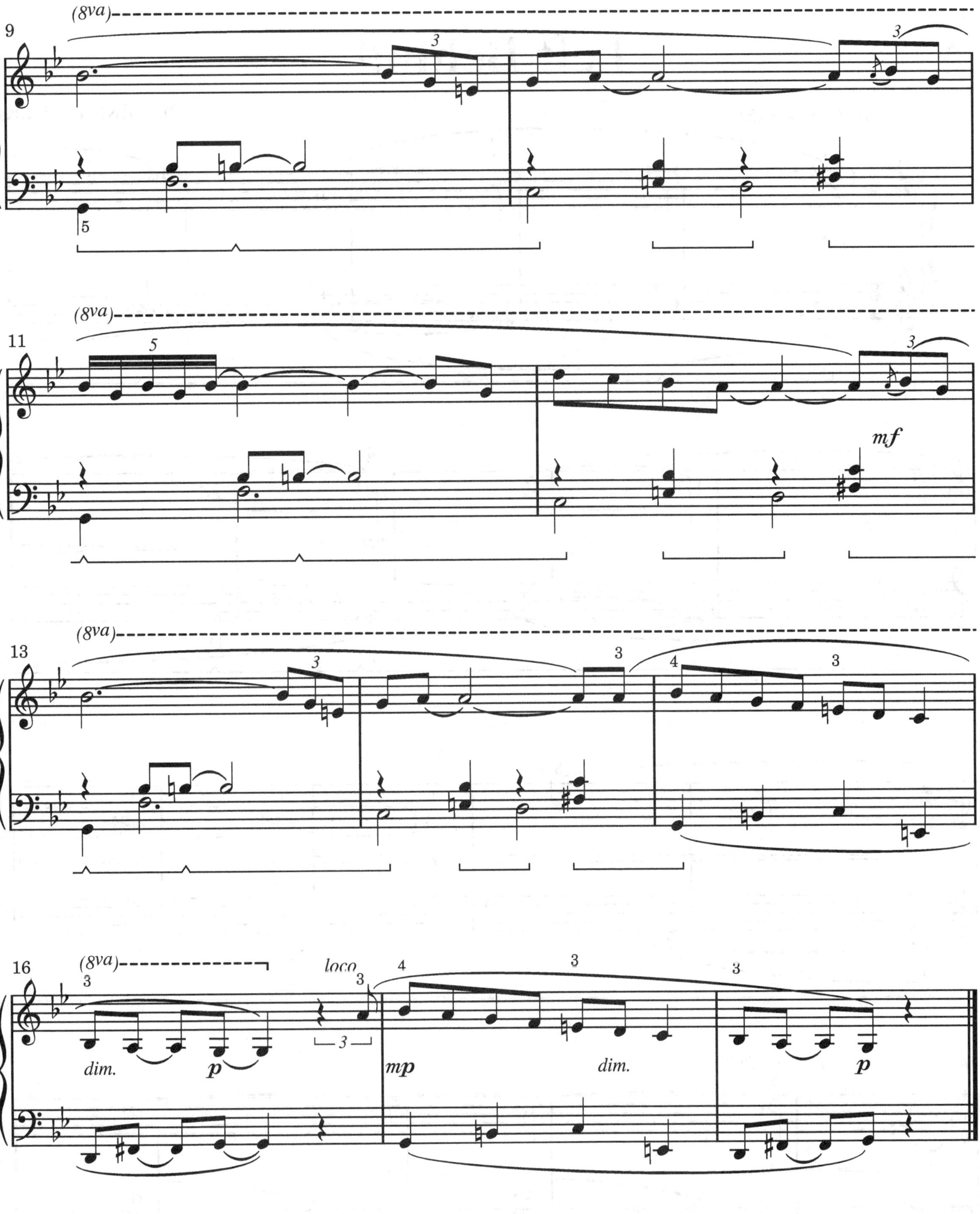
(8va)
mf
loco
dim.
p
mp
dim.
p

2. Note the tempo marking.

Left Behind

Wistfully (♩ = 132)

JEANINE YEAGER

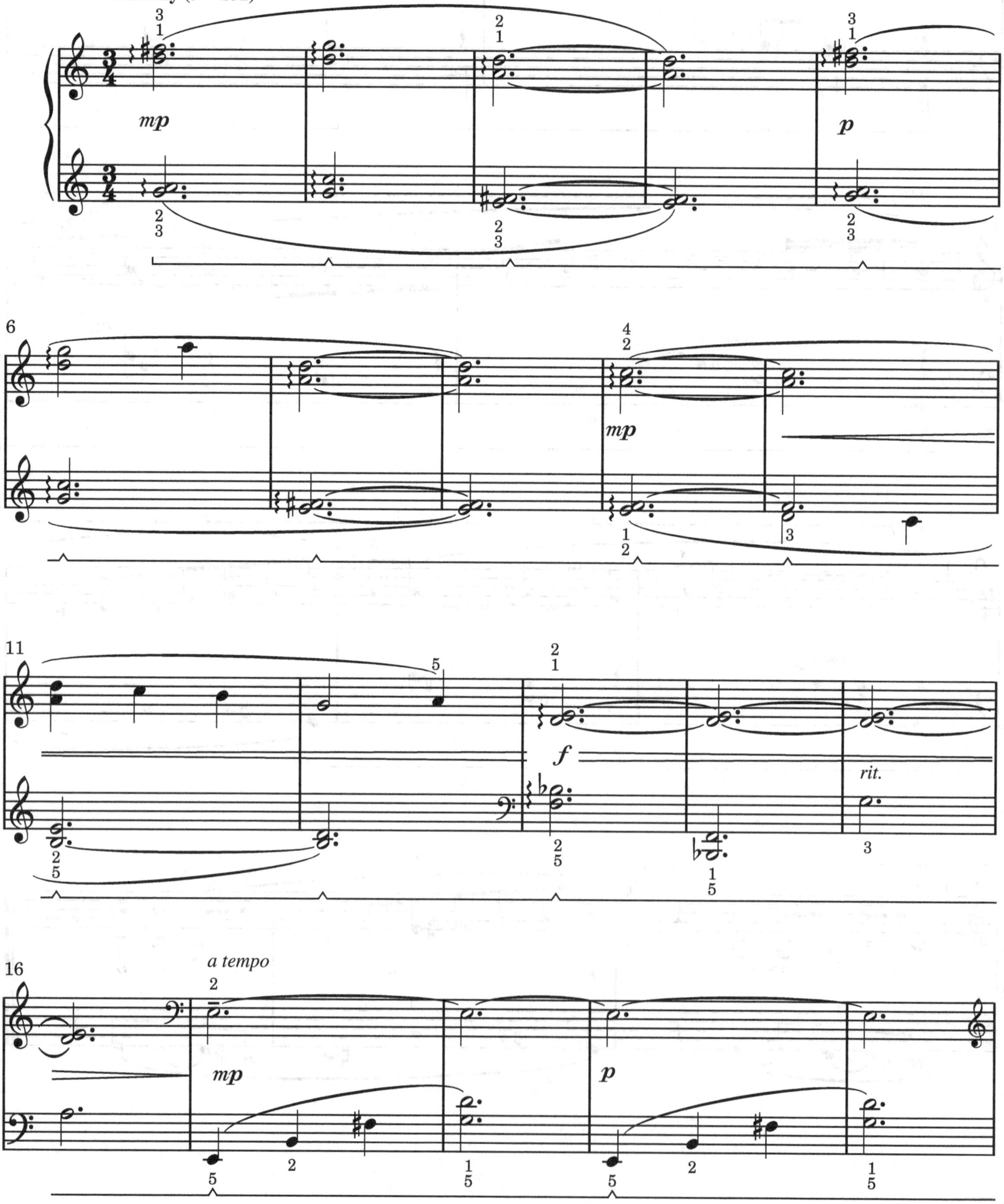

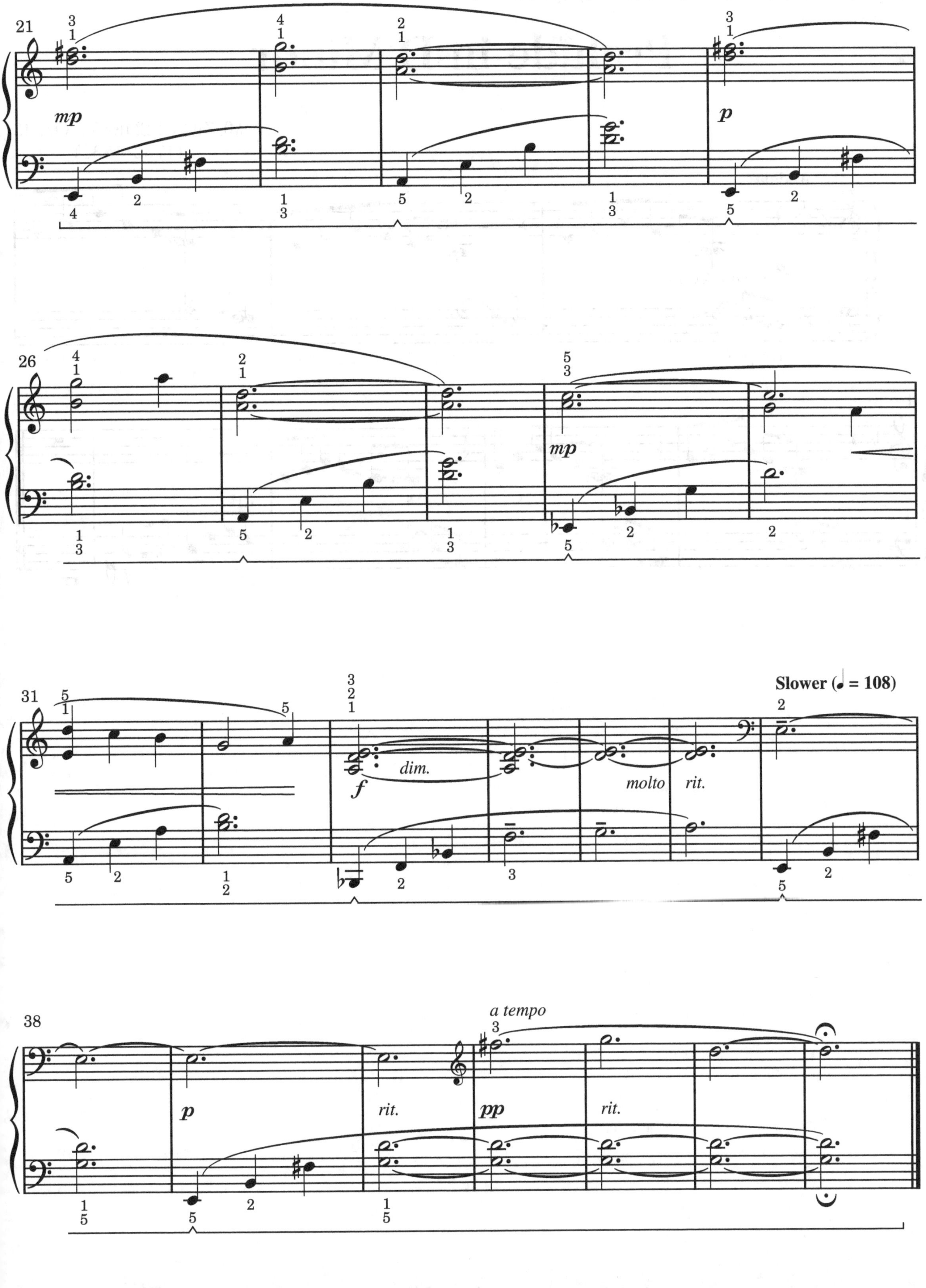

mp
p
mp
dim.
molto rit.
Slower (♩ = 108)
p
rit.
a tempo
pp
rit.

3. Block chord shapes before playing as written.

Prelude in D Minor

MUZIO CLEMENTI, Op. 43
(1752–1832)

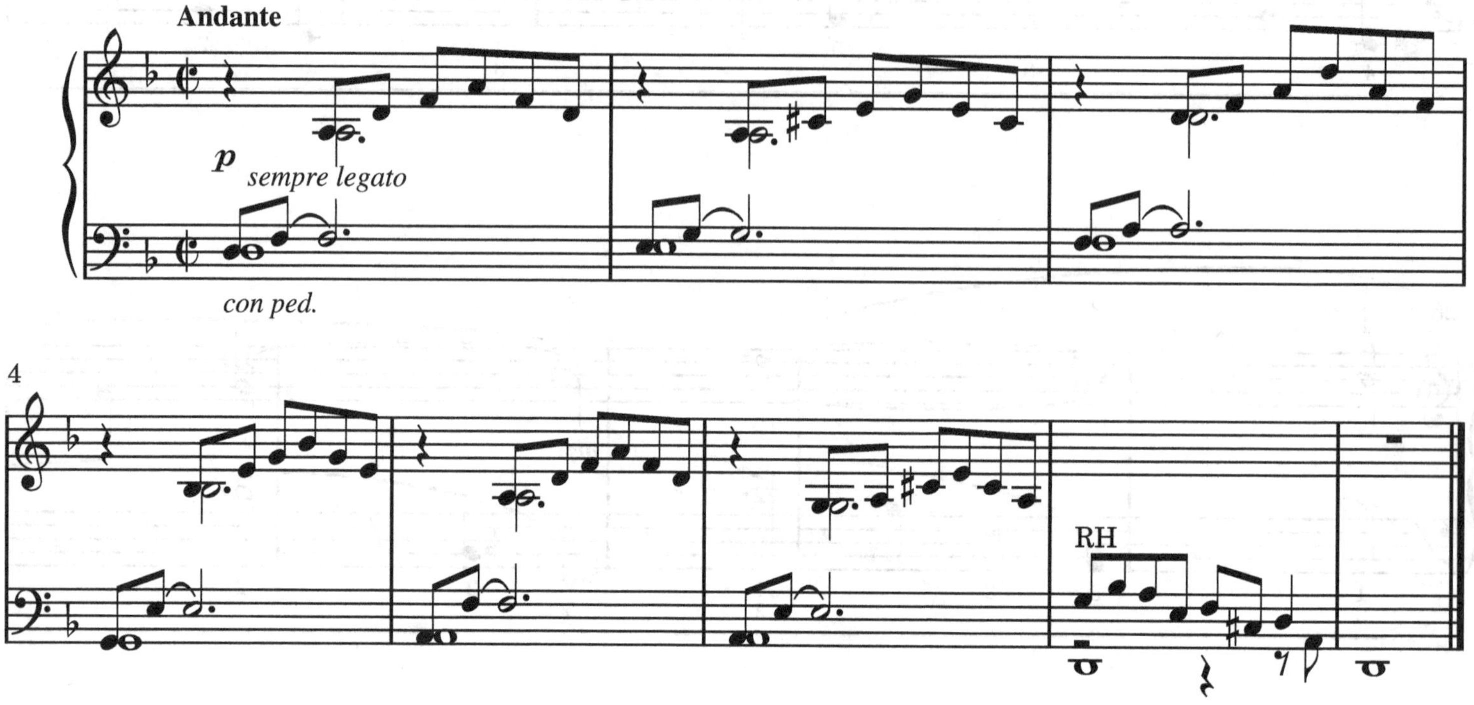

4. Identify the traditional passamezzo progression.

Passamezzo

Italian, 16th Century
Realization by Lynn Freeman Olson

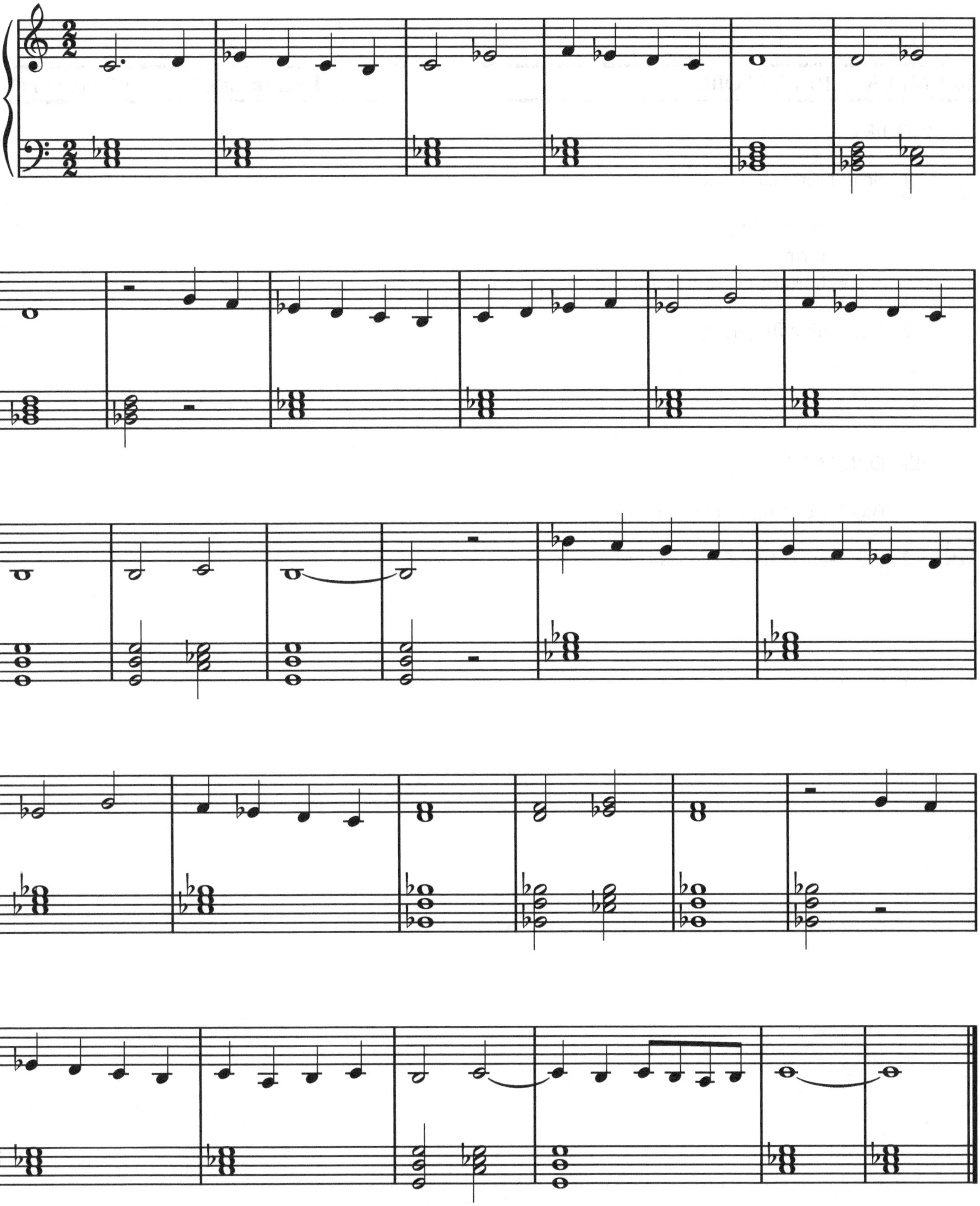

The ii–V7–I Progression

EXEMPLARY REPERTOIRE **Lemonade** Lynn Freeman Olson

INQUIRY

1. Scan *Lemonade*. Observe:
   - chord shapes
   - form
   - harmonic progression
2. Determine fingering.

PERFORMANCE

1. Block right-hand chord shapes.
2. Play as written. Count aloud.

(This page has been left blank to avoid a difficult page turn.)

Lemonade

LYNN FREEMAN OLSON

14
17
f
20
p
23
mf
26

TOPICS TO EXPLORE AND DISCUSS

- Jean-Louis Gobbaerts
- Anton Diabelli
- Gigue
- Maurice Ravel

SKILLS AND ACTIVITIES

TECHNIQUE

1. Review all white-key major scales (C, D, E, G, A).

RH:	1	2	3	1	2	3	4	1	2	3	1	2	3	4	5
LH:	5	4	3	2	1	3	2	1	4	3	2	1	3	2	1

2. Play *Pleasant Morning*.

Pleasant Morning

STREABBOG (JEAN-LOUIS GOBBAERTS)
(1835–1886)

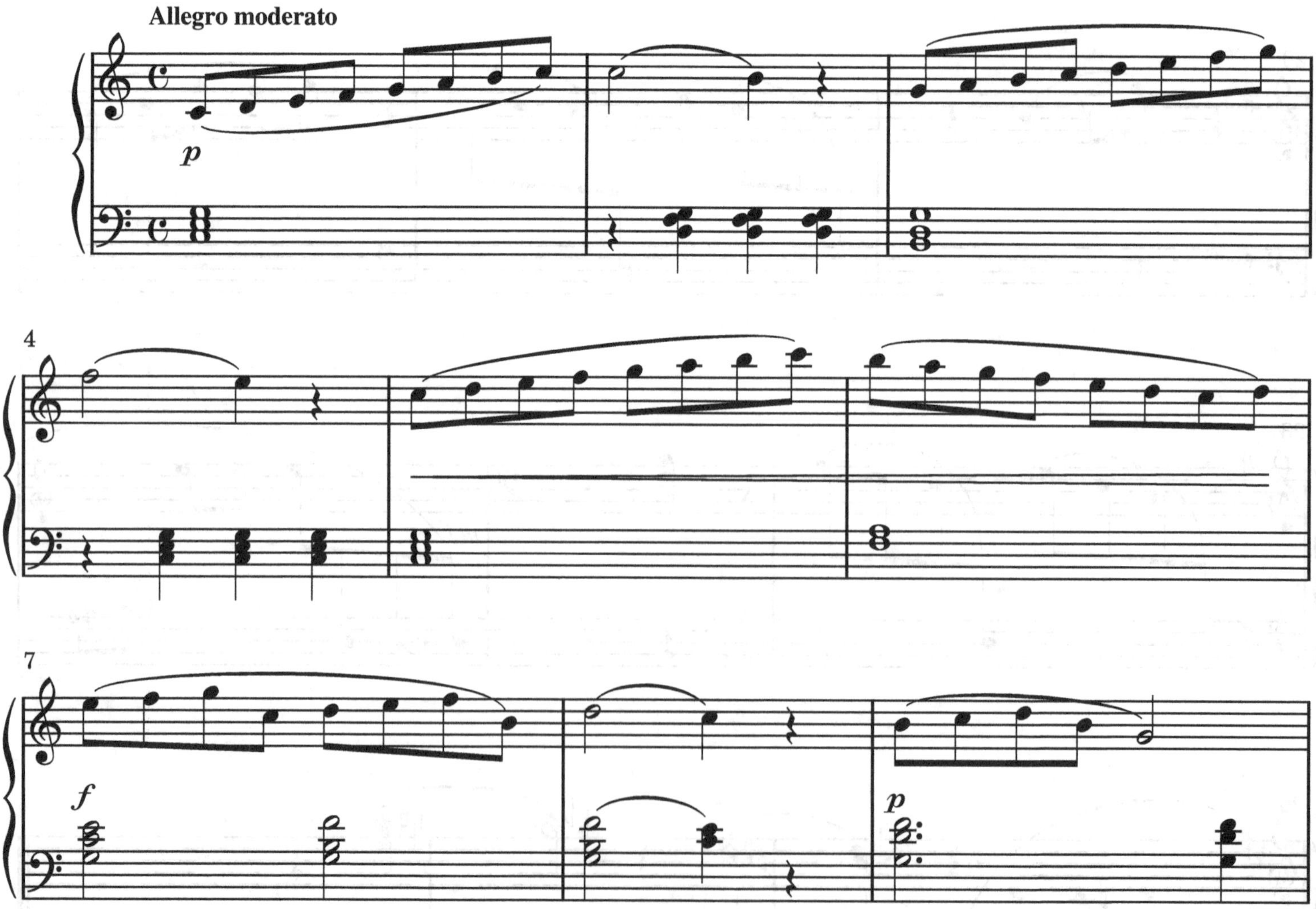

Go to the PDM Web site for additional scalar work.

READING

1. The alto clef positions middle C on the third line of the staff.

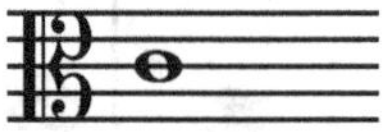

Play the following viola excerpt using alto clef.

String Quartet in E-Flat Major

(Viola excerpt)

WOLFGANG AMADEUS MOZART
(1756–1791)

2. Before playing, look for chord outlines and scalar passages.

String Quartet in G Major

(Viola excerpt)

WOLFGANG AMADEUS MOZART
(1756–1791)

3. Play the following viola line from *Bassa imperiale*, then choose a partner and play as an ensemble.

Bassa imperiale

ANONYMOUS
18th Century

Go to the PDM Web site for additional alto clef reading.

4. Think key signature as you play through these minor key examples.

a.

P. PERIN

b.

Andantino

c.

S. RAMAWY

Con Spirito

d.

Geschwindt

e.

K. RICHMOND

Zierlich

KEYBOARD THEORY

1. The most basic type of authentic cadence is twofold: dominant to tonic. The dominant area is strengthened by preceding it with the subdominant or substituting another chord for the subdominant (such as the supertonic—ii).

   The ii–V7–I cadence appears frequently. For smooth voice leading (and because melodic content often dictates), the form is commonly ii6–V7–I.

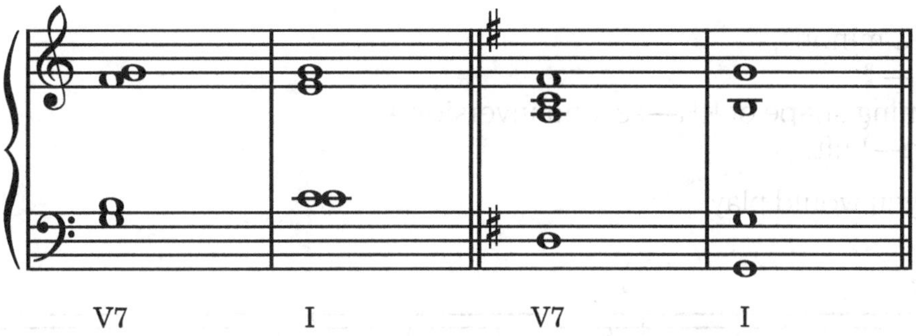

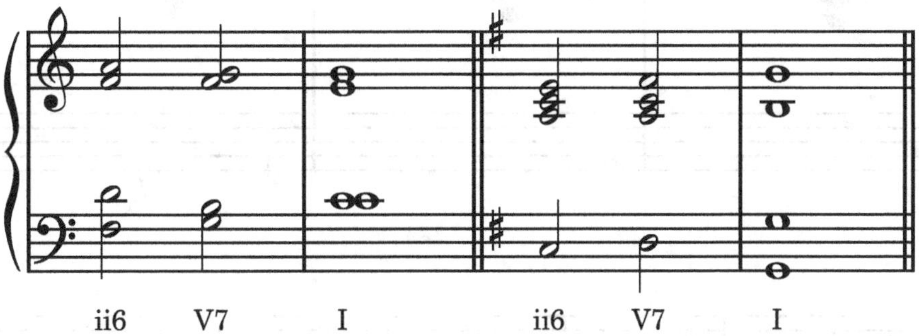

2. Play ii6–V7–I progressions in the following keys. Your teacher will set the tempo and give a measure of rest between each new key:

   A E♭ D A♭ G D♭

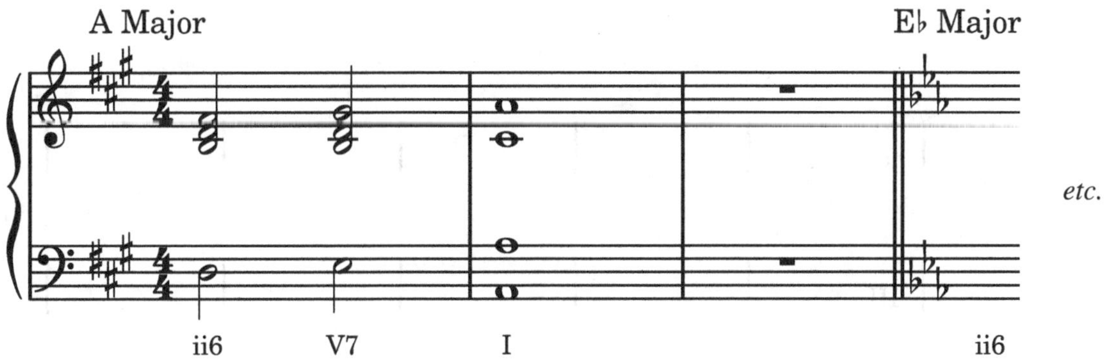

Go to the PDM Web site for additional drill of ii–V7–I.

3. As a class, create three minor key progressions. Play the progressions in keyboard style paying close attention to voice leading. Regardless of meter or choice of rhythm, you should demonstrate two four-bar phrases. Your choices will include:

   - remainder of harmonies
   - key signature
   - meter
   - beginning shape of right hand
   - tempo (choose a term you don't often see)

   Example: i | VI | iv | V7 | ii°6 | V7 | V^6_5 | i ||

   Key—C minor
   Meter—$\frac{3}{4}$
   Beginning shape of RH—second inversion
   Tempo—Luftig

   Then you would play:

a. i | i6 | | | | | | ||

b. i | III | | | | | | ||

c. i | VI | | | | | | ||

HARMONIZATION

1. Follow the suggested styles.

   a. Two-handed strumming style

   b. Extended broken chord

FRANZ SCHUBERT
(1797–1828)

Go to the PDM Web site for tutorial.

c. Modified keyboard style

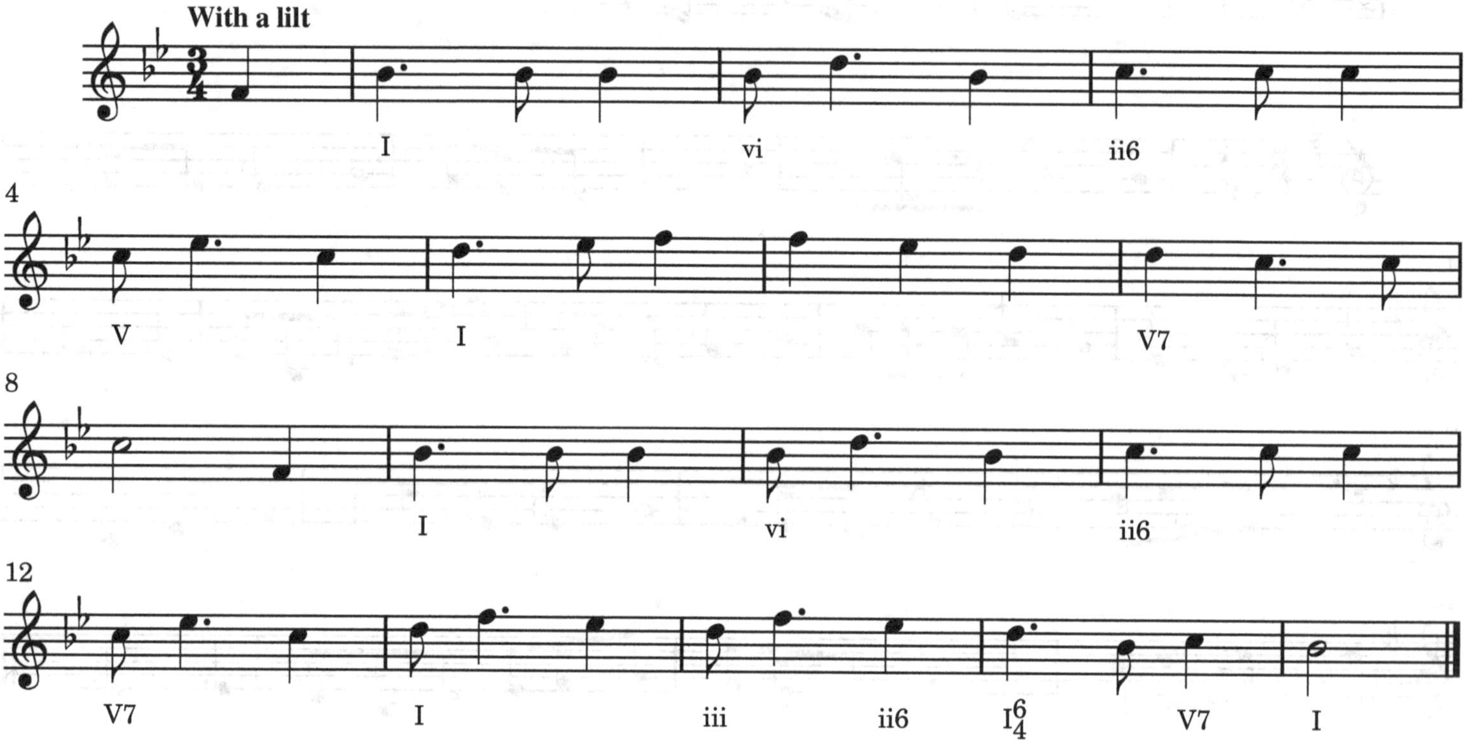

Go to the PDM Web site for tutorial.

d. Left-hand chords with right-hand melody

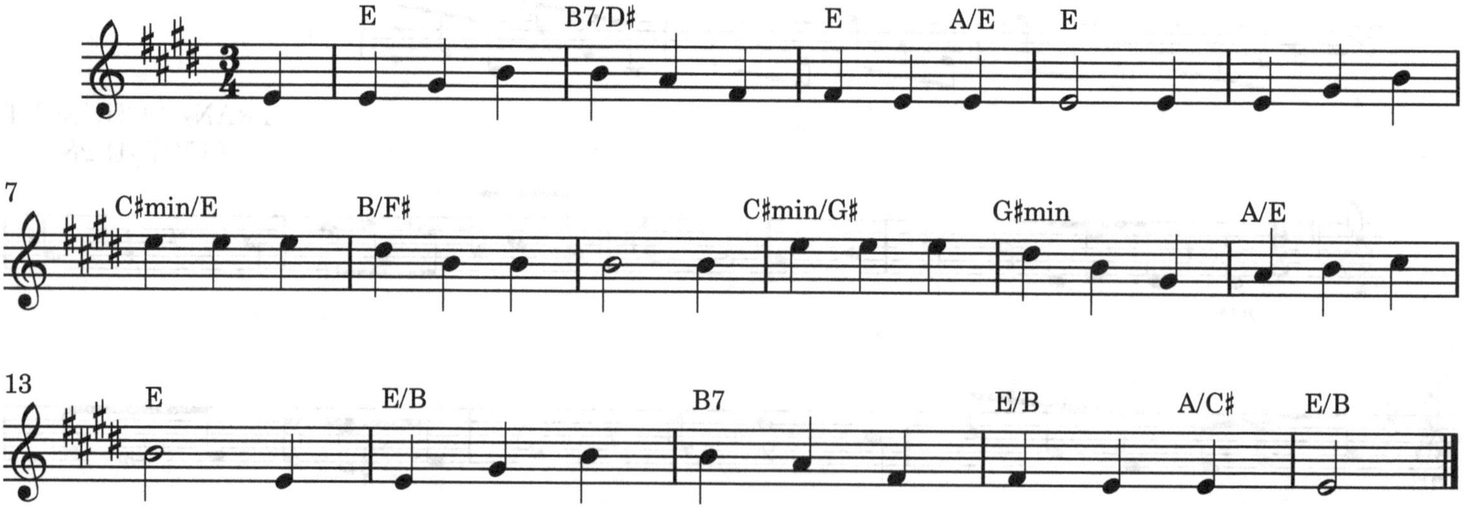

e. Use a two-handed accompanimant.

etc.

American

Go to the PDM Web site for tutorial.

f. Two-handed accompaniment with alternating bass

United States

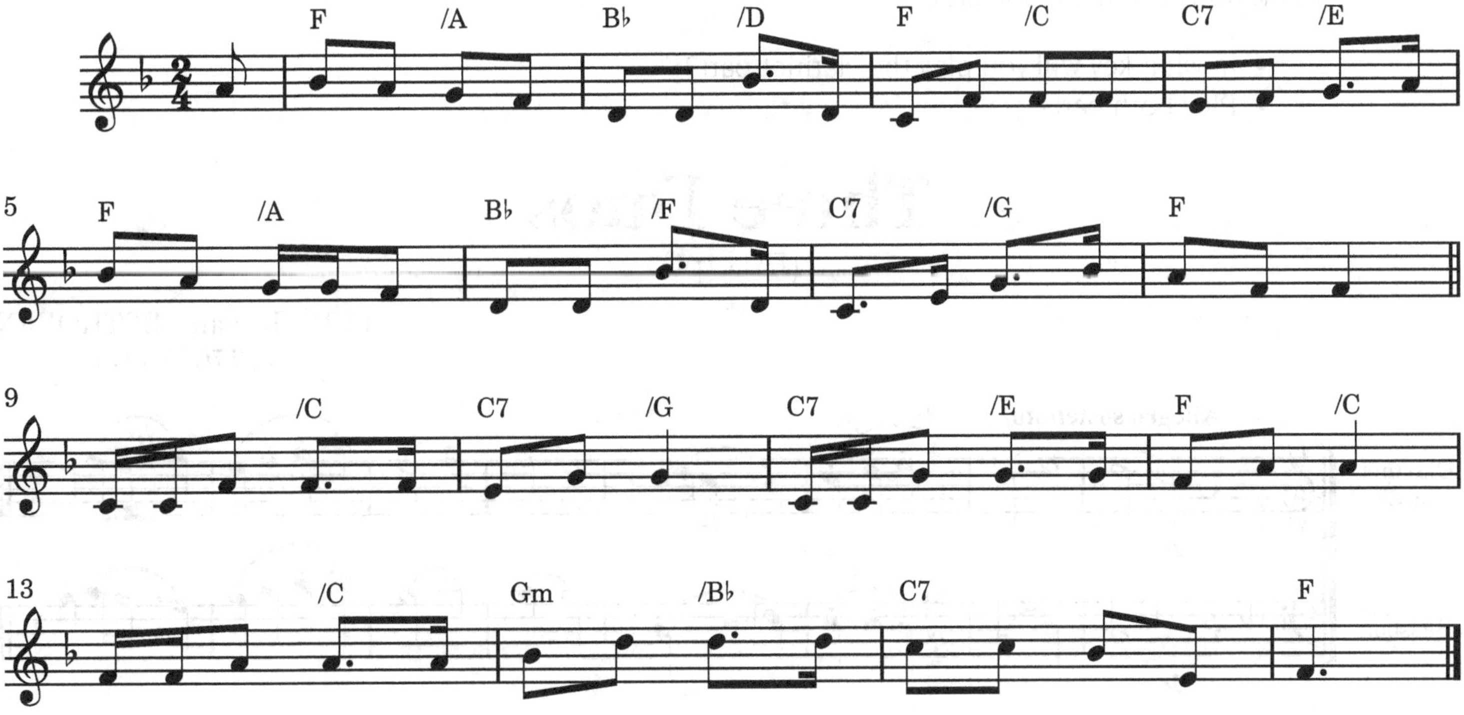

Go to the PDM Web site for tutorial.

TRANSPOSITION

1. Play the following as a round in the key written. As the fourth group plays the last measure of the melody, the teacher will call for a new key. From that point on, at the downbeat of the last measure in each phrase, a new key will be called. Continue until the fourth group has played the melody two more times.

To Portsmouth!

MELVILL

2. With all transposing instruments, *think in concert key* rather than transposing each note. For clarinets in B♭, think down a whole step.

- In what key will you play the clarinet part?
- Play both parts.

Three Duos

(Excerpt)

LUDWIG van BEETHOVEN
(1770–1827)

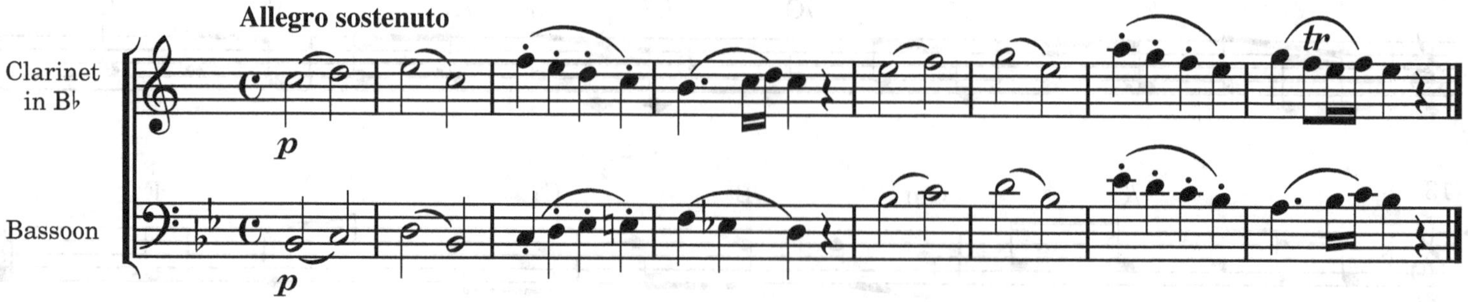

3. Think in the key of G.

4. In what key will you think?

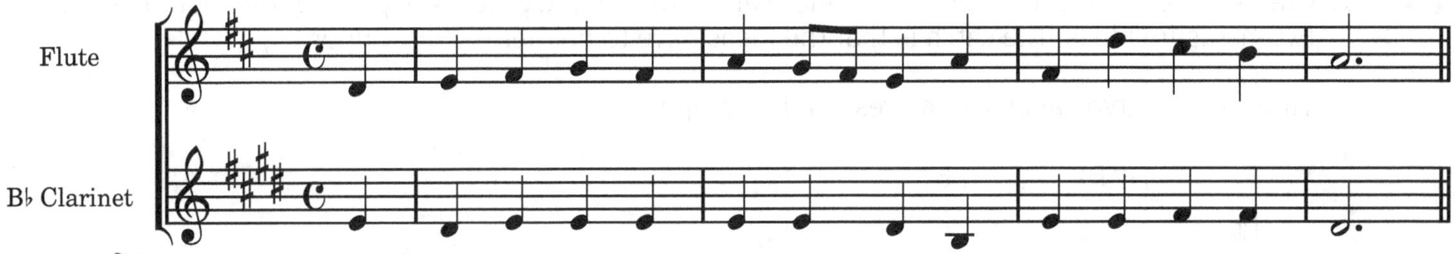

Go to the PDM Web site for additional clarinet examples.

5. The following will be transposed the interval of a tritone.

a. Transpose *up* to A minor.

CYNTHIA BENSON

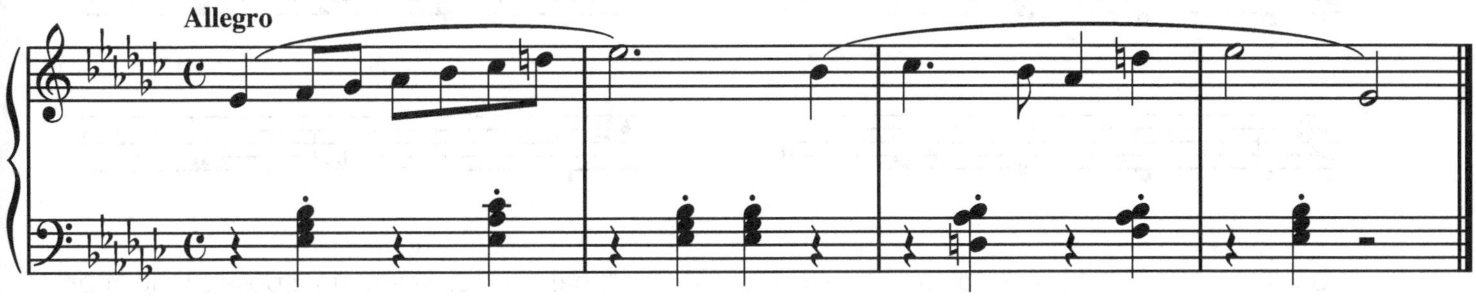

b. Transpose *up* to E minor.

KEVIN RICHMOND

c. Transpose *down* to G major.

OWEN LOVELL

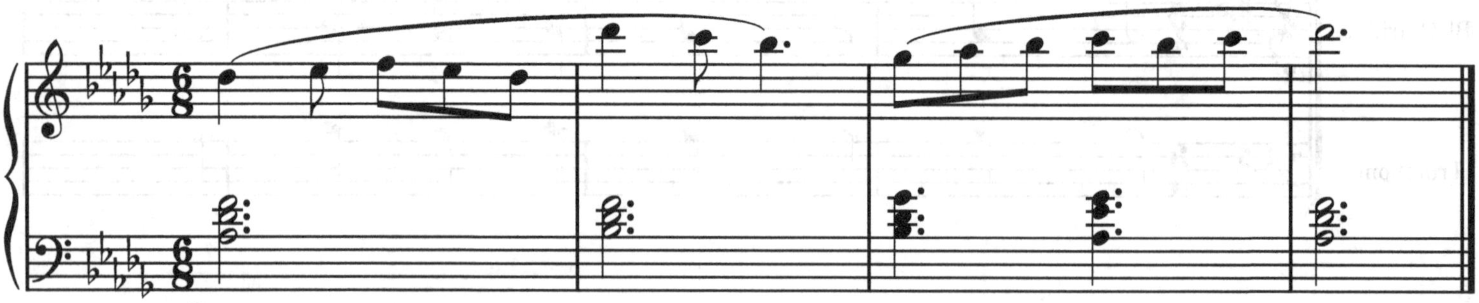

Go to the PDM Web site for additional tritone transpositions.

IMPROVISATION

1. The ascending blues scale is formed by adding one note to the blues pentascale—flat 7.

2. Creating a bass line for a chorus of blues can be the simple process of putting together one- and two-measure ideas. The catch is that the ideas have to be there to draw upon!

   Think about a typical blues progression in F major:

F	B♭	F	F
B♭	B♭	F	F
C	B♭	F	F (or C turn-around for another chorus)

   Use these one-bar ideas for bars 1, 2, 9, or 10. In the case of playing two choruses these could be used for bars 11 and 12 as well. Simply transpose the idea(s) to the harmonies of C and B♭.

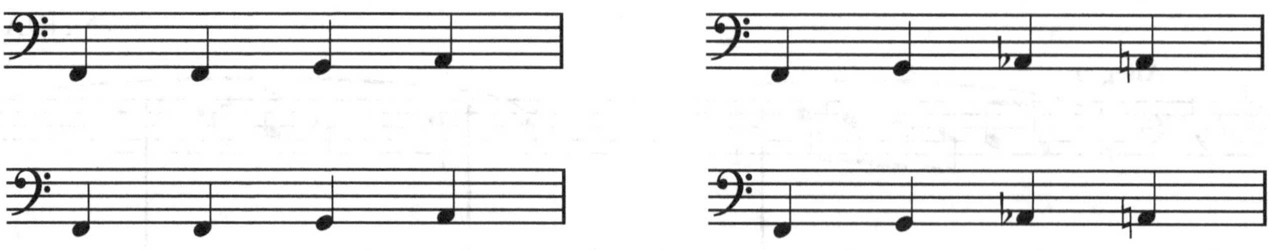

   Use two-bar ideas for measures 3–4, 5–6, 7–8, and the "final" 11–12. Again, transpose to the appropriate harmony. These are nothing more than ascending and descending Mixolydian modes.

3. Play two choruses of blues in your choice of F or G. In the first chorus, improvise on the expanded blues scale while playing left-hand tritones. In the second chorus, improvise a walking bass while playing right-hand tritones. *The octave placement of your tritones should not change—always mid-range.*

(This page has been left blank to avoid a difficult page turn.)

COMPOSITION

1. Compose a piece in the style of *Etude* by Schytte (page 208). Think about:
   - imitation
   - sequence
   - easily defined harmonic structure
   - static rhythm

Be prepared to trade compositions on the due date and play what you receive. Therefore, "do unto others. . . !"

Go to the PDM Web site for representative student compositions.

ENSEMBLE

1. Choose a partner and perform *Allegro in E Minor.*

Allegro in E Minor

ANTON DIABELLI
(1781–1858)

7
ff
ff
p
p
10
cresc.
cresc.
13
f
f
ff
ff

Sleeping Beauty's Pavane

from *Mother Goose Suite*

(Secondo)

MAURICE RAVEL
(1875–1937)

Lento (♩ = 58)

Sleeping Beauty's Pavane

from *Mother Goose Suite*

(Primo)

MAURICE RAVEL
(1875–1937)

1. Be very "aware" of your right-hand thumb. Also, listen for proper note durations in the right-hand upper voice. Balance of melodic and supporting elements are essential.

Meditation

ALEXANDRE TANSMAN
(1897–1986)

13
17
rallentando
a tempo
pp
20
23
rallentando
ppp

2. Be prepared for the key change. Take the time to do a harmonic analysis.

Early Spring

GEORGE PETER TINGLEY

Quietly optimistic

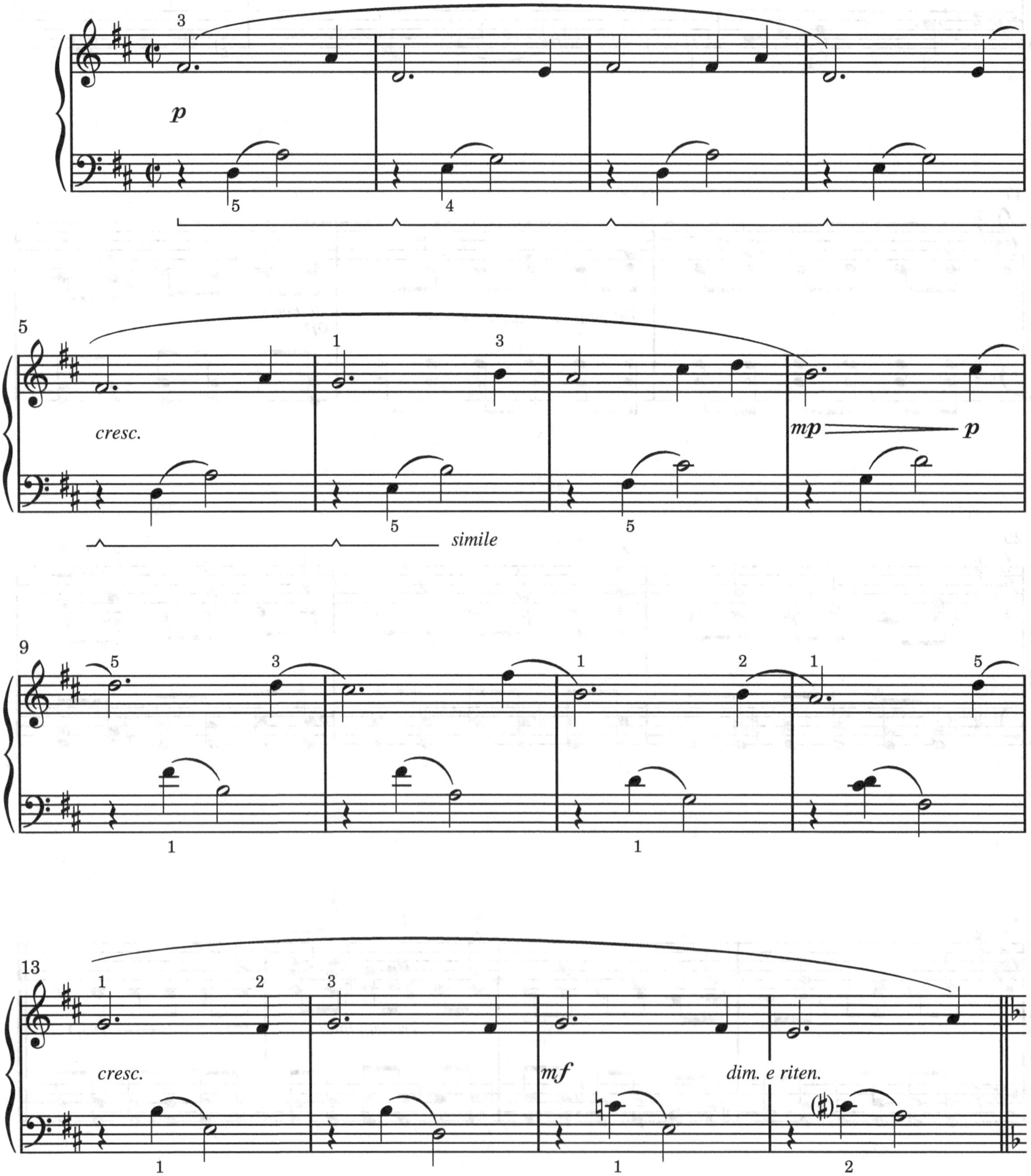

a tempo
p
cresc.
dolce
mf
p
mp
riten.
a tempo
p
rall.

3. A "brisk" tempo is essential.

Gigue

MONA MJOLSNES

p
p
poco
f
dim.

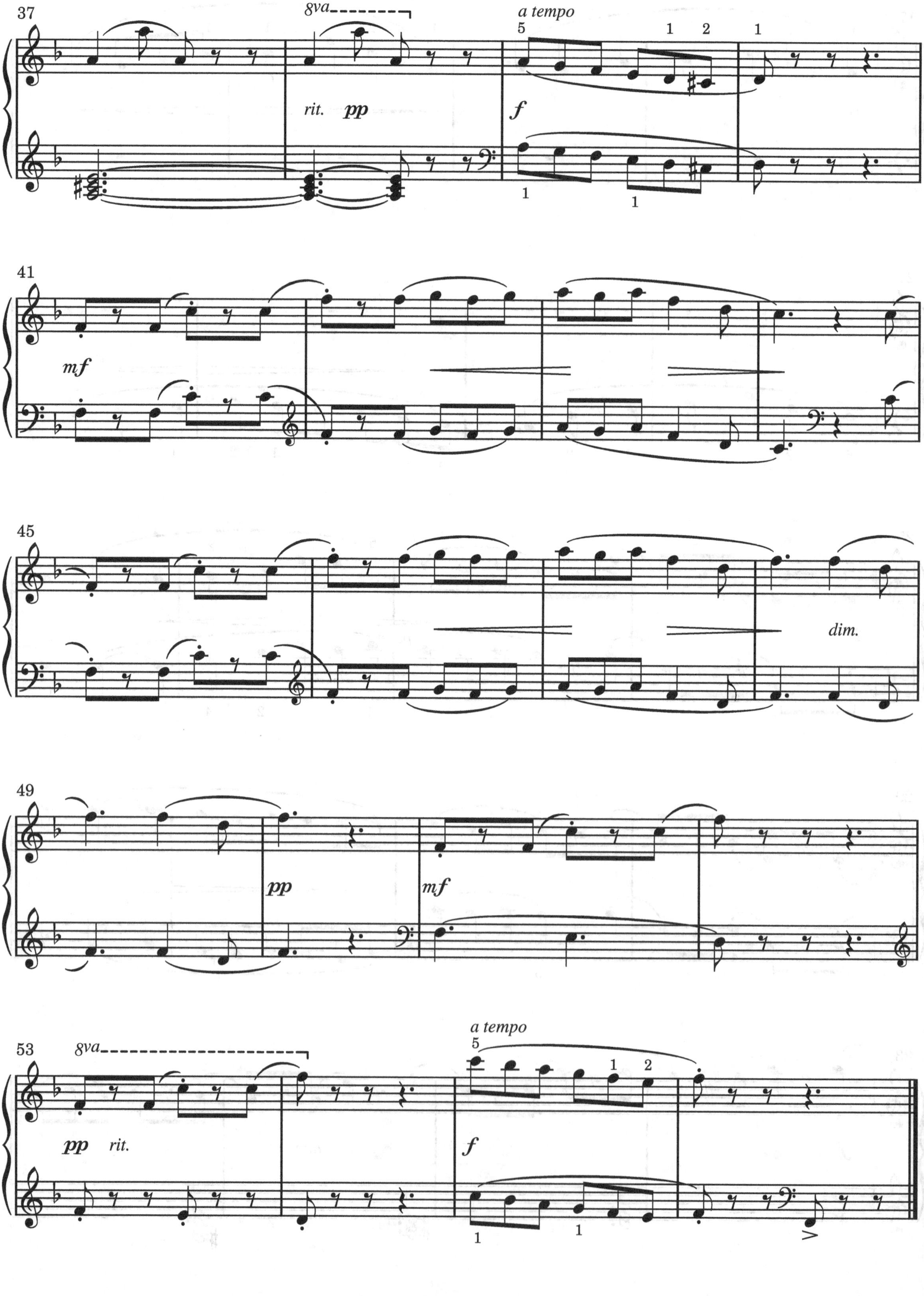
37
8va
a tempo
rit.
pp
f
41
mf
45
dim.
49
pp
mf
53
8va
a tempo
pp
rit.
f

4. Play the Bartók listening for the independent lines.

Mourning Song

from *For Children*, Vol. 2

BÉLA BARTÓK
(1881–1945)

Secondary Dominants/ Styles of Accompanying

EXEMPLARY REPERTOIRE **Gospel Song** Eugenie R. Rocherolle

INQUIRY

1. Scan *Gospel Song*. Observe:
    - double stemming
    - fingering suggestions for last eight measures
    - need for voicing "within the hand"
2. Do a harmonic analysis of *Gospel Song*. It helps to see the harmonic progression rather than just trying to read all of the notes without an understanding of why they are being used.

PERFORMANCE

1. Separate the parts of the score into SATB. As you play your part, sing the pitches on "loo."
2. Spend the time on right-hand alone to be secure with the shifts and the in-hand voicing before attempting to put it together.
3. Play only beats 1 and 3 the first time you put this together (in two instances it will be the second half of beat 2). This will give your hands a chance to become comfortable with the basic harmonic layout of the chords.
4. Play as written. Listen carefully to your foot!

Gospel Song

EUGENIE R. ROCHEROLLE

Go to the PDM Web site.

TOPICS TO EXPLORE AND DISCUSS

- Eugenie R. Rocherolle
- Alessandro Scarlatti
- Polytonality

SKILLS AND ACTIVITIES

TECHNIQUE

1. Review all minor scales (c, d, e, g, a), all forms.

RH:	1	2	3	1	2	3	4	1	2	3	1	2	3	4	5
LH:	5	4	3	2	1	3	2	1	4	3	2	1	3	2	1

Go to the PDM Web site for technical study.

2. Play the following broken-chord extensions.

a.

b.

c.

d.

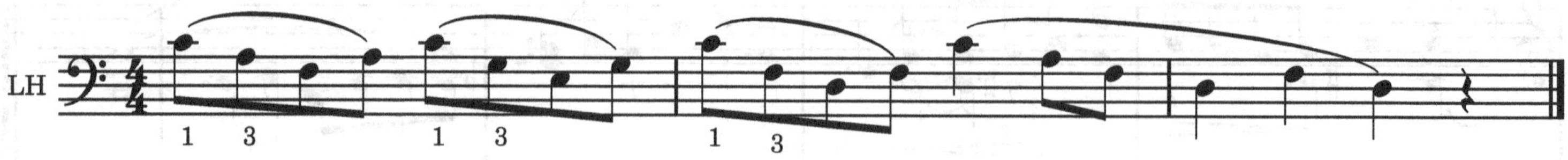

e.

f.

3. Notice the range of each arpeggiated figure. Determine a fingering that will accommodate that range. Spend a bit of preparation time with the final cadence.

Etude

MARTHA HILLEY

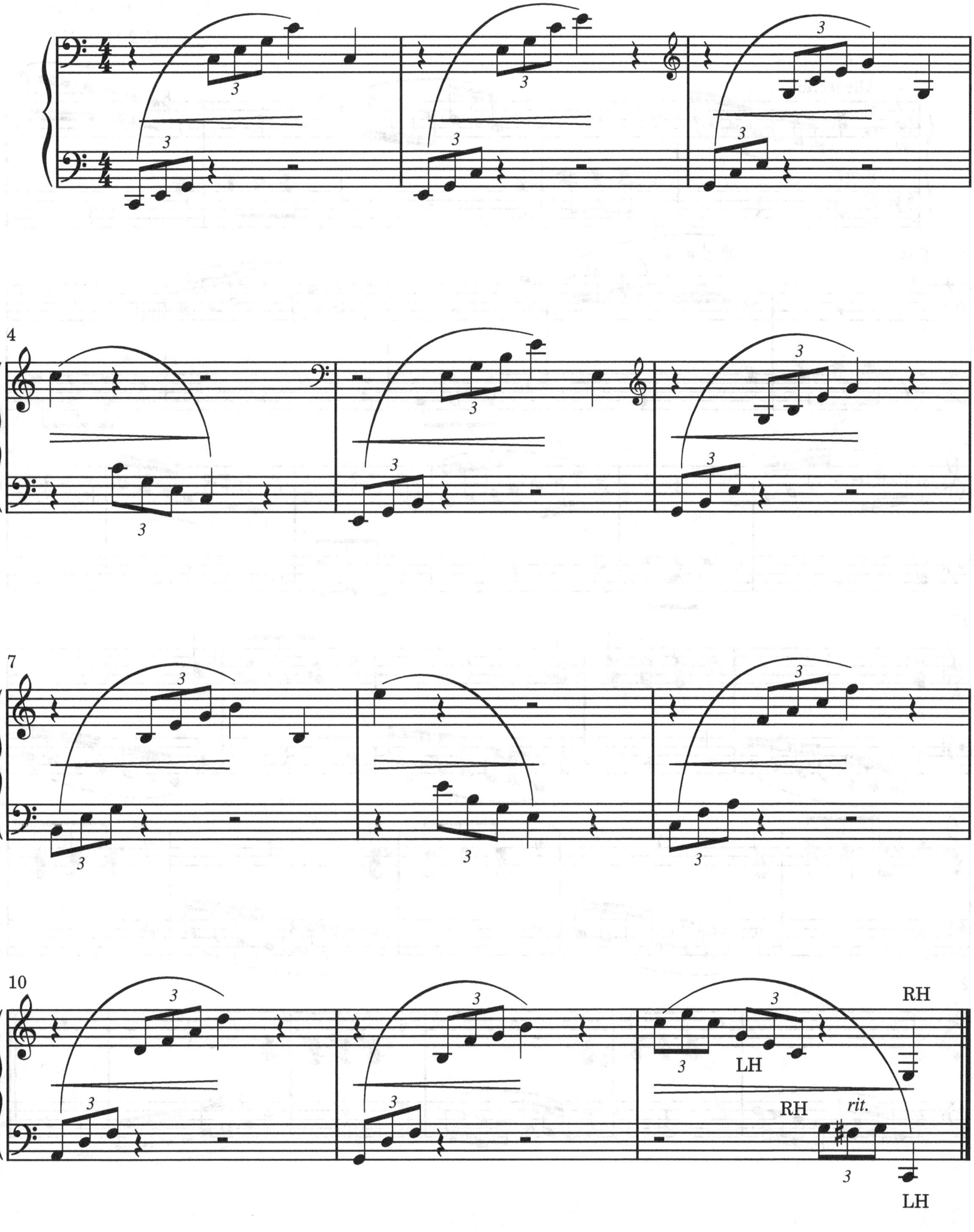

4. Using traditional scale fingerings, mark the beginning and crossover fingerings for measures 5, 21, 23, and 25.

Etude in C

CORNELIUS GURLITT
(1820–1901)

READING

1. Determine chord shapes of arpeggios.

Wiedersehen

CORNELIUS GURLITT, Op. 117, No. 24
(1820–1901)

2. Play through these viola parts.

a. Your teacher or a classmate should play the accompaniment.

Adapted

3. Try it at about 126. Your teacher will play the piano part.

Adapted

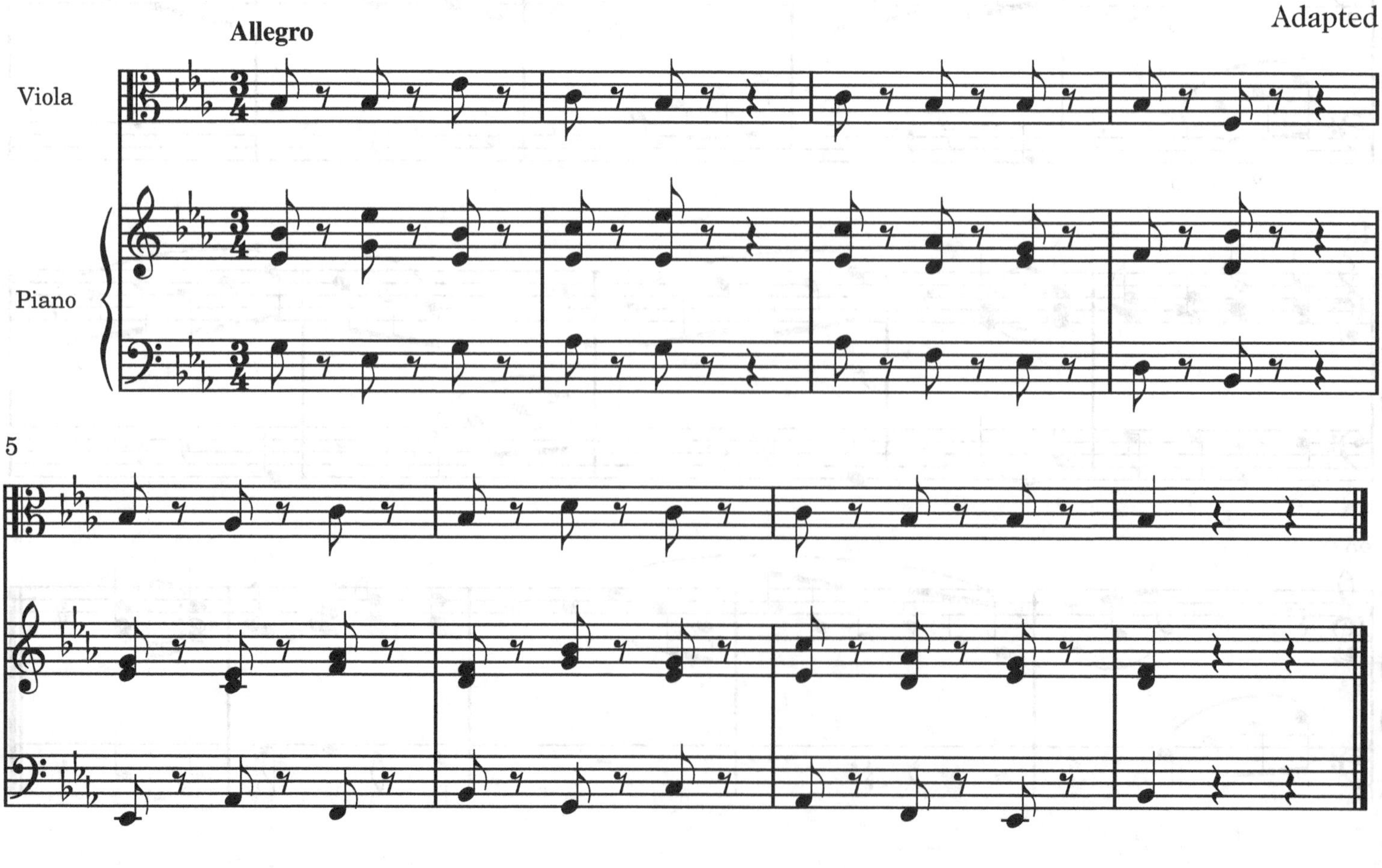

4. This one is for the singers in class!

Adapted

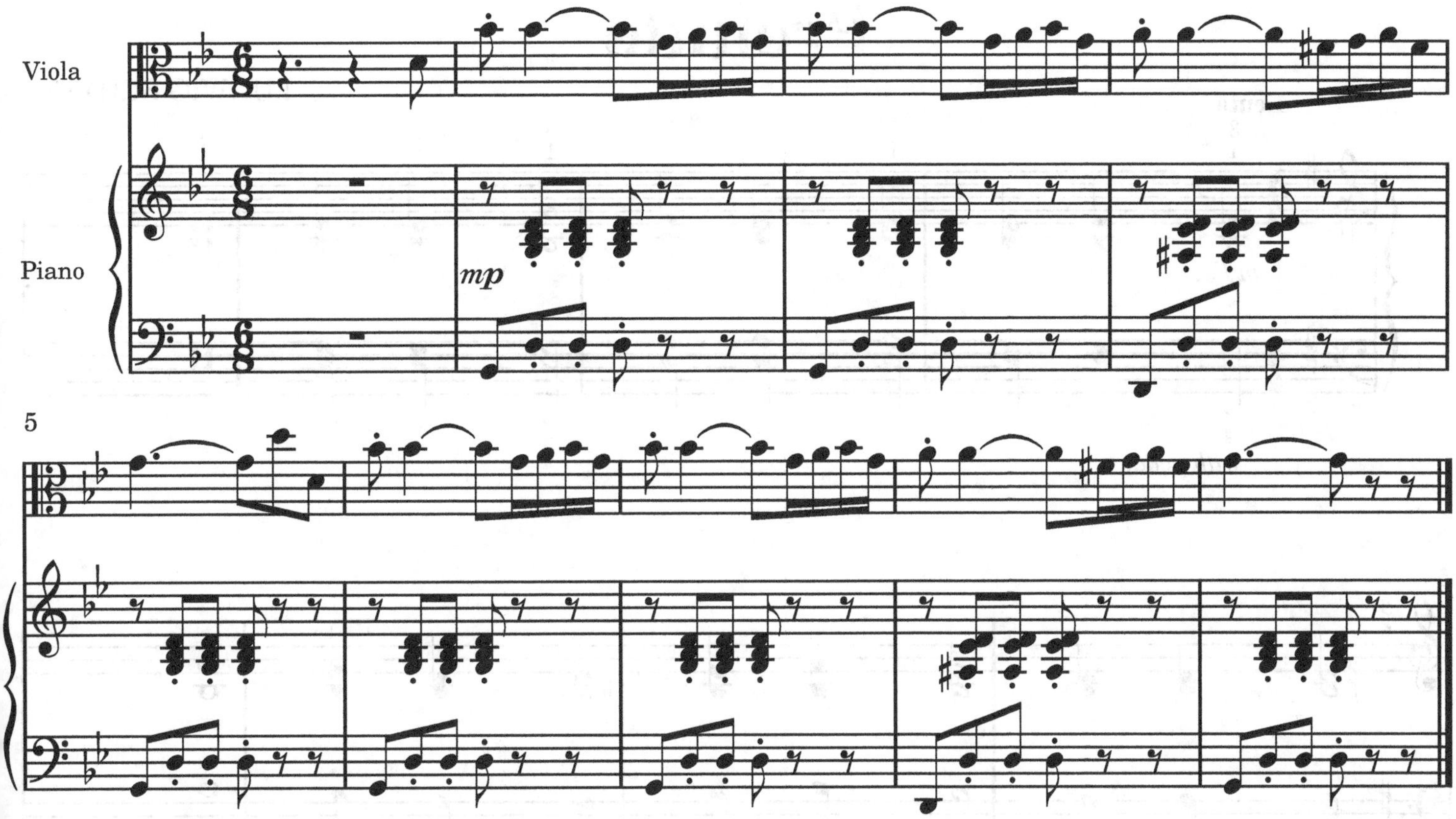

5. Let the use of repetition make this easier for you to read. A classmate can play the piano accompaniment.

Adapted

6. Locate a singer in your class and accompany this excerpt from B*ist du bei mir.*

J. S. BACH
(1685–1750)

7. Be an efficient reader by noticing common tones.

Prelude

LUGWIG SCHYTTE

Go to the PDM Web site for additional reading material.

KEYBOARD THEORY

1. Play the chord of resolution for each secondary dominant. Thinking of each key in parentheses as the tonic, analyze and play the secondary dominant and its chord of resolution.

Example:

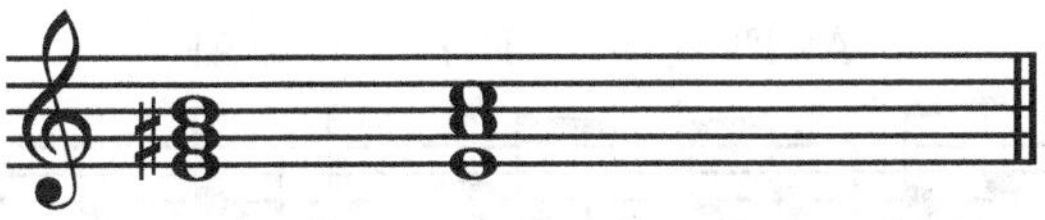

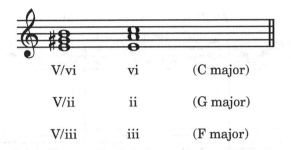

V/vi	vi	(C major)
V/ii	ii	(G major)
V/iii	iii	(F major)

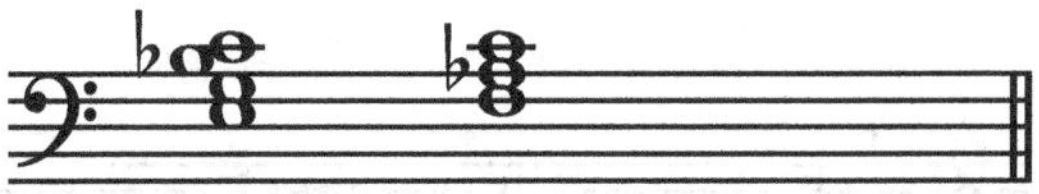

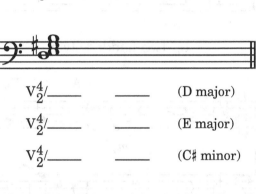

V^6_5/ii	ii	(E♭ major)
V^6_5/____	____	(D♭ major)
V^6_5/____	____	(A♭ major)

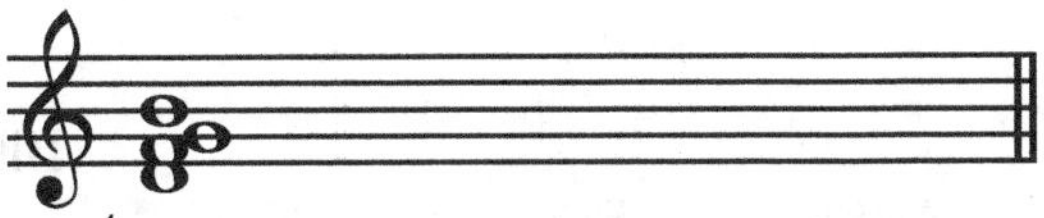

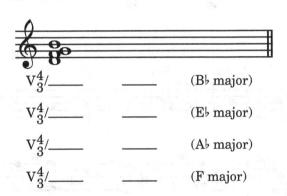

V^4_3/____	____	(B♭ major)
V^4_3/____	____	(E♭ major)
V^4_3/____	____	(A♭ major)
V^4_3/____	____	(F major)

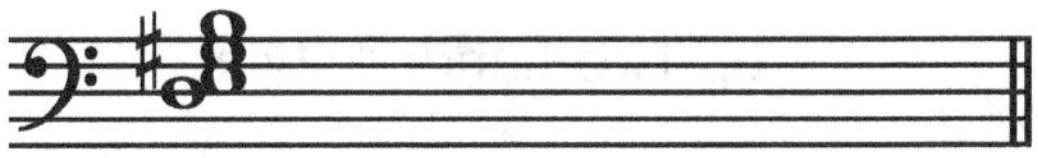

V^4_2/____	____	(D major)
V^4_2/____	____	(E major)
V^4_2/____	____	(C♯ minor)

2. Take the first example and extend the progression to the I chord. Look at the two possible resolutions of the V7.

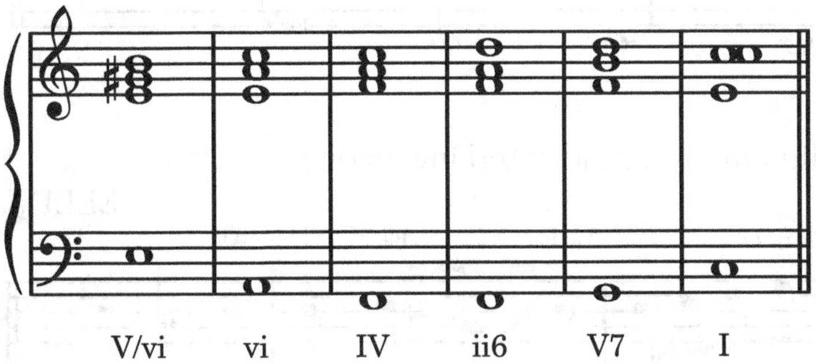

V/vi vi IV ii6 V7 I

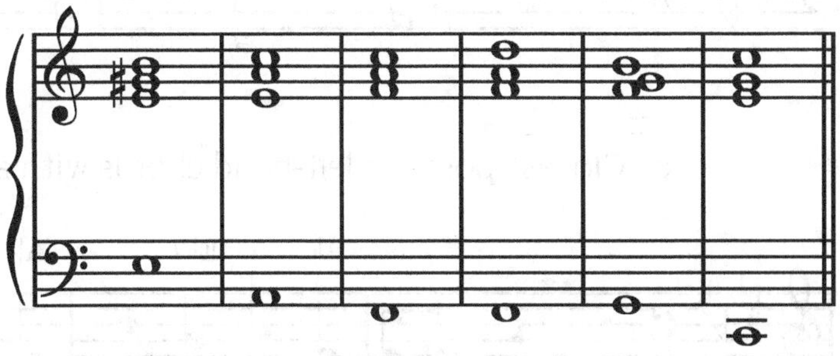

V/vi vi IV ii6 V7 I

Go to the PDM Web site for extensive drill on secondary dominants within harmonic progressions.

HARMONIZATION

1. There are several possible harmonization styles for the following melody:

   a. Keyboard style

VINCENZO BELLINI
(1801–1835)

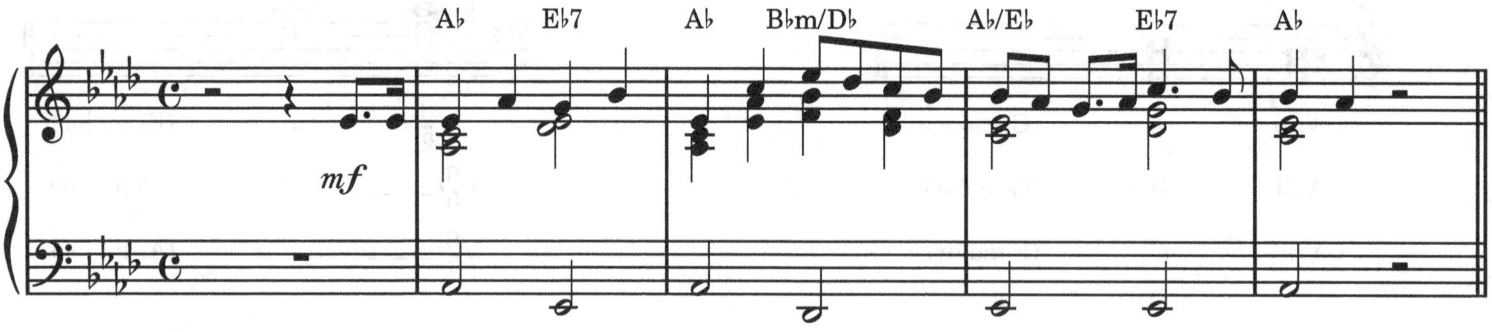

   b. Two-handed style

BELLINI

   c. Closest-position left-hand chords with an adjustment for indicated inversions

BELLINI

2.

   a. Use closest-position left-hand chords. In what measure is the secondary dominant?

THOMAS MORLEY
(1557–1602)

Go to the PDM Web site for a tutorial.

b. An accompaniment should complement the melody and support the harmonic rhythm. The following item has been harmonized for you. Do the choices, both harmonically and rhythmically, make sense?

TÜRK

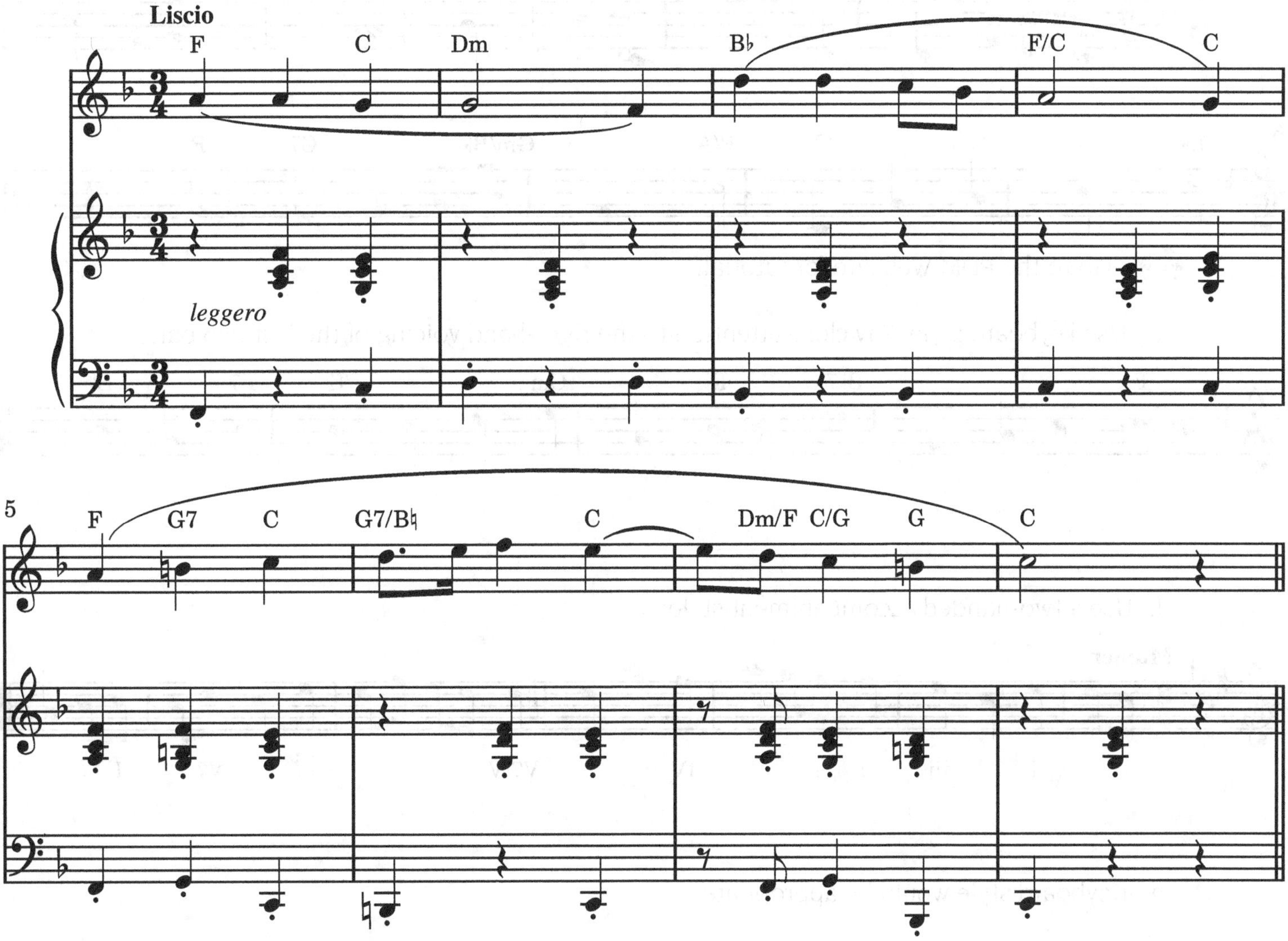

c. Modified keyboard style

ANTON RUBINSTEIN
(1829–1894)

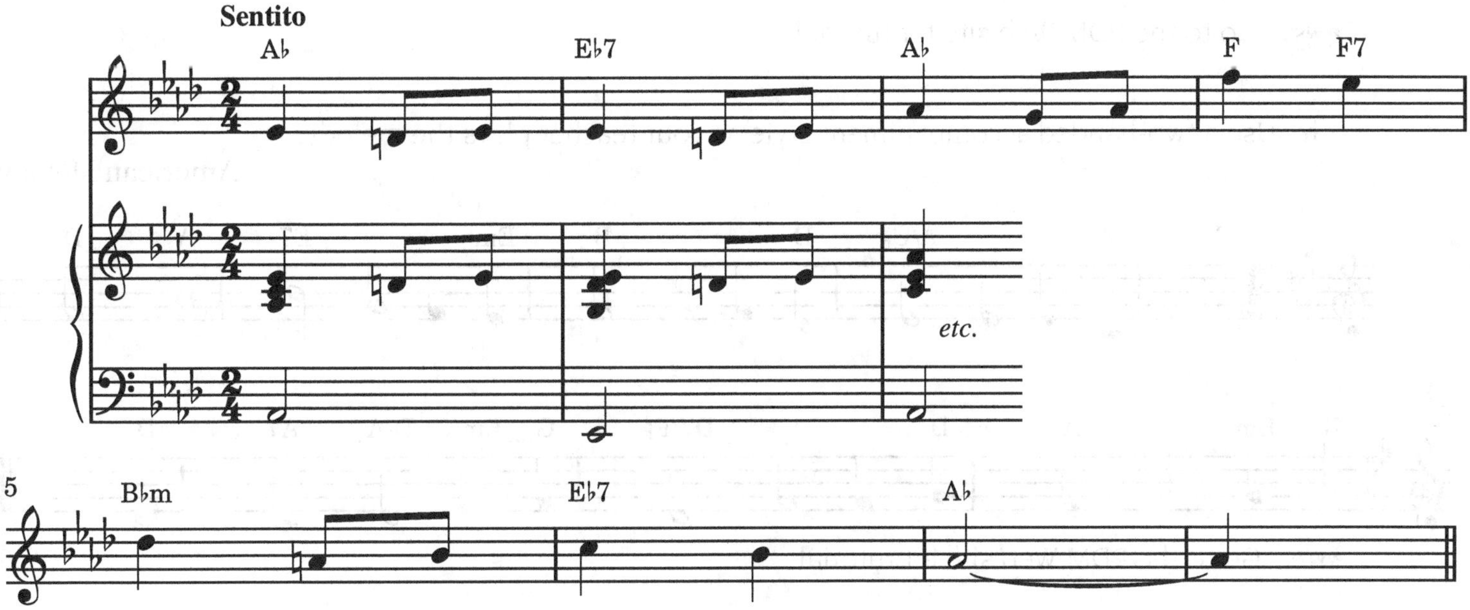

d. Use a two-handed accompaniment style as you sing or your teacher plays the melody. Be sure you choose an appropriate range for your accompaniment.

JAMES LYNAM MOLLOY

Go to the PDM Web site for tutorial.

e. Use keyboard style. Pay close attention to the right-hand voicing of the last two bars.

f. Use a two-handed accompaniment style.

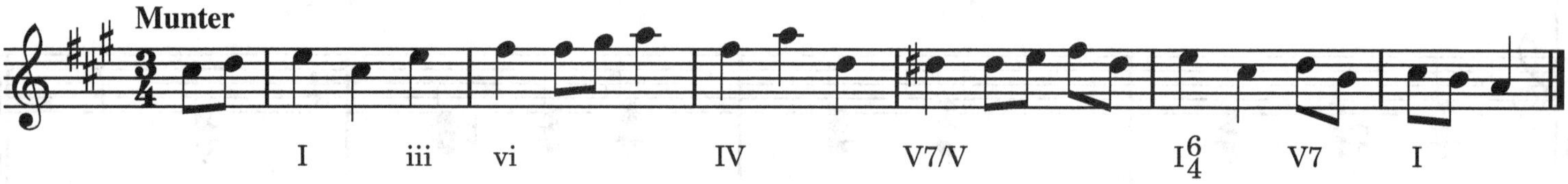

g. Keyboard style would be appropriate.

Go to the PDM Web site for tutorial.

h. Use a two-handed accompaniment style as your teacher plays the melody.

American Melody

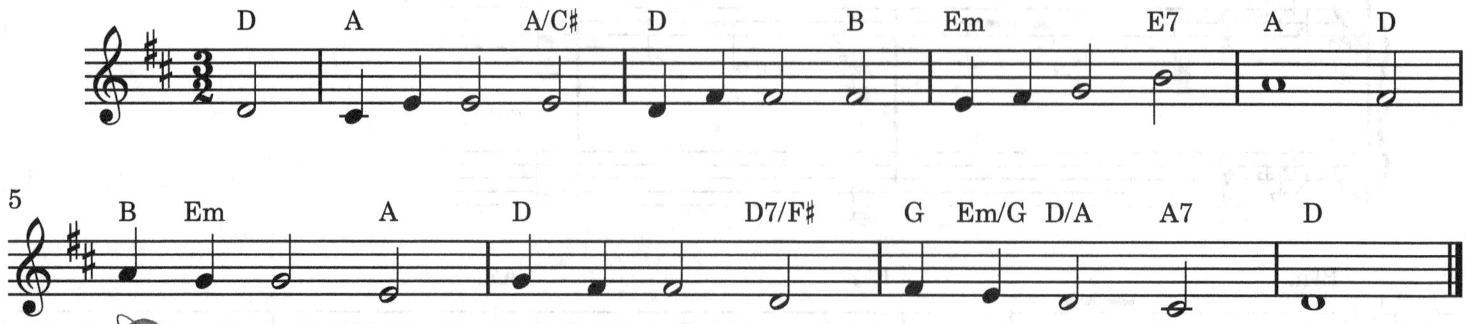

Go to the PDM Web site for tutorial.

3. Complete the harmonization in the three styles indicated.

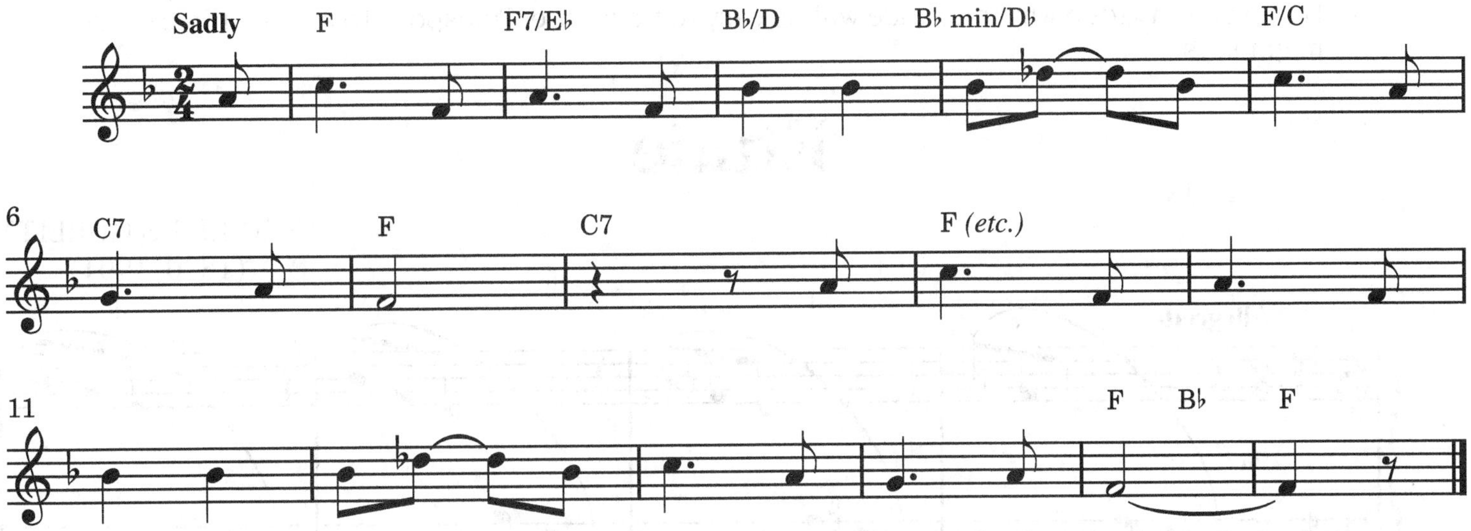

a.

b.

c.

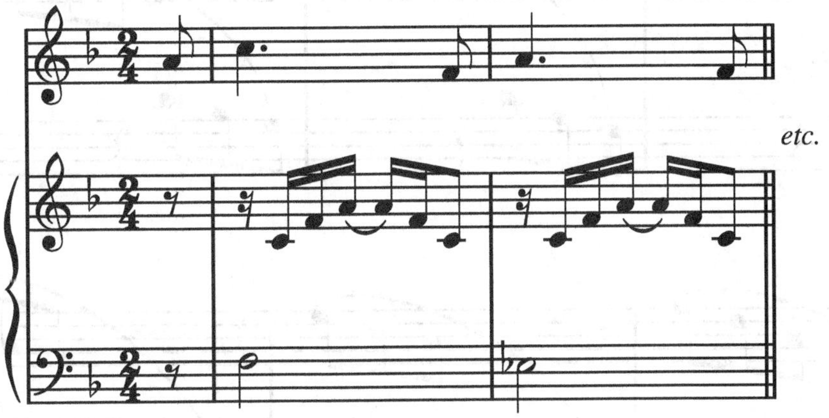

TRANSPOSITION

1. Discover as a group why this etude will be easy to transpose. Transpose to at least three other major keys.

Etude

CORNELIUS GURLITT
(1820–1901)

2. The following are to be transposed the interval of a tritone. It is so much easier if you follow the steps.

   a. Transpose *up* to A major.

   b. Transpose *down* to C major.

CARLA DAVIS

   c. Transpose *up* to B♭ major. Think about key and function before you start.

KEVIN RICHMOND

   d. Label with Roman numerals, then transpose *down* to E♭ major.

Go to the PDM Web site for additional tritone transpositions.

3. Choose a partner and play the following:

a. Think B♭ major.

b. Think G major.

c. In what major key will you think?

HAYDN
(Adapted)

d. Play both parts on this one.

HAYDN
(Adapted)

Go to the PDM Web site for additional clarinet examples.

(This page has been left blank to avoid a difficult page turn.)

IMPROVISATION

1. It was fairly common practice in eighteenth-century music to vary recurring materials by adding figuration to the written score. In addition to increased ornamentation of the trill and mordent variety, it was natural for the performer to "fill in" tones, especially in the small skips. On a repeat, for example:

might well become

could become

Rhythmic variations were common also. A single held chord or tone could be given new vigor through repetition

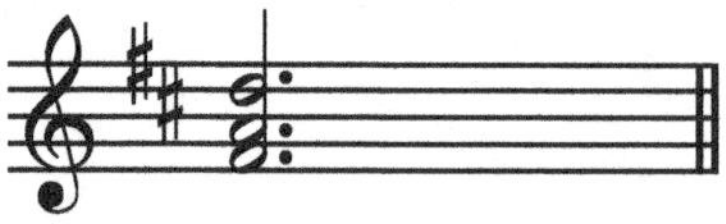
could become
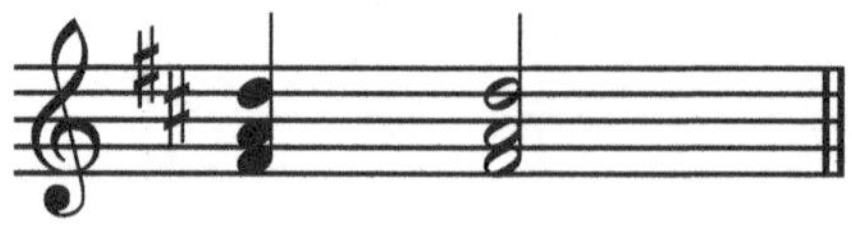

and "straight" rhythms could be "bent" to provide a new buoyancy. In many cases, these dotted rhythms were played in a "lazy" or rounded manner when a gentle lilt was appropriate.

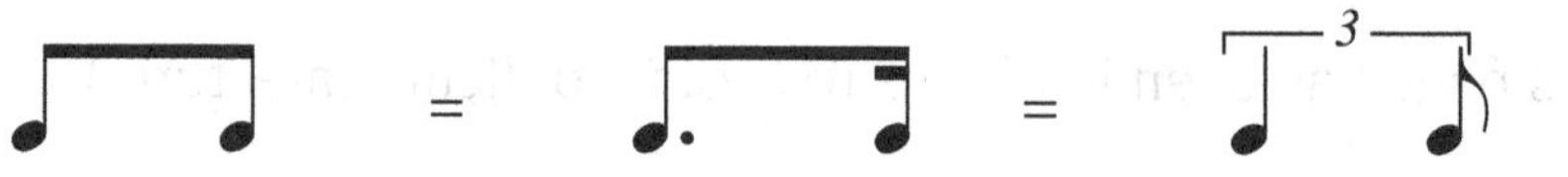

(notated) (performed)

Following the original version of the Krieger *Minuet*, we have suggested some ways to ornament the patterns. Use these ideas and vary them. This practice is called "melodic ornamentation," and, as in all such matters, your own sense of style and taste should be your main guide.

Minuet

JOHANN KRIEGER
(1651–1738)

Possible melodic ornamentation for the A section:

Possible melodic ornamentation for the B section:

In both examples notice the use of sequence in the melodic ornamentation—just as Krieger used sequence in his score.

1. Return to *Gospel Song* (page 261). Convert your Roman numeral analysis to letter names.
   - Play an improvised *obligato* as your teacher or a classmate plays the score as written.
   - Notice how the music becomes more "involved" in measure 9 and on. It would be appropriate if your improvisation complemented the score. Perhaps chord tones only—for the most part—in bars 1–8 then add non-chord tones for the last eight bars.

Go to the PDM Web site for tutorial.

ENSEMBLE

1. Perform the following once as written. Perform again with these options:
   - Parts 2 and 3 become one part.
   - On the repeat Part 1 should play a solo improvisation based on the harmonic structure; the second ending as written may be used for the close of the solo improvisation.

The ii–V Doodle

MARTHA HILLEY

2. Note that the two middle staves are to be played as one part.

Alexander's Ragtime Band

IRVING BERLIN
(1888–1988)
Arr. S. Ogilvy

13
f
17
21
mf

f

COMPOSITION

Compose an original minuet in Baroque style (refer to *Minuet* by Krieger, page 278). At the time of performance, add melodic ornamentation to the repetition of the A and B sections.

Go to the PDM Web site for representative student compositions.

SUBSEQUENT REPERTOIRE

Chromatizone Rag

ANN COLLINS

8va

1. As a class determine a fingering that will support a "seamless" effect.

Aria

ALESSANDRO SCARLATTI
(1660–1725)

2. What compositional tonality has Persichetti used? What about the measures where this tonality is not used?

Prologue

VINCENT PERSICHETTI
(1915–1987)

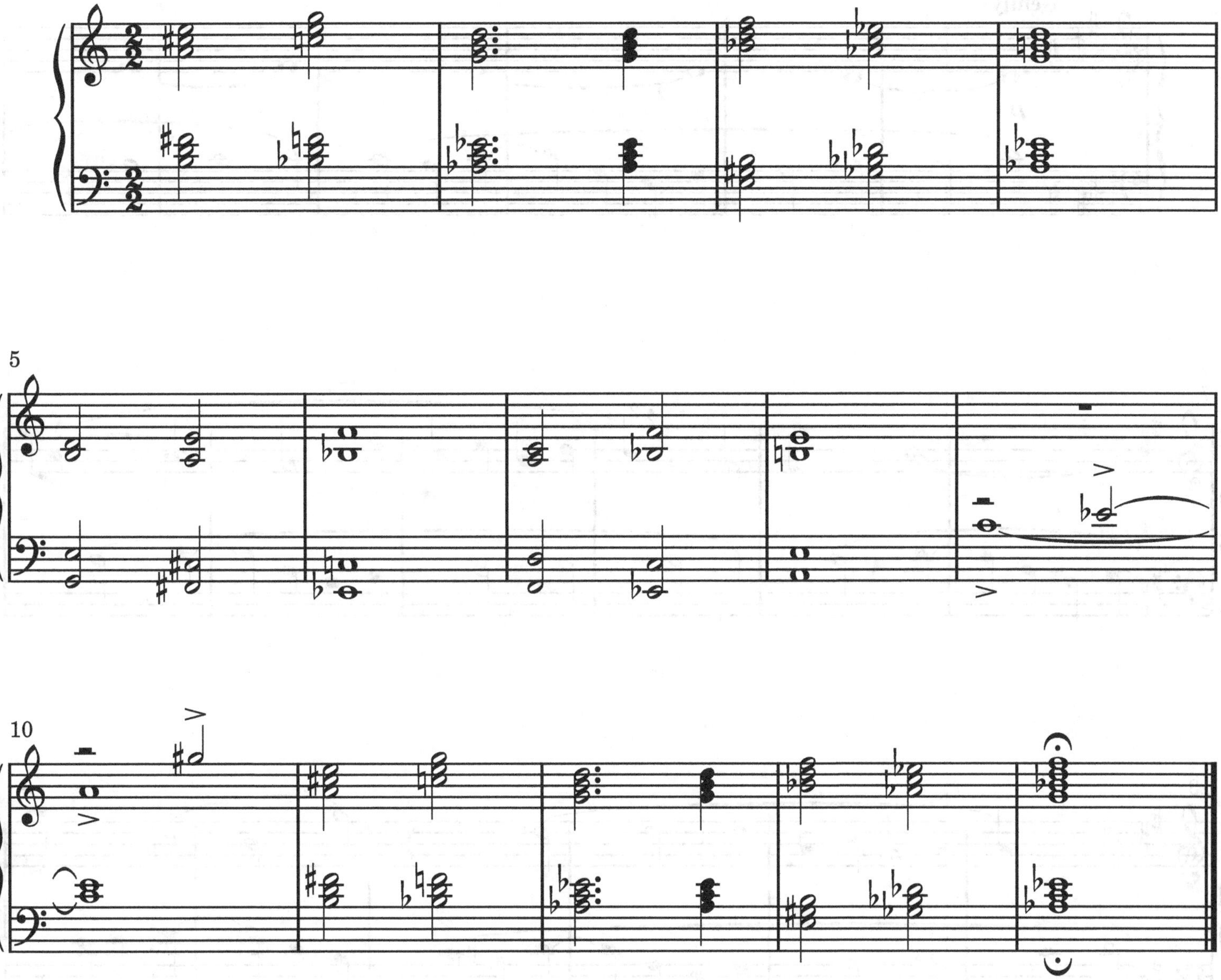

3. Careful subdivision of the pulse will ensure success in bars 21–22 and 30–31. Be very aware of phrasing.

Two Voices Singing

JOSEPH SCRIVENER

25
pp
31
p
36
41
mf
46
pp

Harmonic Implications of Common Modes

EXEMPLARY REPERTOIRE

Lydian Nocturne Robert D. Vandall

INQUIRY

1. Scan the piece. Observe:
    - broken chord accompaniment
    - clef changes
    - octave placement
    - Lydian scalar passages
    - pedal indication in last measure

PERFORMANCE

1. Determine a fingering for the left-hand accompaniment figure. Experiment until you find one that is comfortable for your hand.
2. Start your practice with bars 11–18. Why?

(This page has been left blank to avoid a difficult page turn.)

Lydian Nocturne

ROBERT D. VANDALL

Moderately slow; freely, expressively

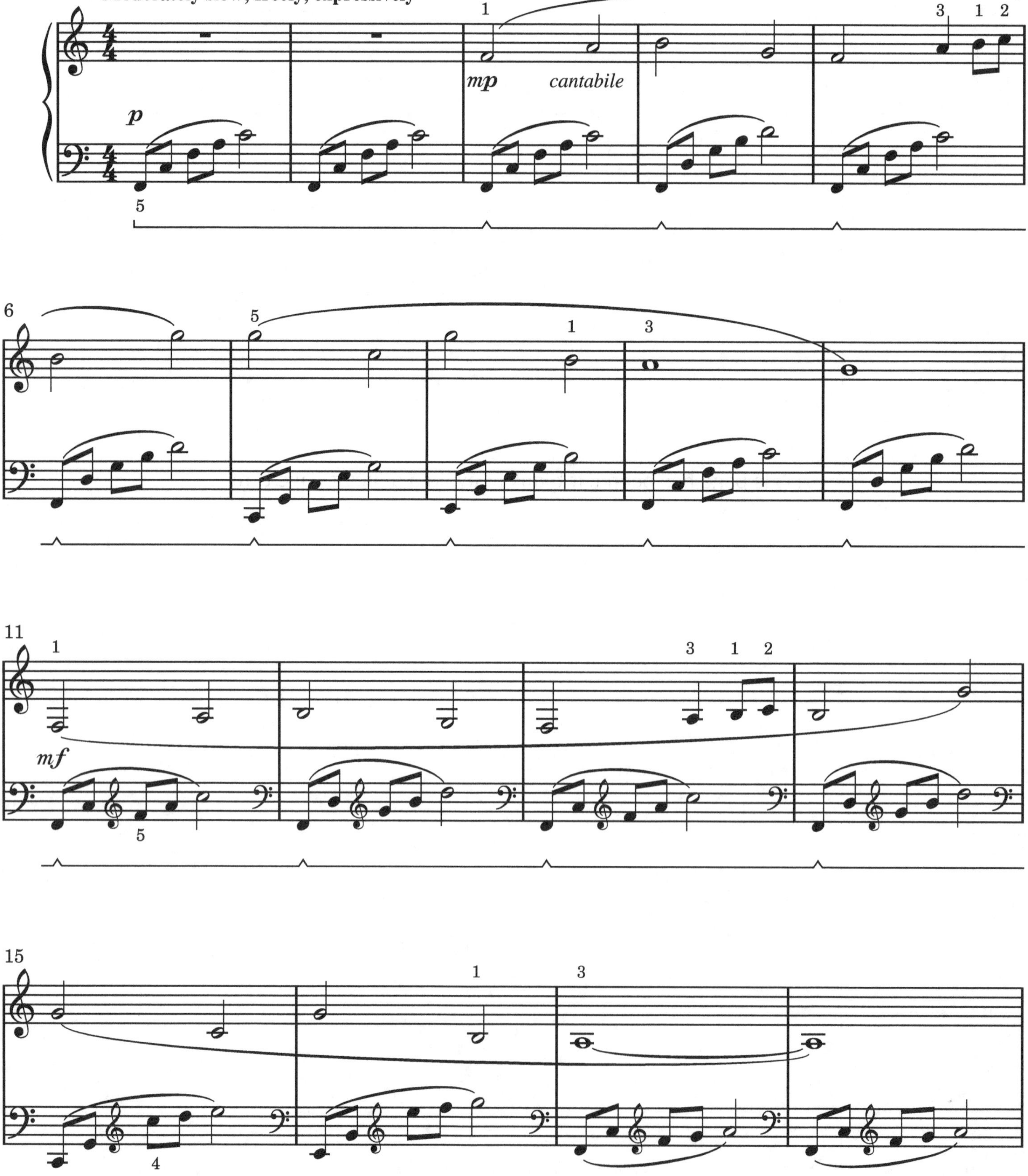

19
8va
p
cresc.
f
23
mf
dim.
27
(8va)
a tempo
rit.
mp
31
loco
rit.

TOPICS TO EXPLORE AND DISCUSS

- Robert D. Vandall
- Frank Lynes
- Carl Orff
- Johann Pachelbel

SKILLS AND ACTIVITIES

TECHNIQUE

The following is traditional F major/minor scale fingering (2 octaves)

RH:	1	2	3	4	1	2	3	1	2	3	4	1	2	3	4
LH:	5	4	3	2	1	3	2	1	4	3	2	1	3	2	1

Away from the keyboard on a flat surface, play the scale upward and downward. Say "1's" when thumbs play together. Now play on the keyboard, slowly and steadily.

Play the F major and three forms of F minor scales.

Go to the PDM Web site for further drill in F minor scales.

READING

1. Play both parts. Think about the octave placement of the parts in the first measures. It is suggested that you play the first seven beats with the right hand, then split on the second beat of the third bar.

Duo in C Major

JOHANN GEORG ALBRECHTSBERGER
(1736–1809)

2. Play Violin II and Viola together. Notice parallel and oblique motion.

String Quartet in E-Flat Major

(Violin II and viola excerpt)

WOLFGANG AMADEUS MOZART
(1756–1791)

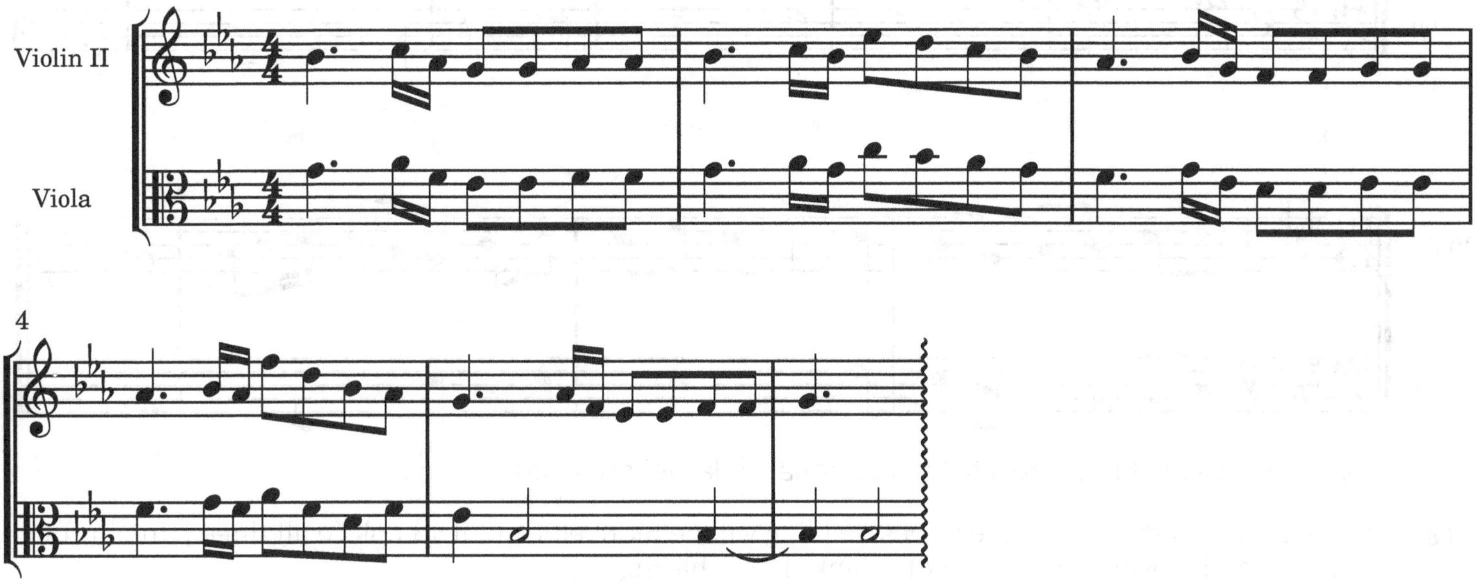

3. Before playing, look for parallel and contrary motion between the parts.

String Quartet in G Major

(Viola and cello excerpt)

WOLFGANG AMADEUS MOZART
(1756–1791)

Molto Allegro

4. Play both parts.

a.

b.

Go to the PDM Web site for additional viola clef exercises.

5. Even though there are three staves, reading will be more efficient if you place all three parts in your right hand. It will make it easier to think chord shapes.

JEAN SIBELIUS
(1865–1881)

6. How would you group this example? What keeps you from playing it all in one hand? What is unusual about the first downbeat? The last bar?

7. Probably best suited for two hands.

8. Let the use of consecutive thirds between the baritone parts help you.

9. Look for chord shapes, common tones, and parallel movement.

10. This example has rhythmic challenges.

Go to the PDM Web site for additional vocal open score.

KEYBOARD THEORY

1. The harmony in modal music is diatonic to the particular scale. Modes can be divided into major and minor categories.

Major	**Minor**
Ionian	Dorian
Lydian	Phrygian
Mixolydian	Aeolian

The harmonies resulting from building triads on modal scale tones tend to diffuse the strong traditional sense of tonic. For example, in Dorian, Mixolydian, and Aeolian modes, the dominant is a minor triad; in Phrygian, the dominant is diminished.

Play diatonic triads for the following modal scales.

Example:

D Phrygian:

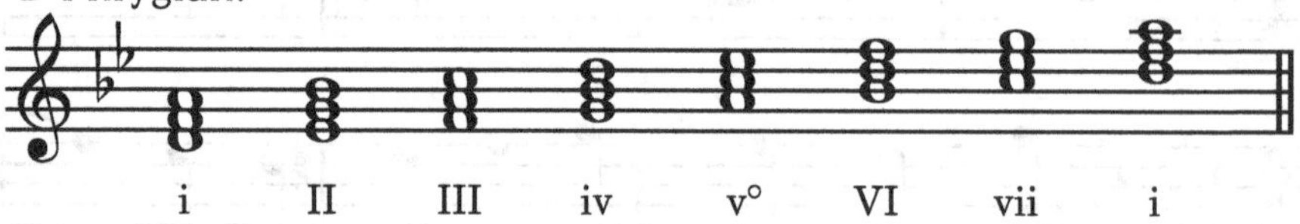

A Dorian

B♭ Mixolydian

E Lydian

C Phrygian

Go to the PDM Web site for additional examples.

2. In the following examples, indicated harmonies represent progressions characteristic of the mode. Complete each harmonization using chords that will highlight the mode.

It is occasionally appropriate to harmonize modal melodies in ways not associated with eighteenth-century common practice because of the special characteristics of certain modes. Although modal harmonies should use only pitches from the mode in question, occasional accidentals (such as a raised 7th or a lowered 6th) may occur as the tasteful choice.

HARMONIZATION

1. Use left-handed broken-chord accompaniment.

2. On what mode is the following American melody based?

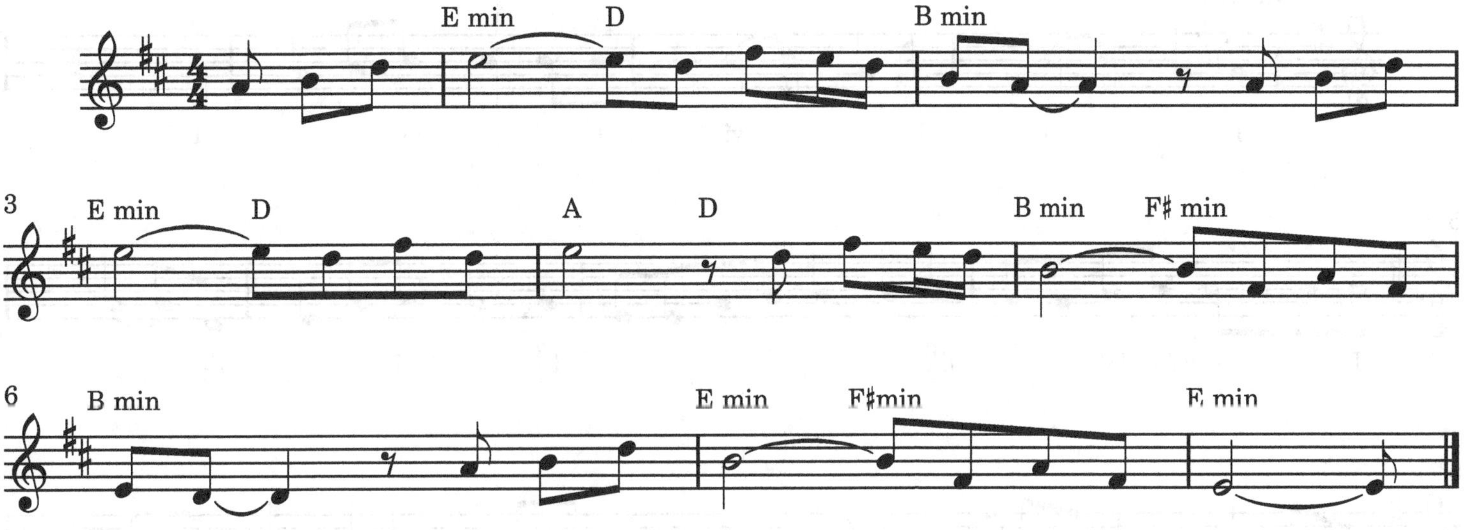

Harmonize using a "strumming" style of accompaniment:

3. Use keyboard style.

FRANZ SCHUBERT
(1797–1828)

Go to the PDM Web site for tutorial.

4. Choose an appropriate style.

American

Go to the PDM Web site for tutorial.

5. Complete in the style indicated. Plan carefully for measures 7 and 15.

AMILCARE PONCHIELLI
(1834–1886)

6. Determine the tonality and then use a left-hand broken chord style.

7. Use a "modified" keyboard style—chords only on the beats indicated.

8. Use a "boom-chick-chick" two-handed accompaniment.

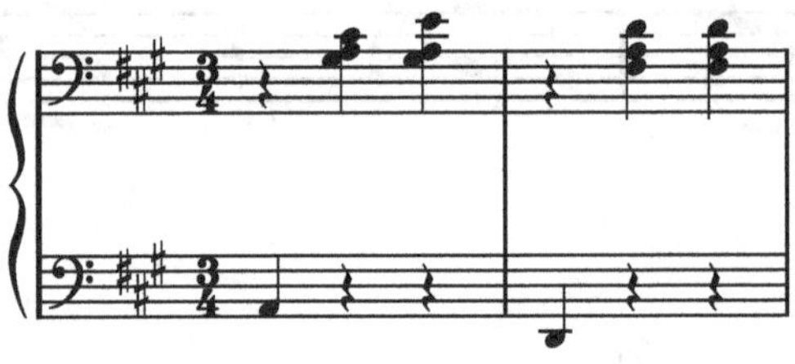

9. Use keyboard style.

TRANSPOSITION

1. The clarinet part must be transposed down a whole step in order to be played on a keyboard. Simply think in the key of B-flat and read intervals.

    - Play the clarinet line
    - Play the accompaniment
    - Choose a partner and play as an ensemble

Sonata for B-Flat Clarinet

(Excerpt)

JOHANN BAPTIST VANHAL
(1739–1813)

Go to the PDM Web site for more B♭ transposing instruments.

2. The following examples are to be transposed the interval of a tritone.

a. Transpose *up* to G major.

KEVIN RICHMOND

b. Transpose *up* to D major.

KEVIN RICHMOND

c. Transpose *down* to C major.

Go to the PDM Web site for additional tritone transposition.

3. A horn in F transposes down a perfect fifth. Work through the following examples. Transposing individual pitches makes this a daunting task. Think in the transposed or new key and then simply read intervals.

a. Think in the key of A major.

b. Think in the key of F major. Ask a classmate to accompany you, then trade parts.

c. Let the non-transposing instrument help you double check the key in which you must play the horn.

d. Use the following opening fingering and the rest of the horn part falls within a five-finger position. Try playing both parts.

e. Choose a partner and let the one playing the flute part set the tempo.

HAYDN
(Adapted)

Go to the PDM Web site for additional French horn examples.

IMPROVISATION

1. Determine the tonal center for each of the following and improvise melodically above the given bass.

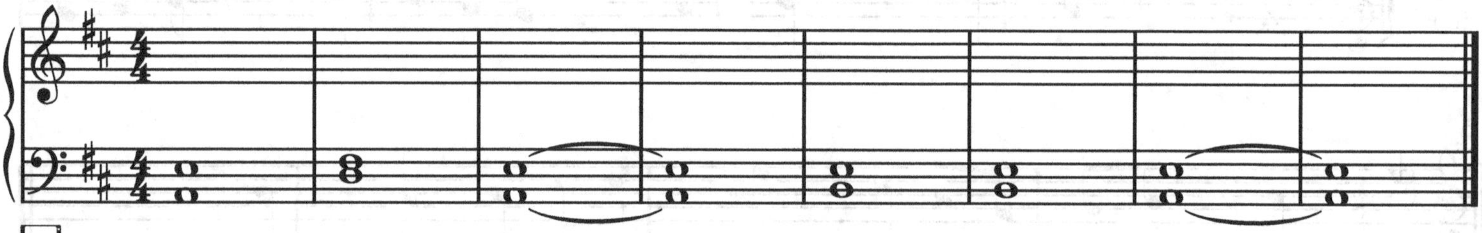

2. In Chapter 9 (Keyboard Theory, page 240) your class created minor progressions. With these progressions you were to demonstrate harmonic content, rhythm, and two four-bar phrases. Return to those progressions and alter them to represent one Dorian, one Phrygian, and one Aeolian progression. Choose a partner and create an improvisation duet—one plays the progressions as a two-handed accompaniment demonstrating harmonic content and rhythm while the other plays a melodic improvisation representing the particular mode.

   For instance, the C minor example could become C Dorian resulting in a diminished vi, a major IV, a minor v, and a minor ii. You should probably retain the accompaniment as shown with the exception of changing the bass note of the vi° to "C" to eliminate doubling of a member of the tritone. A possible melodic improvisation has been added to serve as an example.

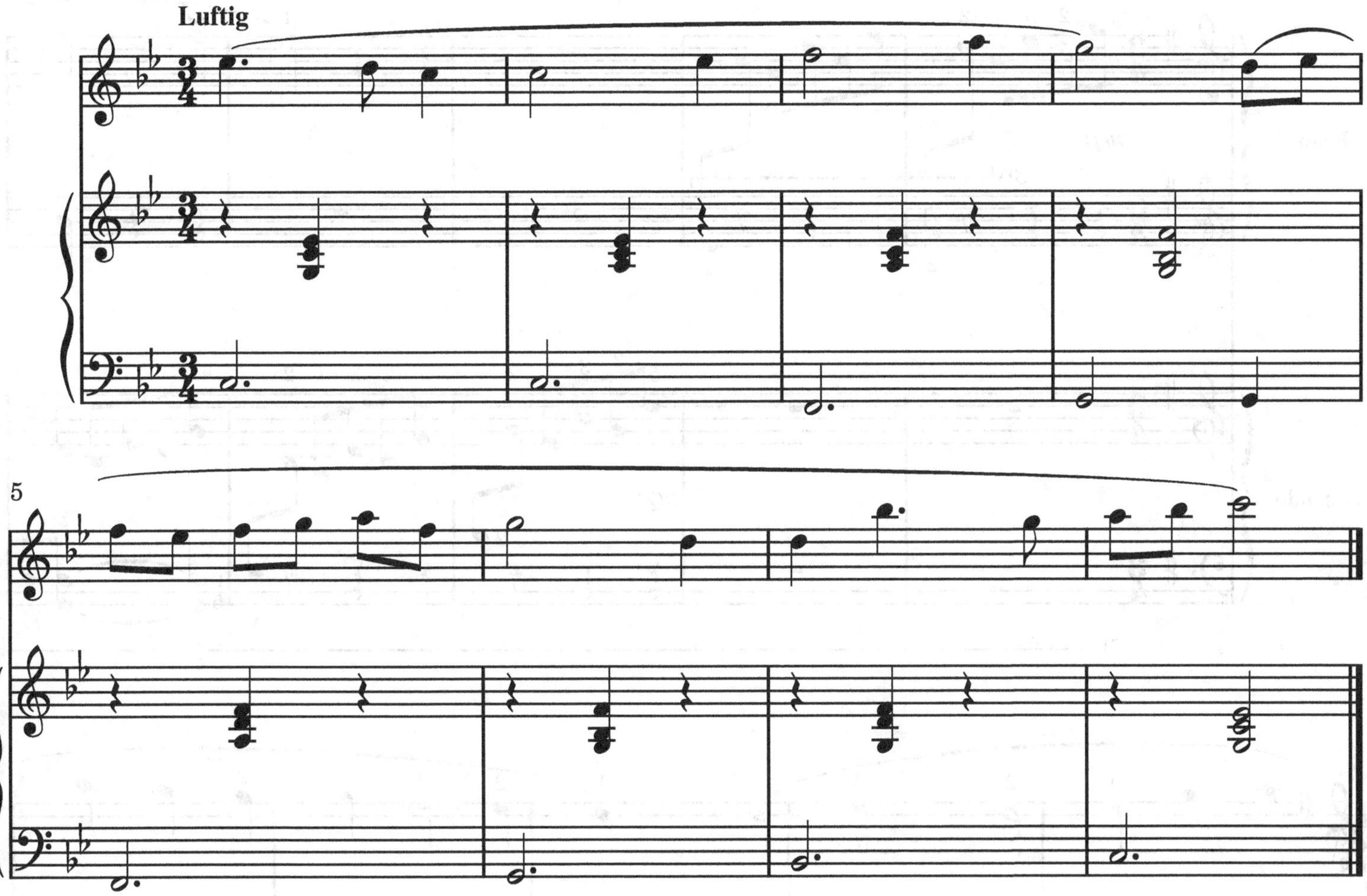

Go to the PDM Web site for further study in modal improvisation.

COMPOSITION

1. Compose an ensemble "in the style" of *Allegretto* (page 312). You may wish to do a harmonic analysis of the Czerny and then pick an alternate key in which to compose your own ensemble. This *is not* simply a transposition of *Allegretto*.

   Notice the following characteristics in the original score:

   - broken chords
   - melodic passing tones and neighbor tones
   - pedal tones
   - closest-position implied harmonies

   Choose a classmate as your duet partner and perform your composition.

Go to the PDM Web site for representative student compositions.

1. Take the time to do a harmonic analysis with particular attention to the Secondo. Chordal content moves to the Primo in bar 21.

It Came Upon a Midnight Clear

E.H. SEARS and R.S. WILLIS
Arr. Leigh Kaplan

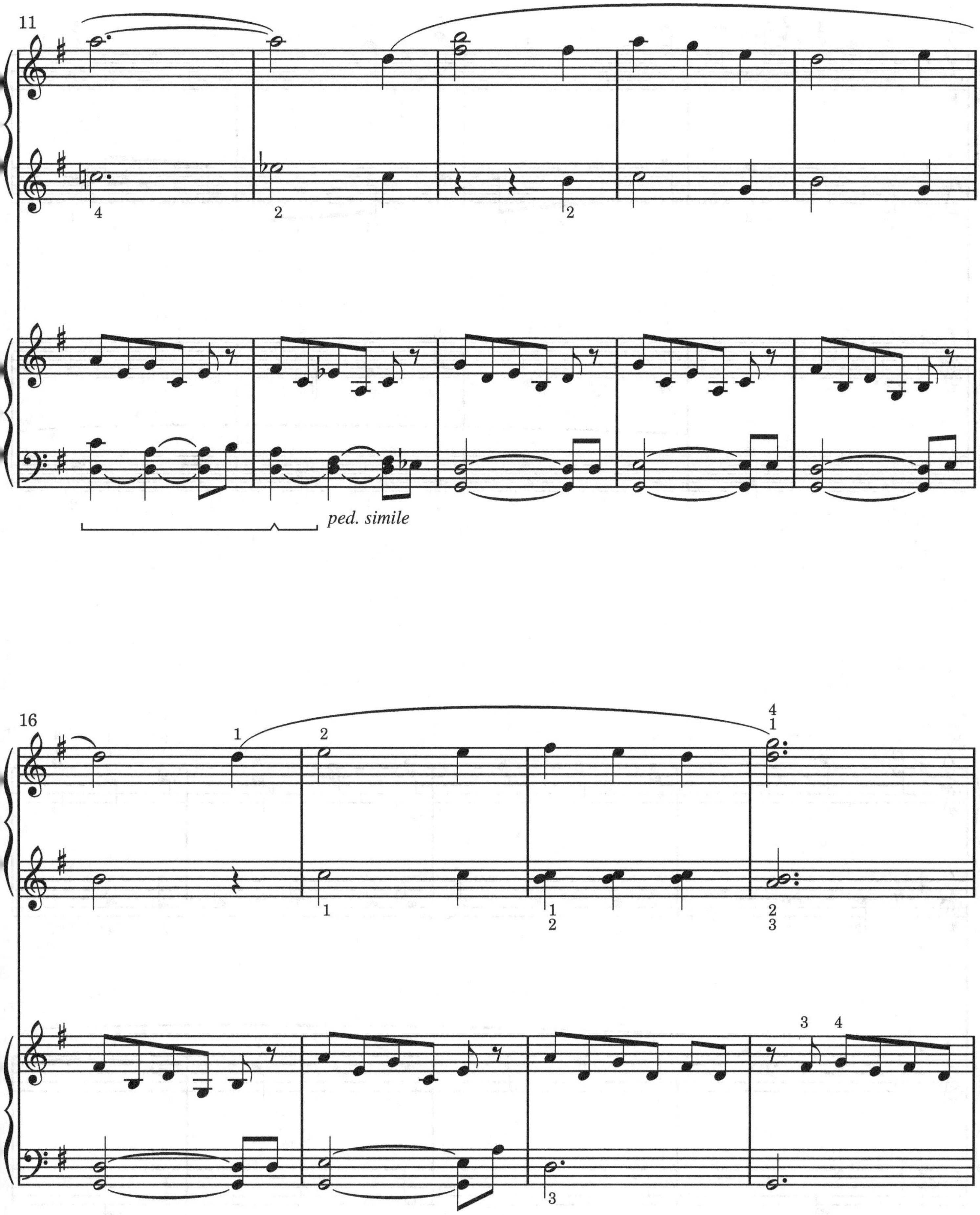
ped. simile

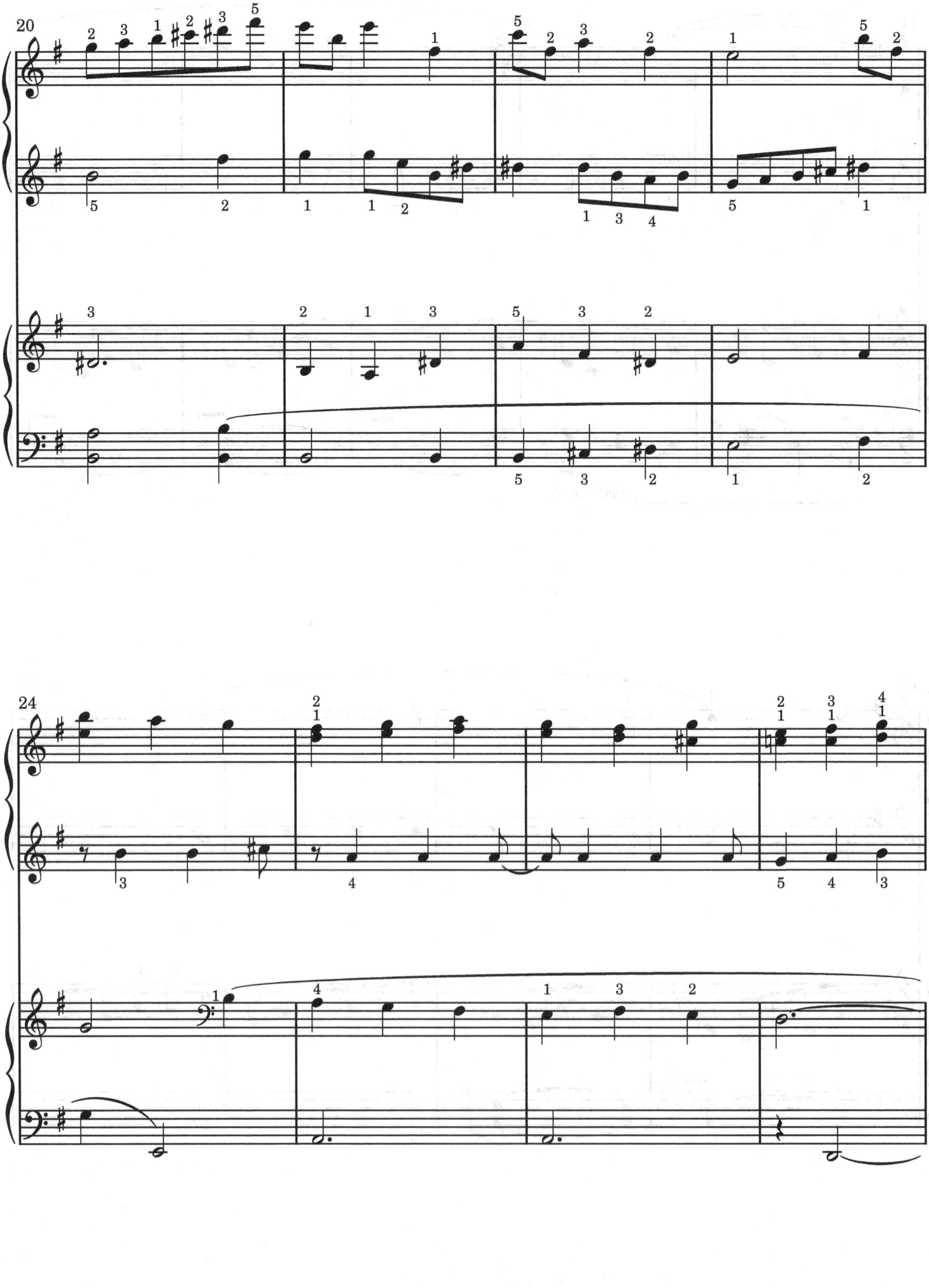
20
24

28
33
8va
rit.
R.H.
rit.

2. Trade parts at each repeat.

Allegretto

Secondo

CARL CZERNY, Op. 824, No. 18
(1791–1857)

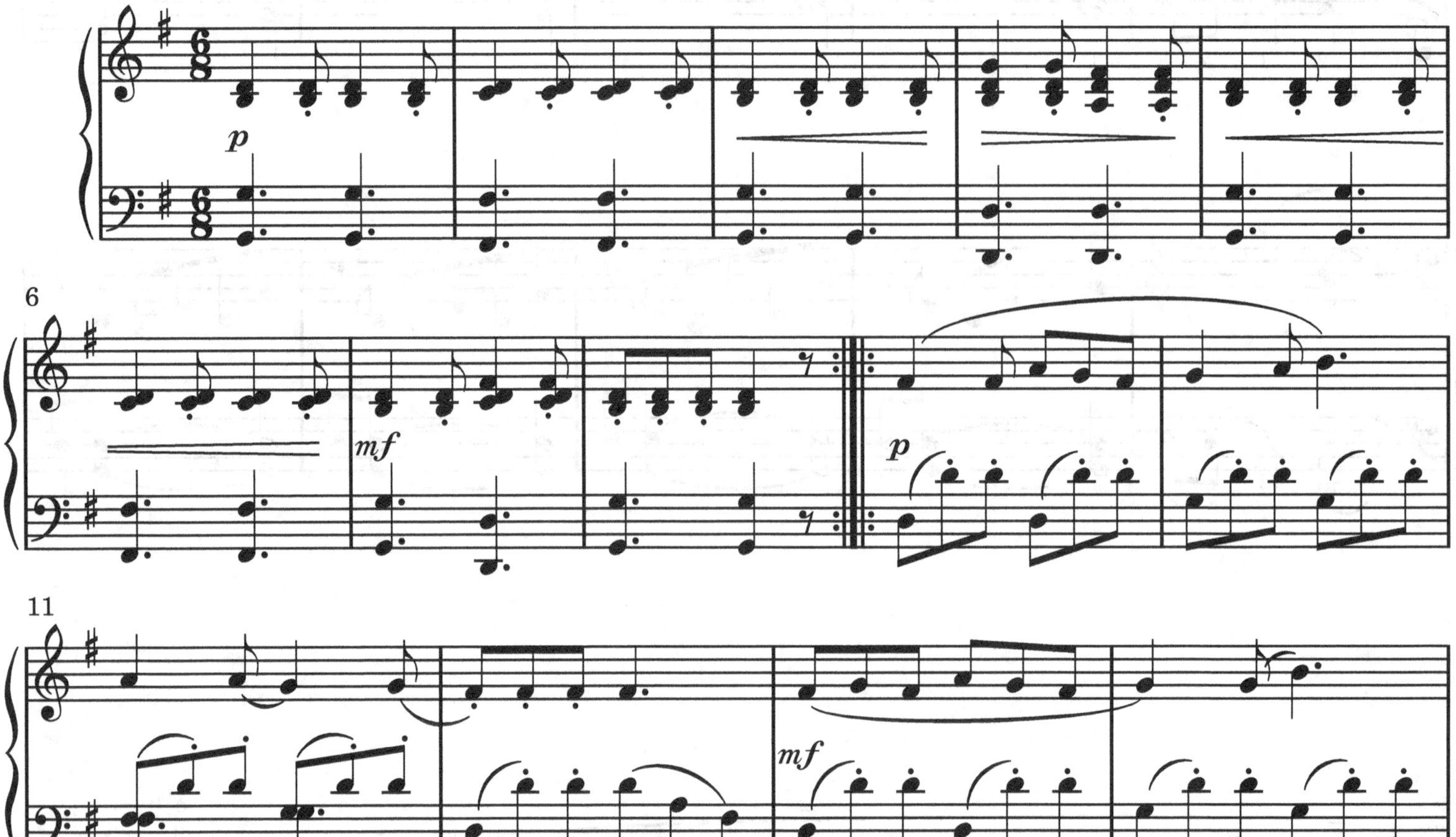

Allegretto

Primo

CARL CZERNY, Op. 824, No. 18
(1791–1857)

SUBSEQUENT REPERTOIRE

1. Beth Ann graduated from UT Austin in May of 2004. She and her husband, Shane, are now graduate students at the University of Cincinnati College-Conservatory of Music (bassoon and french horn).

Minuet

BETH ANN REHNBORG

2. Discuss variable meters and tonal basis before playing. Your tempo must compliment the meter and a feel for one pulse to a bar.

Dance Piece

(1933)

CARL ORFF
(1895–1982)

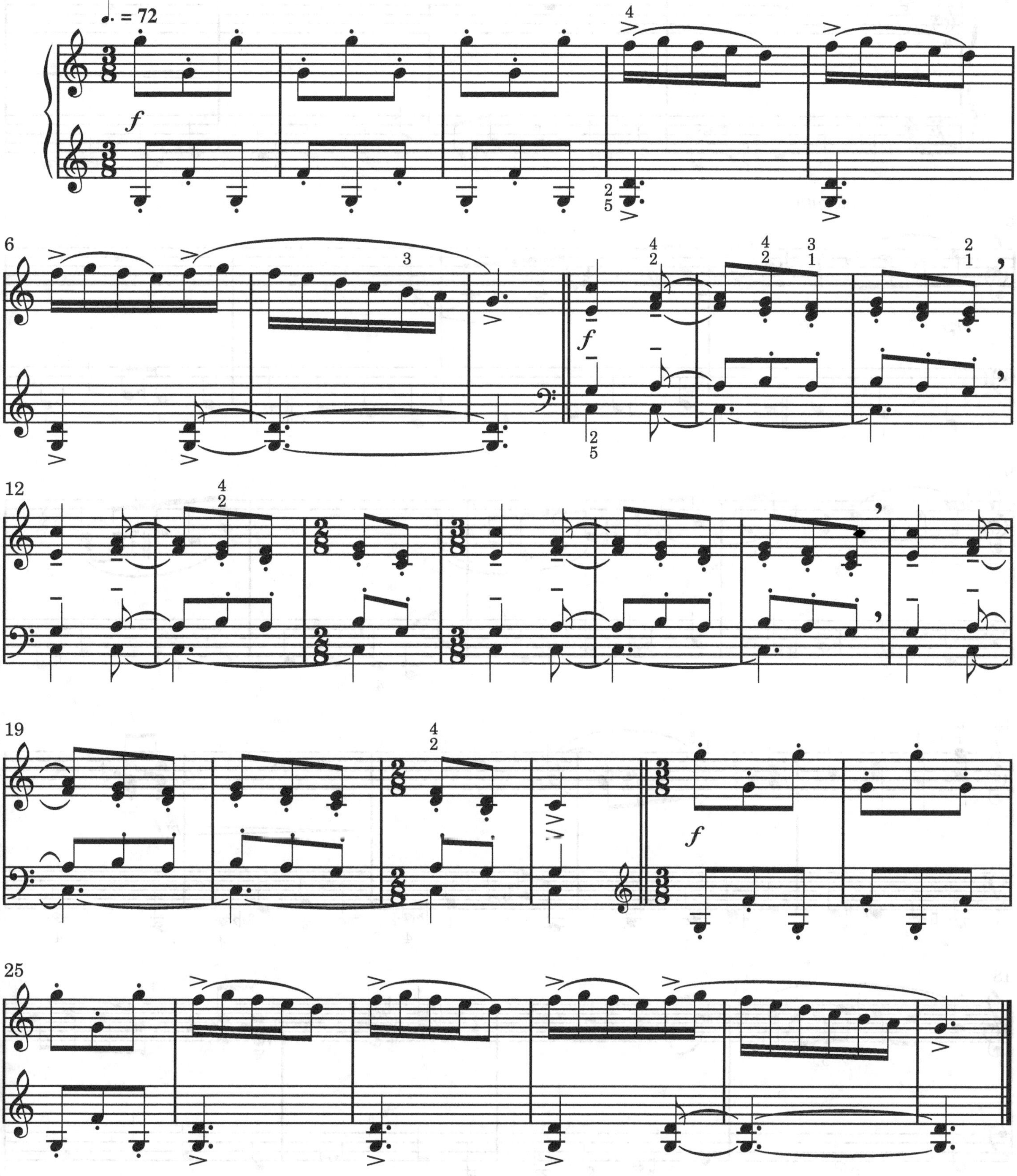

3. You need to be totally relaxed.

The Bass Man Walketh

BILL BOYD

22
26
mp
30
34
38
mf mp

4. In the indication 15 ma, the "ma" is an abbreviation for what?

O Little Town of Bethlehem

LEWIS H. REDNER
Arr. by Catherine Rollin

Moderately and tenderly

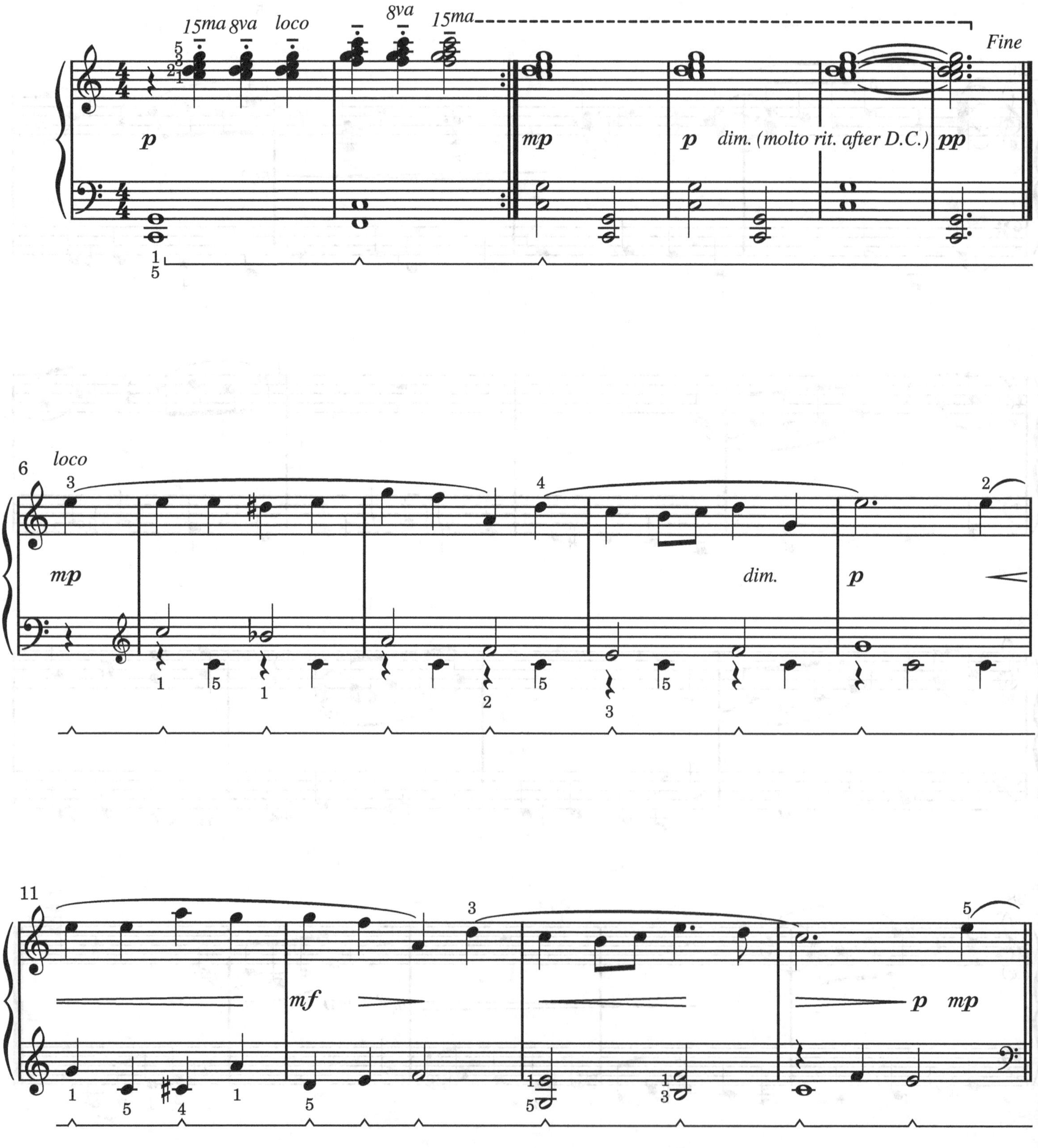

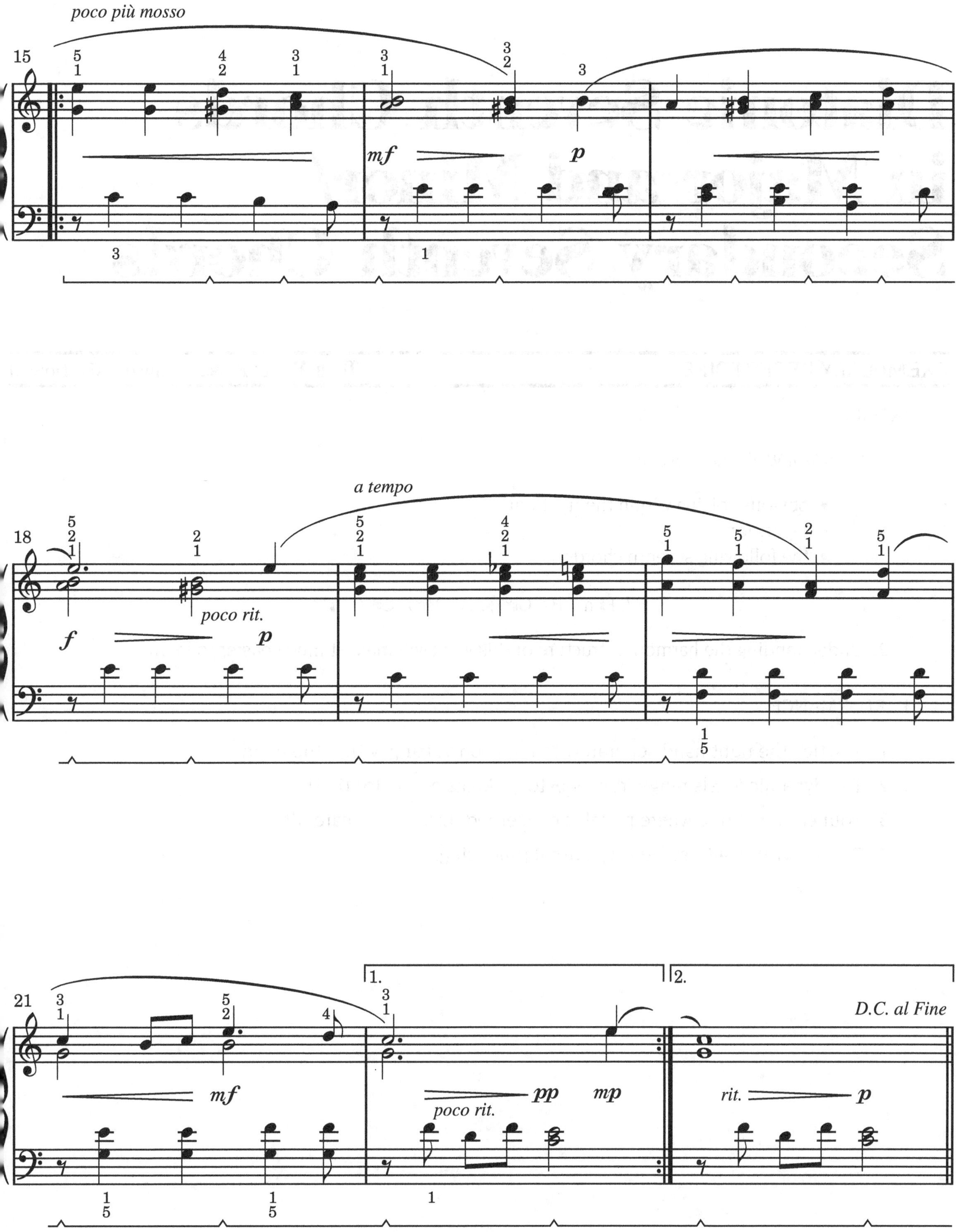
poco più mosso
a tempo
poco rit.
D.C. al Fine
poco rit.
rit.

Diatonic Seventh Chords in Major and Minor/ Secondary Seventh Chords

EXEMPLARY REPERTOIRE **To a Wild Rose** Edward MacDowell

INQUIRY

1. Scan *To a Wild Rose*. Observe:
   - obvious voicing within the right hand
   - repetition
   - the following seventh chords:

     E7, F♯m7, B7, G♯°7, AΔ7, B♯°7, G♯ø7, D♯ø7

2. Understanding the harmonic structure of this work will make it much easier to learn.

PERFORMANCE

1. Practice the right hand separately to focus on voicing within the hand.
2. The dynamic levels range from ***ppp*** to ***f***. Make a plan for that!
3. Your ear must rule where pedal is concerned. Listen very carefully.
4. Play as written *after* some very careful practicing.

(This page has been left blank to avoid a difficult page turn.)

To a Wild Rose

Op. 51, No. 1

EDWARD MacDOWELL
(1861–1908)

25
rit.
a tempo
f
p
30
p
35
41
mp
p
46
pp
ppp

TOPICS TO EXPLORE AND DISCUSS

- Edward MacDowell
- Lead sheets
- William Schuman
- Jackson Berkey

SKILLS AND ACTIVITIES

TECHNIQUE

1. Play the following arpeggio drills.

a.

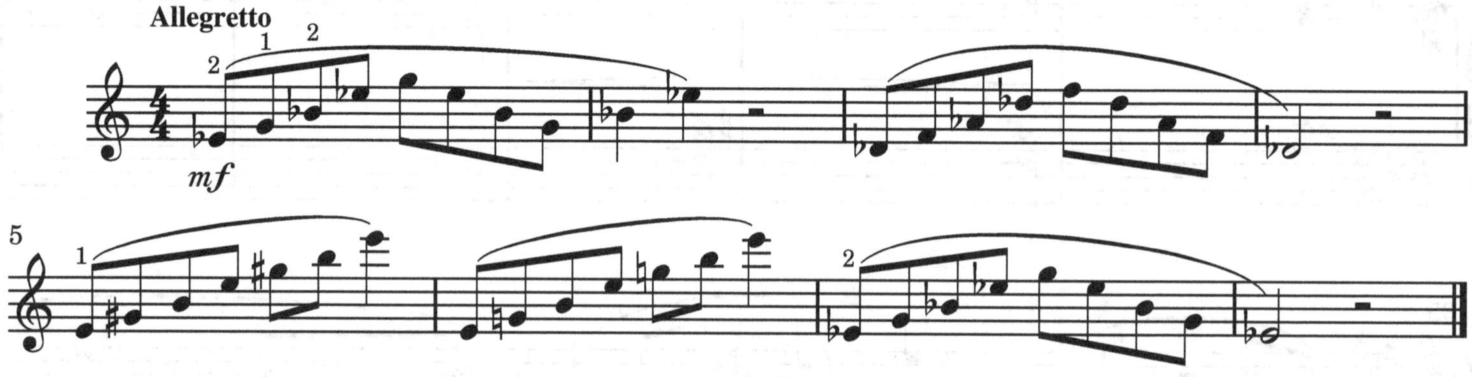

b.

Go to the PDM Web site.

2. A♭/G♯ minor, B♭/A♯ minor, and E♭/D♯ minor scales use the same fingering combinations as their relative majors:

G♭ major

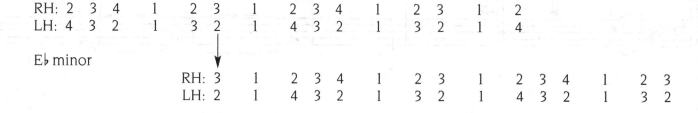

RH: 2 3 4 1 2 3 1 2 3 4 1 2 3 1 2
LH: 4 3 2 1 3 2 1 4 3 2 1 3 2 1 4

E♭ minor

RH: 3 1 2 3 4 1 2 3 1 2 3 4 1 2 3
LH: 2 1 4 3 2 1 3 2 1 4 3 2 1 3 2

READING

1. is a vocal tenor clef. The actual sound is an octave lower than written.

a.

b. Play ST and AT.

c. Play ST, AT, and SA.

2. Play the following viola excerpts.

a. Not too fast

SCHUBERT

b.

HAYDN
Op. 76, No. 5

c.

MOZART
K. 465

d.

e.

Go to the PDM Web site for additional viola plus one exercises.

3. Before playing, look for parallel and contrary motion between the parts. Play different combinations of two parts.

String Quartet in G Major

(Excerpt, violin II, viola, cello)

WOLFGANG AMADEUS MOZART
(1756–1791)

4. Play the vocal lines of the Mozart excerpt as your teacher plays the accompaniment.

Die Zauberflöte

(Excerpt)

WOLFGANG AMADEUS MOZART, K. 620
(1756–1791)

5. Lots of doubled pitches. Be aware!

6.

Psalm 31

(Excerpt)

FRANZ JOSEPH HAYDN
(1732–1809)

7. Look for chord shapes.

Cantata No. 27

J. S. BACH

8. Notice parallel motion in Baritone parts.

9. Look for chord shapes and common tones.

a.

b.

c.

d.

e.

f.

Go to the PDM Web site for additional hymn tune excerpts.

KEYBOARD THEORY

1. In a major key, diatonic 7th chords fall into one of four categories.

Major 7th	Minor 7th	Major-Minor 7th	Half-Diminished 7th
I7	ii7	V7	vii^ø7
IV7	iii7		
	vi7		

Play the diatonic 7th chords in each white-key major scale as shown. Use the keys of C, D, E, F, G, and A.

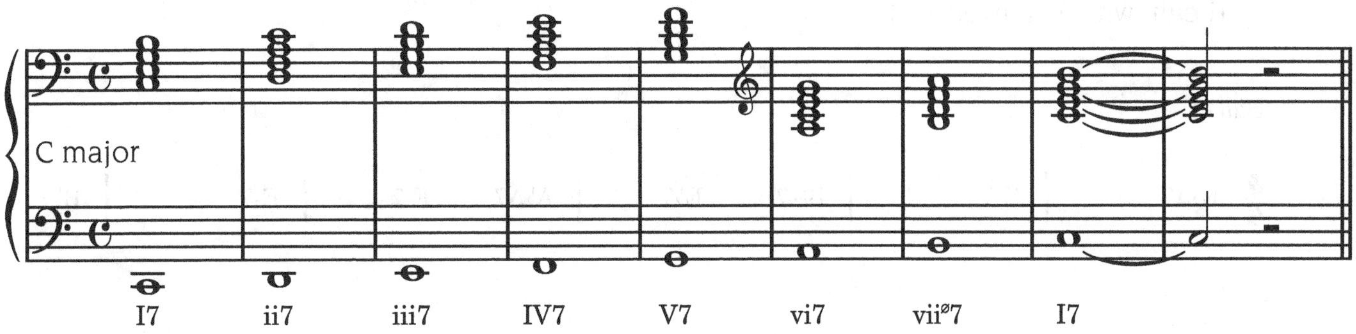

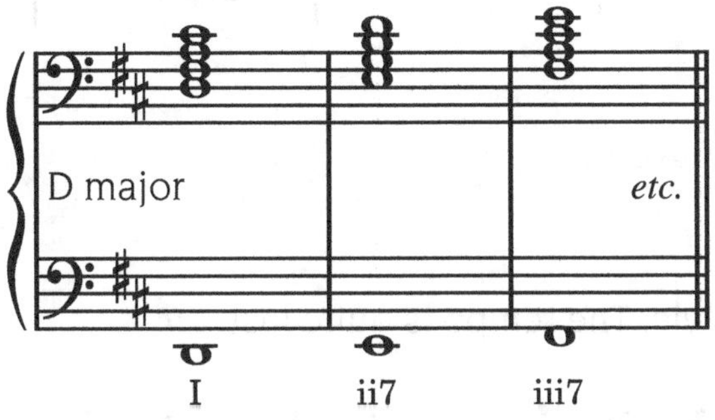

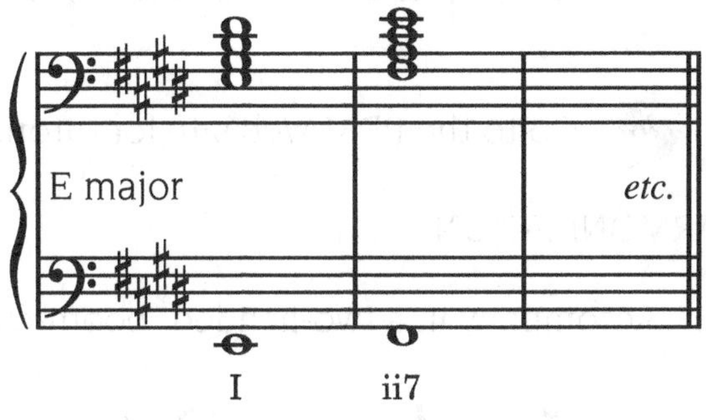

2. Play the following 7th chords in C minor. Notice the raised 7th degree in the i7 (creating a minor-major 7th chord).

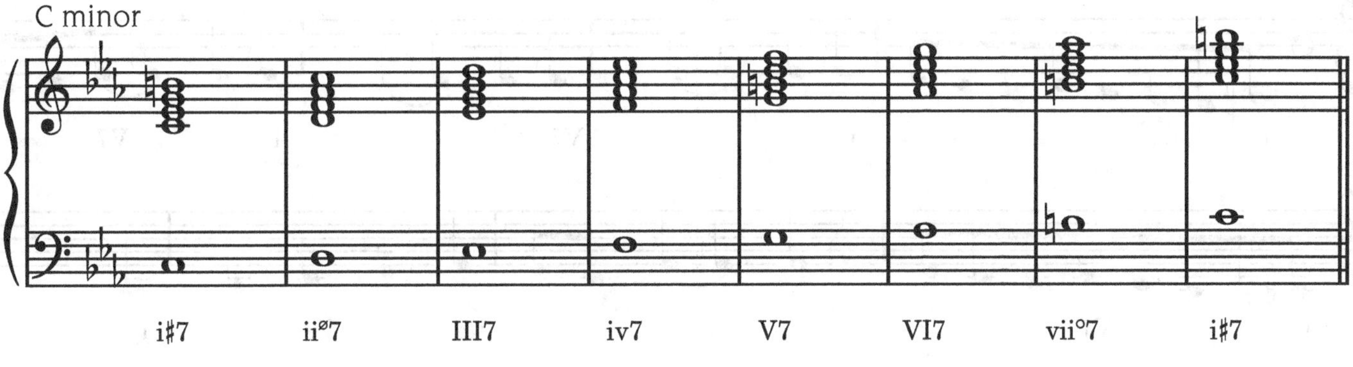

3. There are many ways to write lead sheet notation of 7th chords.

Key of C:	I7	C Δ7 or C maj 7
	ii7	D-7 / D min 7
	iii7	E-7 / E min 7
	IV7	F Δ7 / F maj 7
	V7	G7
	vi7	A-7 / A min 7
	vii^{ø}7	B-7♭5 / B min 7♭5

A designation of G^{sus} or G^{sus}C is a suspended 4th above the root. A triad with an added 6th is shown as C6 (CEGA).

4. Play the following progression in a relaxed tempo, keyboard style. Use common tones between chords. Begin with root position (once you get past measure 3, you are home free!).

(begin with 1st inversion)

(begin with 2nd inversion)

(begin with 3rd inversion)

Ballad

4/4 E♭Δ7 | C-7 | B♭-7 E♭7 | A♭Δ7 F-7 | F-7 | B♭7 |

C-7 C-7/B♭ | A♭Δ7 A♭Δ7/G | F-7 | B♭7 | E♭Δ7 | E♭6 ||

Go to the PDM Web site for tutorial.

HARMONIZATION

1. Accompany in a two-handed "boom-chick" style. The tempo is quite fast.

Joshua Fit da Battle of Jericho

Spiritual

2. Accompany *Myrtilla* in a similar manner, varying the pattern as necessary for faster harmonic changes. Furnish missing harmonies before playing.

Myrtilla

THOMAS ARNE
(1710–1778)

Go to the PDM Web site for tutorial.

3. Complete in the style indicated.

Take Me Out to the Ball Game

ALBERT VON TILZER
Words by Jack Norworth

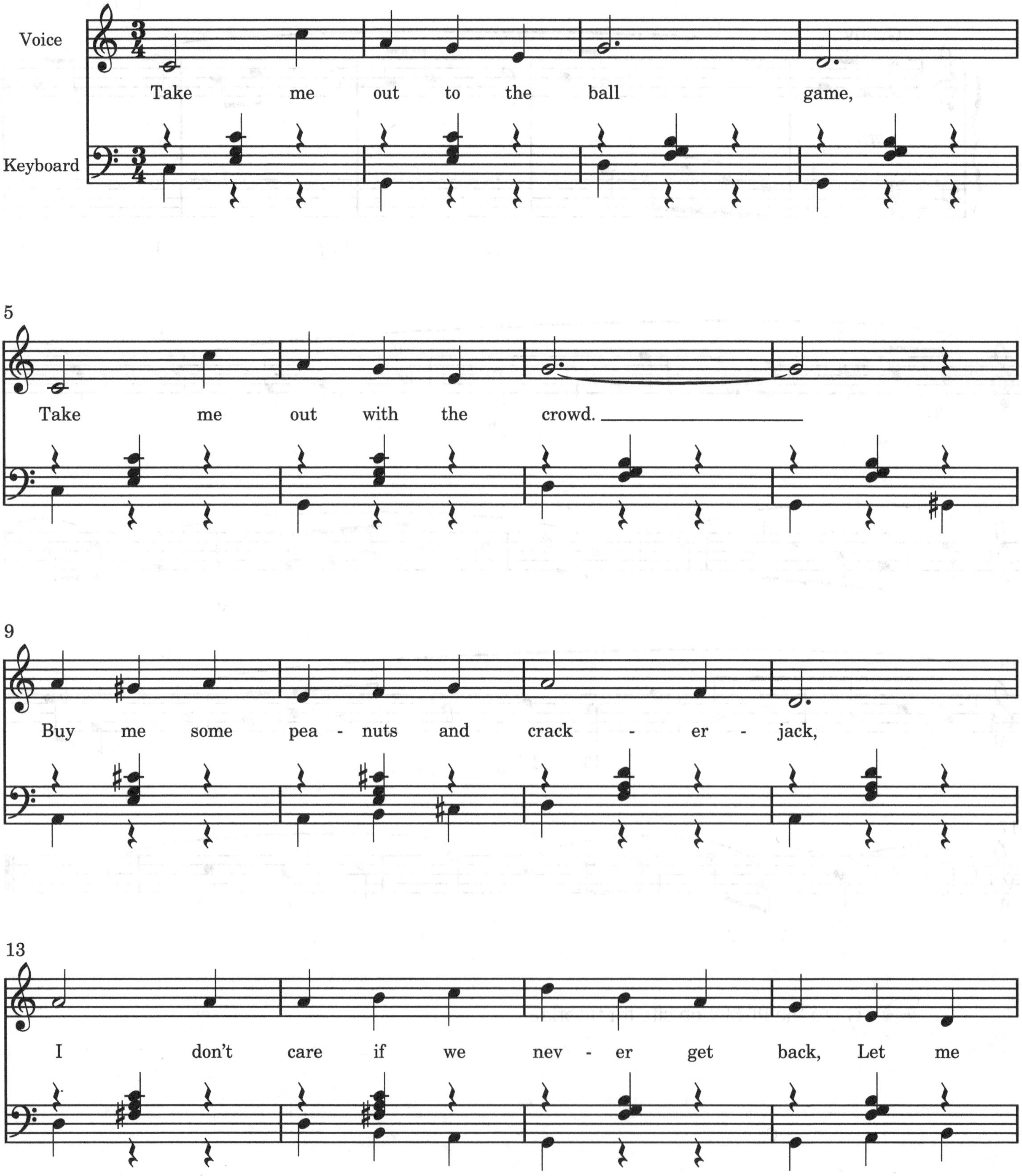

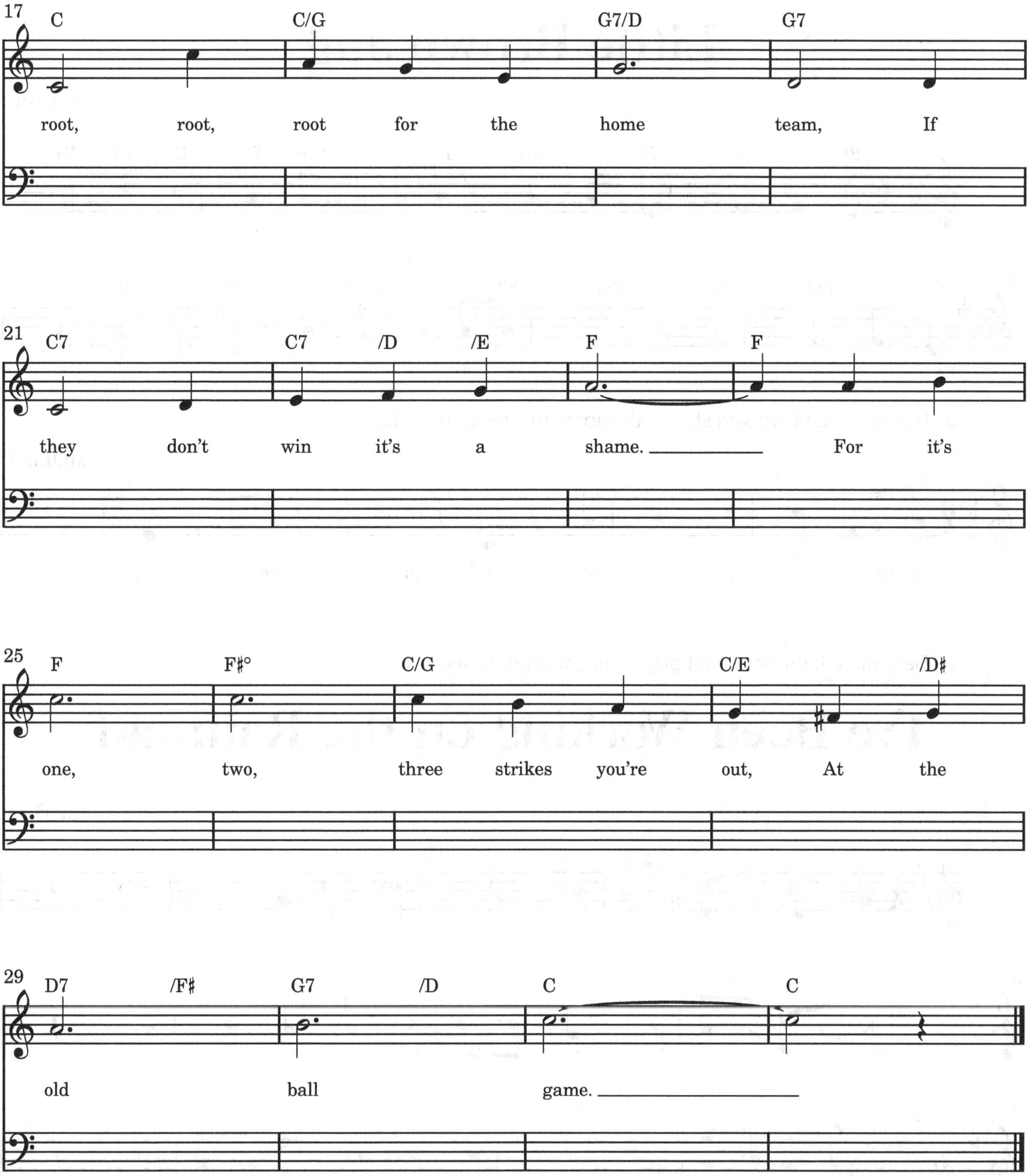
17
C C/G G7/D G7
root, root, root for the home team, If
21
C7 C7 /D /E F F
they don't win it's a shame. For it's
25
F F♯° C/G C/E /D♯
one, two, three strikes you're out, At the
29
D7 /F♯ G7 /D C C
old ball game.

4. Use a two-handed accompaniment—keep it staccato with lots of "daylight."

Little Brown Jug

J. E. WINNER

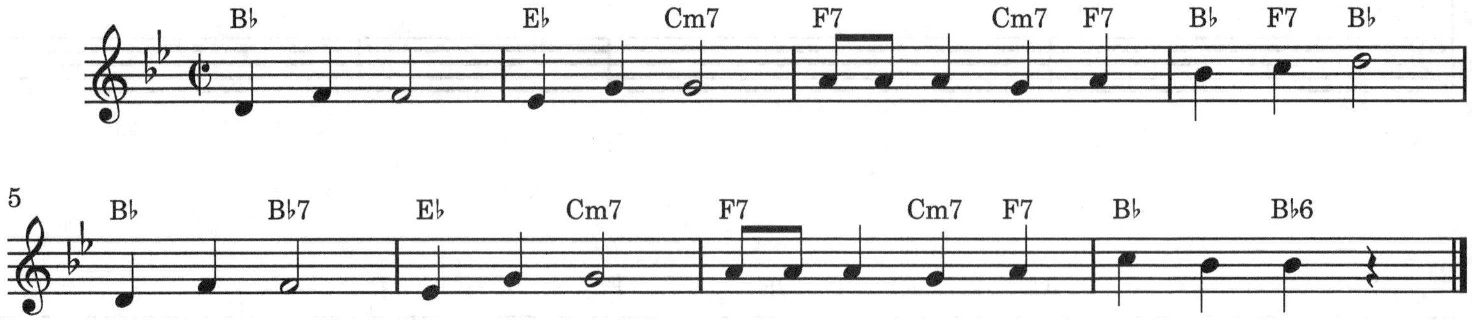

5. Use modified keyboard style with chords mostly on downbeats.

J. L. MOLLOY

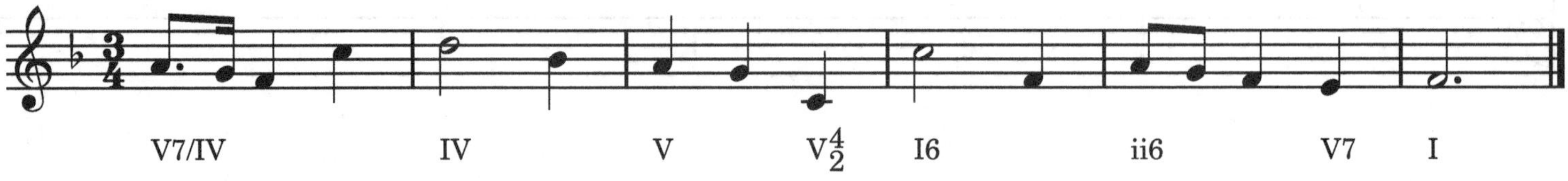

6. Determine harmonies and play in an appropriate style.

I've Been Working on the Railroad

American

Go to the PDM Web site for tutorial plus prime vista harmonization.

TRANSPOSITION

1. The following examples are to be transposed the interval of a tritone. Remember to follow the steps.

a. Transpose *up* to B♭ major.

b. Transpose *down* to G major.

KEVIN RICHMOND

c. Transpose *down* to F major.

SANDRA RAMAWY

d. Transpose *down* to A major.

CARLA DAVIS

e. Transpose *down* to C major.

Go to the PDM Web site for additional tritone transposition.

2. Your singer has a cold—play this down a 4th in the key of D major.

Salti de terza

NICOLA VACCAJ
(1790–1848)

Andantino

13
ti - glio vo - la in grem-bo al cac - cia - tor, vo - la in grem-bo al cac - cia - tor.

Go to the PDM Web site for further assistance with this transposition.

3. Ask a classmate to accompany you. Then switch parts. Think in the key of F major.

B♭ Clarinet
Piano

5

4. Try both parts.

Horn in F
Trombone

5

IMPROVISATION

1. Improvise a two-handed pattern for each basic movement.

(Marching)

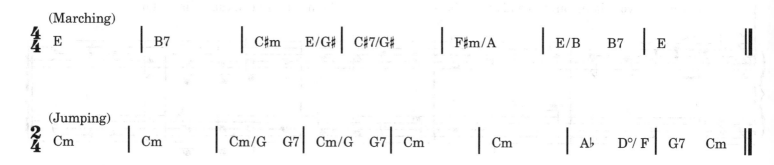

4/4 E | B7 | C♯m E/G♯ | C♯7/G♯ | F♯m/A | E/B B7 | E ||

(Jumping)

2/4 Cm | Cm | Cm/G G7 | Cm/G G7 | Cm | Cm | A♭ D°/ F | G7 Cm ||

2. As a class, create major key progressions that include secondary dominants. Play the progressions in keyboard style paying close attention to voice leading. Regardless of the choice of meter or rhythm, you should demonstrate two four-bar phrases. Your choices will include:

- remainder of harmonies
- key signature
- meter
- beginning shape of right hand
- tempo (choose a term you don't often see)

Example: I | V/vi | vi | IV | V/ii | ii | V7 | I |

- Key— E♭ Major
- Meter—$\frac{2}{4}$
- Beginning shape of RH—first inversion
- Tempo—Vite

Then you would play:

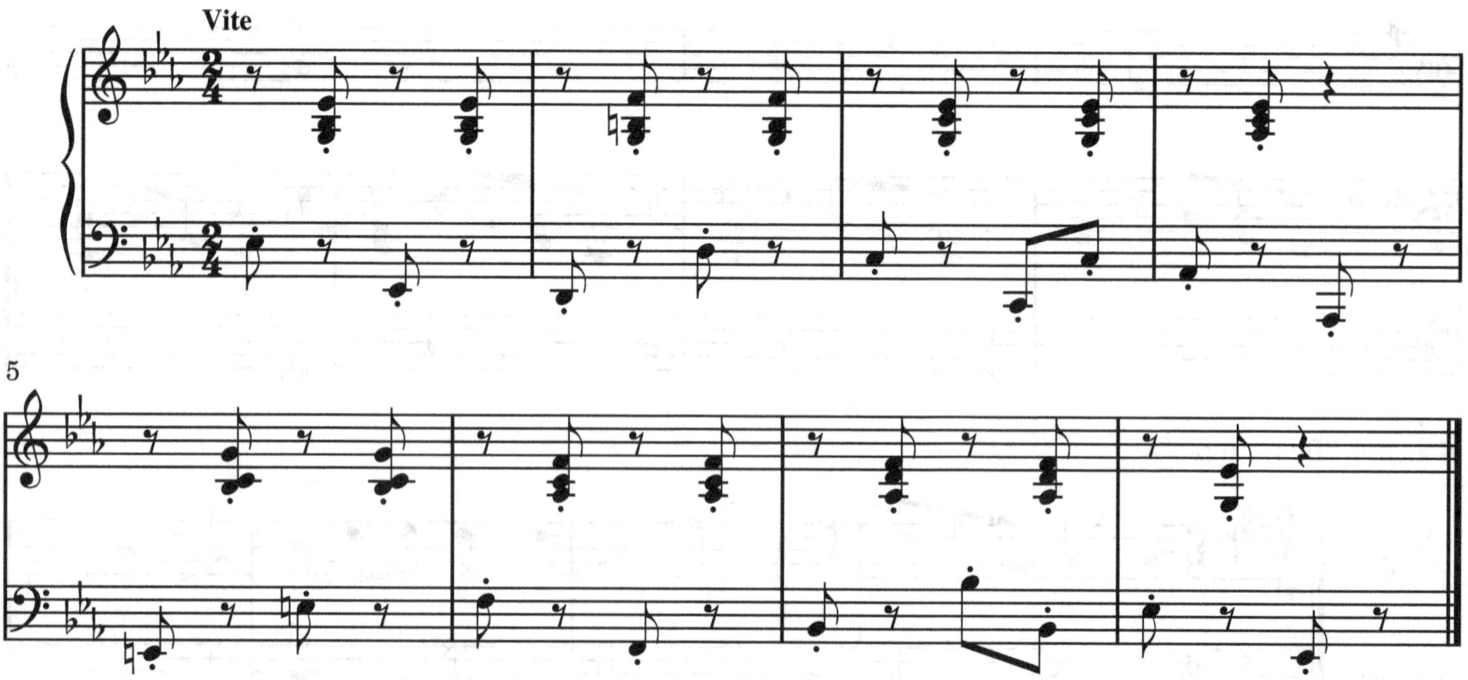

Go to the PDM Web site for additional improvisation.

(This page has been left blank to avoid a difficult page turn.)

COMPOSITION

1. Using diatonic seventh chords, arrange one of your favorite folk songs. The arrangement should be completely notated. Trade compositions with your classmates.

Go to the PDM Web site for representative student compositions.

ENSEMBLE

1.

Andantino con Grazia

Secondo

CARL CZERNY
(1791–1857)

Andantino con Grazia

Primo

CARL CZERNY
(1791–1857)

2. Each part has some challenging "moments" but the end product is worth the effort.

Amazing Grace

Secondo

Traditional
Arr. Leigh Kaplan

(Secondo)

Amazing Grace

Primo

Traditional
Arr. Leigh Kaplan

(Primo)

1. Syncopation reigns! The eighth notes are even.

Carnival in St. Thomas

GLENDA AUSTIN

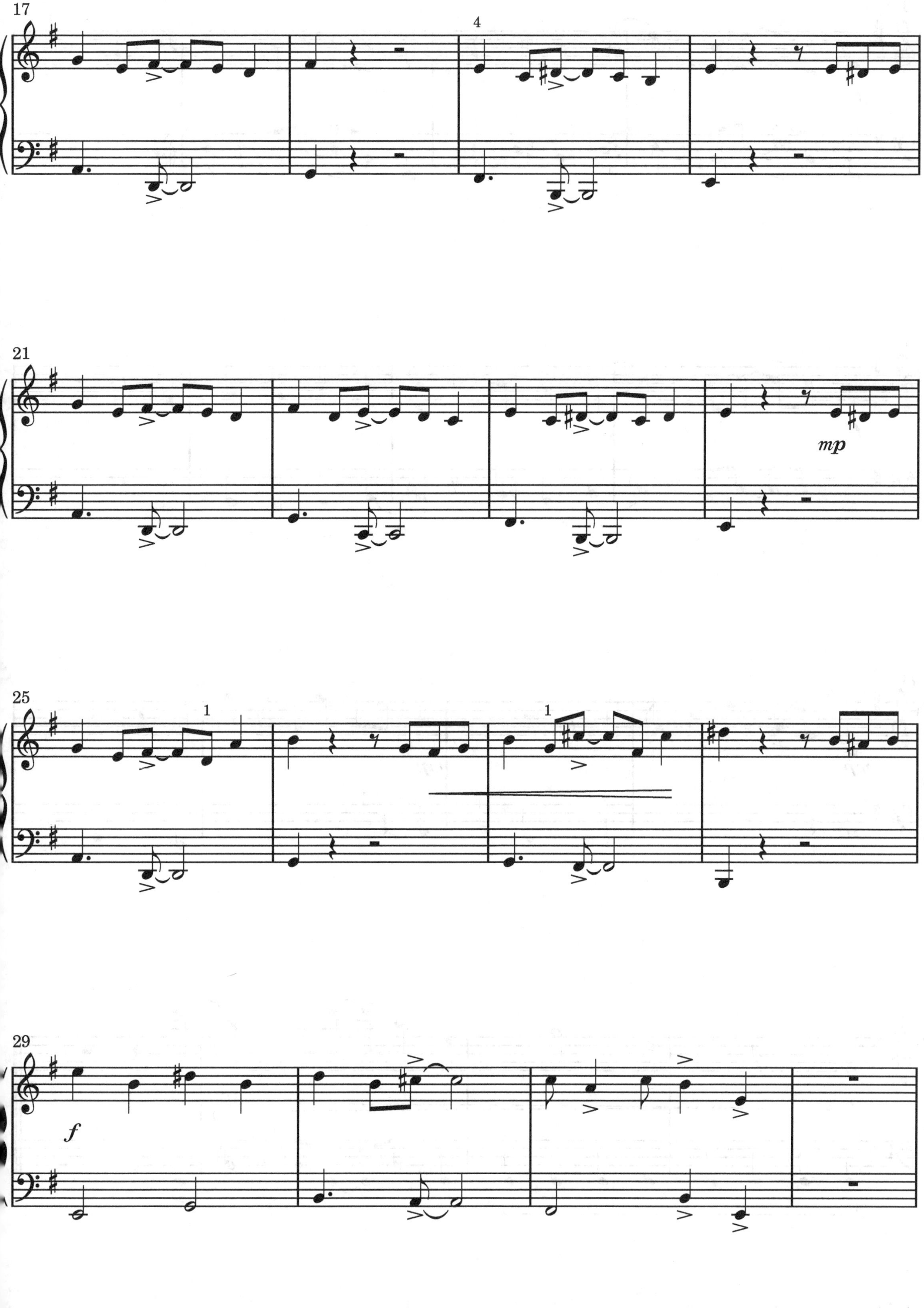
17
4
21
mp
25
1
1
29
f

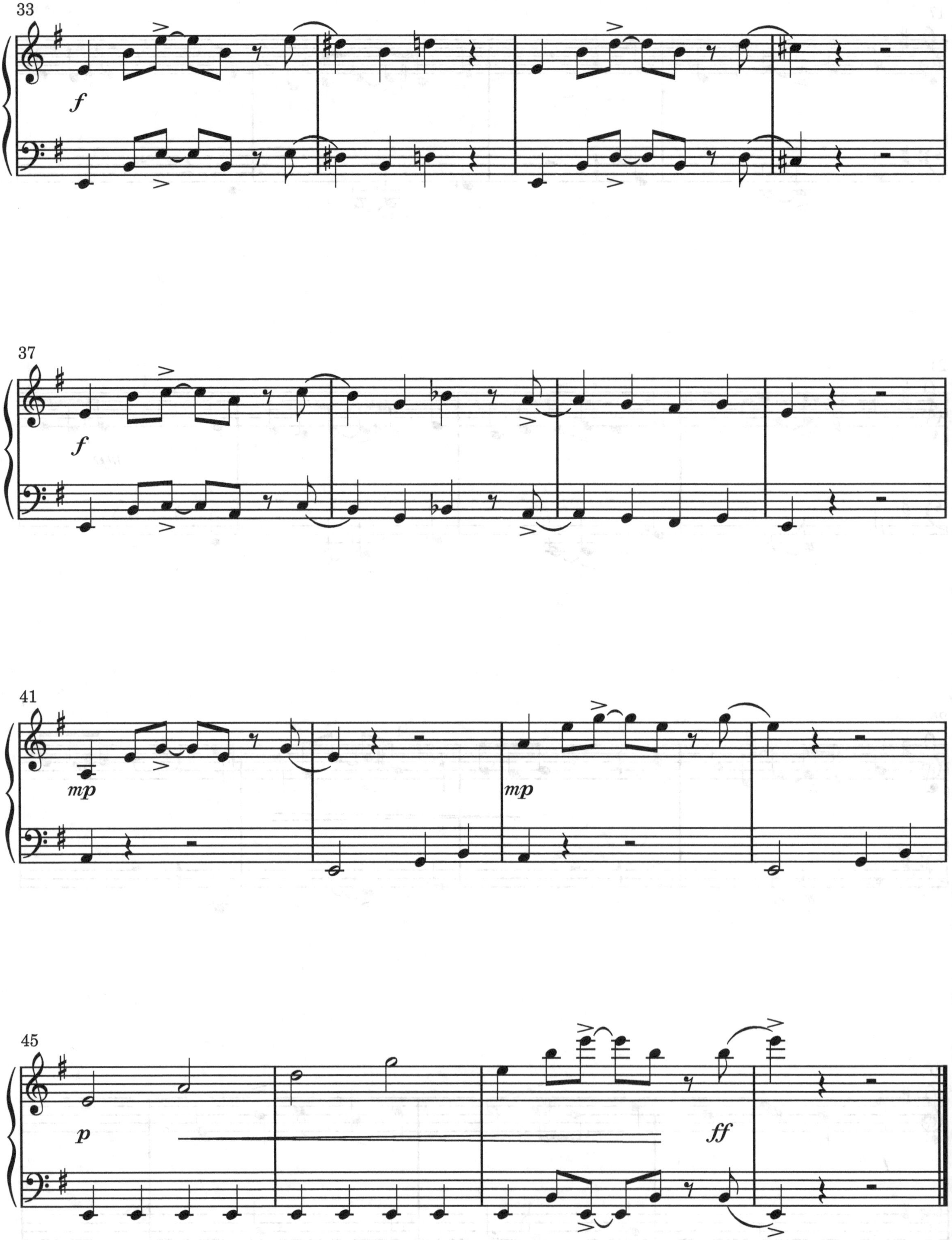
33
f
37
f
41
mp
mp
45
p
ff

2. Plan chord shapes silently. Note that the pedal is generally used throughout when performing.

II

from *Three-Score Set*

WILLIAM SCHUMAN
(1910–1992)

3. The subtle melodies within a melody are really wonderful—don't miss them.

Sunday Morning Fire

JACKSON BERKEY

Very much at peace (♩ = ca. 66)

"Sunday Morning Fire" is taken from Jackson Berkey's longer piano collection *Cape May Preludes*, published by SDG Press (catalog #SDG 99-204).

The complete collection is recorded by the composer on SDG Records, SDG CD2000. Visit www.berkey.com for more information.

4. Add melodic ornamentation on the repeats.

Minuet

GEORG PHILIPP TELEMANN
(1681–1767)

Altered/Borrowed Triads

EXEMPLARY REPERTOIRE — **Prelude** Samuil Maykapar

INQUIRY

1. Scan *Prelude*. Observe:

   - clef change
   - obvious voicing within the right and left hands
   - placement of the melody
   - couplings in the form: 2 + 4 + 4 + 2 + 2 + 1 + 1 + 2
   - harmonic progression
   - ♯iv°7 versus vii°7/V
   - borrowed ii°7
   - countermelody in bars 5–6, 9–10, and 17–18
   - indicated articulation . . . .—what does it mean?

2. Note the use of syncopated pedal (legato pedal). The sound should be seamless yet clear.

PERFORMANCE

1. The dynamic levels range from ***ppp*** to somewhere around ***mp***. If you start too softly you will find yourself with nowhere to go.

2. Your ear must rule where pedal is concerned. Listen very carefully. I sound like a broken record but so much of your pedaling decisions must come at the moment of playing and this is done through active listening.

3. Play as written *after* some very careful practicing.

Prelude

SAMUIL MAYKAPAR
(1867–1938)

Andantino

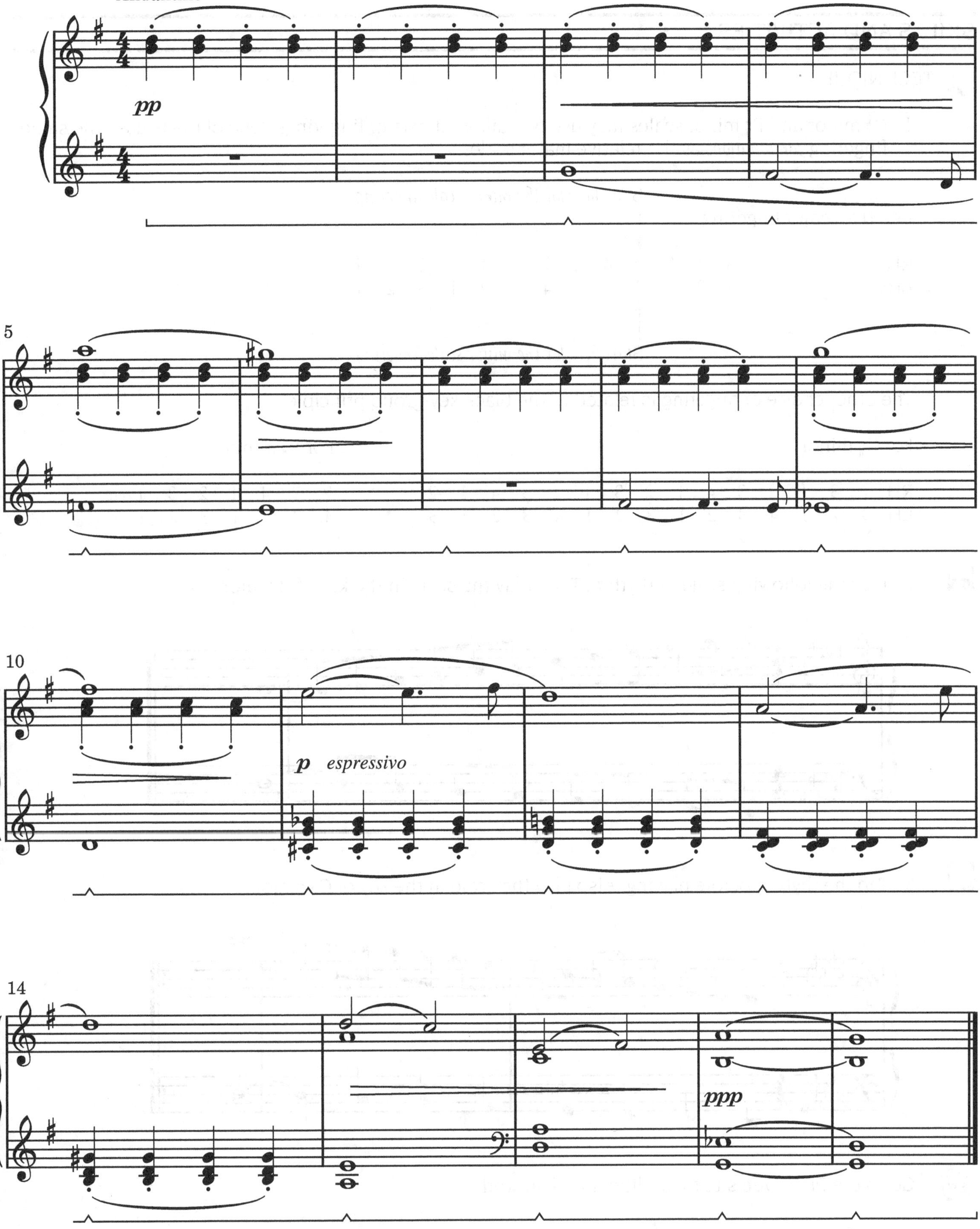

TOPICS TO EXPLORE AND DISCUSS

- Samuil Maykapar
- Franz Anton Hoffmeister
- Karol Kurpinski
- William Catania

SKILLS AND ACTIVITIES

TECHNIQUE

1. C♯ minor and F♯ minor scales may use two different sets of fingerings. One of these uses the same fingering *combinations* as the relative major scale:

Relative major fingering: *Start here for the minor scale fingering* (↓ above the sixth finger number, RH 3)

RH:	1	2	3	1	2	3	4	1	2	3	1	2	3	4	1
LH:	5	4	3	2	1	3	2	1	4	3	2	1	3	2	1

Start here for the minor scale fingering (↑ below the sixth finger number, LH 3)

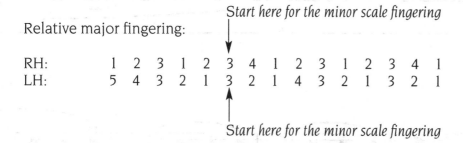

The other choice of fingering is related to the black-key-group principle:

For C♯ minor

RH:	2	3	1	2	3	4	1	2	3	1	2	3	4	1	2
LH:	3	2	1	4	3	2	1	3	2	1	4	3	2	1	3

For F♯ minor:

2	3	4	1	2	3	1	*etc.*
4	3	2	1	3	2	1	

2. Play the following scale in rhythm. Then play the scale in the key of B major.

3. Tap the rhythm before playing. Also play the scale in the key of G♭ major.

Go to the PDM Web site for additional scalar work.

READING

1. The tenor clef positions middle C on the fourth line of the staff. Play the following bassoon excerpt.

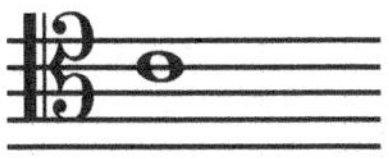

2. Play the following violoncello excerpt as your teacher plays the accompaniment.

Sicilienne

(Excerpt)

GABRIEL FAURÉ, Op. 78
(1845–1924)

3. Think about a left-hand fingering for measures 2–5 before you play.

4. Play all three parts of the following.

a.

b.

Adapted from Alexander Hume

c.

Go to the PDM Web site for additional SAT and SAB examples.

5. Think fingering before you start each item.

a.

CARLA DAVIS

b.

Adapted from Mazas

c.

Go to the PDM Web site for additional SAT and tenor clef exercises.

6. Scan each example quickly. Look for:

- common tones
- chord shapes
- consecutive intervals (3rds, 6ths)
- key signatures
- rhythmic challenges

a.

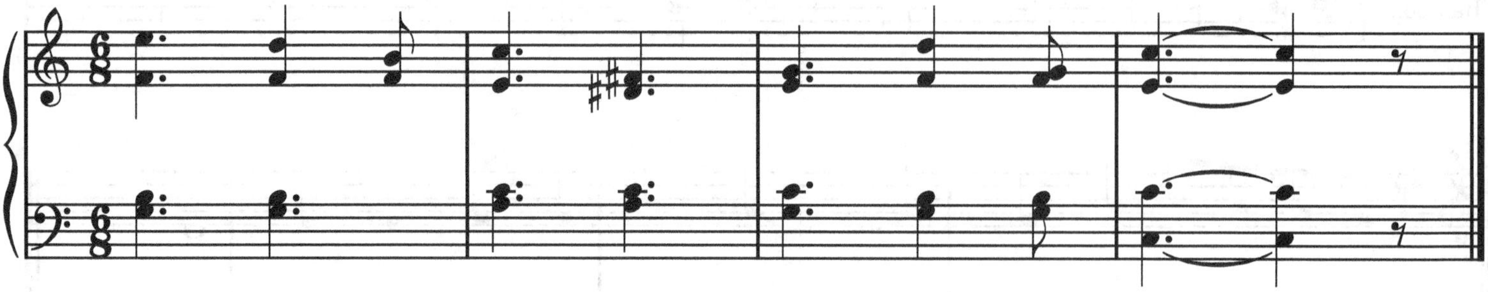

b.

c.

d.

KEYBOARD THEORY

1. Borrowed chords use notes that are accidentals in the major key but would be diatonic in a minor key. The following example shows the borrowed triads most often used in a major key.

D major

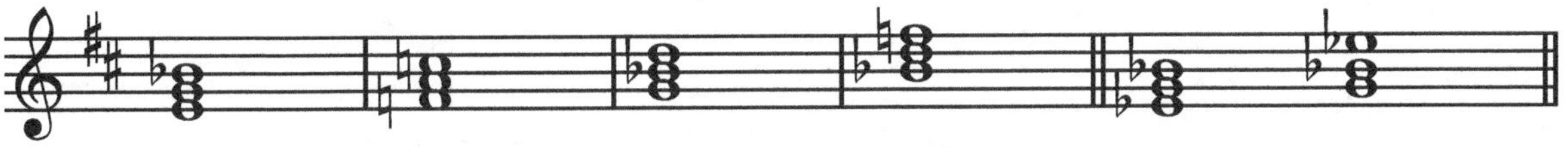

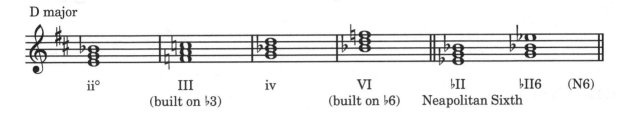

ii° | III (built on ♭3) | iv | VI (built on ♭6) | ♭II Neapolitan Sixth | ♭II6 (N6)

2. Play the following progressions using borrowed triads.

A major

3/4 I | I6 | ♭II6 | V^6_5/V | I^6_4 | V7 | I | I :|| also key of F

D major

4/4 D /C♯ | B min /A | G /F♯ | E min /D | A/C♯ A7 | D D/F♯ | E♭/G A7 | D :||

G major

3/4 I | iii | IV | I | ♭VI | ♭III | V7 | vi | iv | ii°6 | I^6_4 V7 | I :||

also key of B♭

Go to the PDM Web site for a tutorial on these progressions.

HARMONIZATION

1. Use a two-handed "boom-chick-chick" accompaniment.

2. Use keyboard style.

3. Use keyboard style.

4. Use a traditional two-handed "root-chord" style.

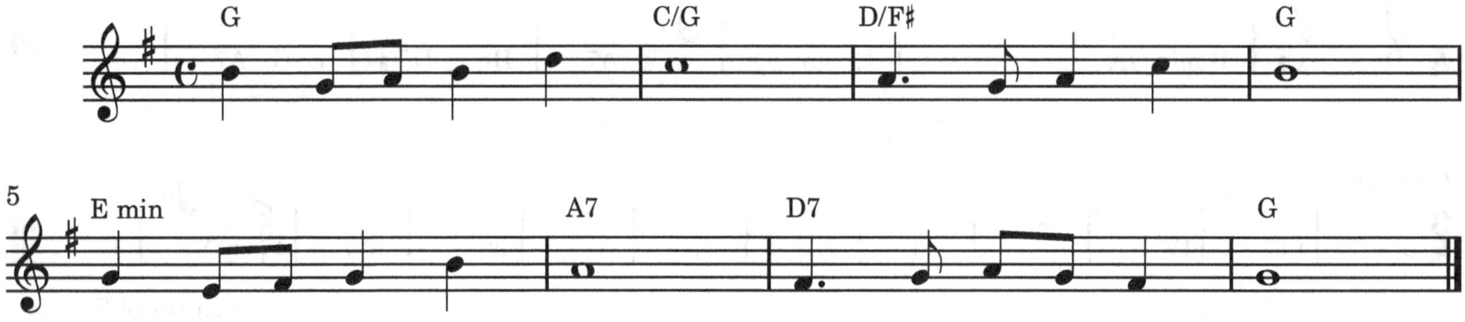

5. Harmonize the following and include vi, V7/IV, V7/V, and III. Play the verse by ear. Use keyboard style.

Go to the PDM Web site to hear verse.

6. Use a two-handed "root-chord" accompaniment for this folk tune.

American

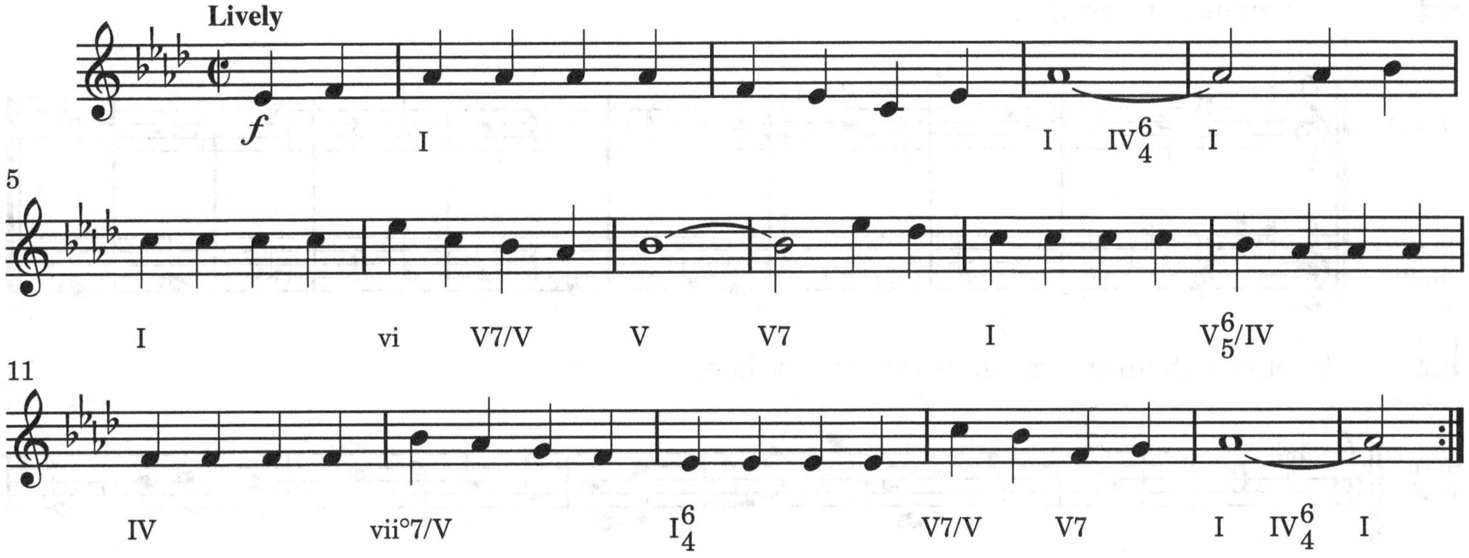

7. Play a two-handed accompaniment using the following progression.

F major

4/4 I | V7 | I V7/IV | IV ♯iv°7 |

I$^6_4$ | V7 vii°7/vi | vi ii7 V7 | I ||

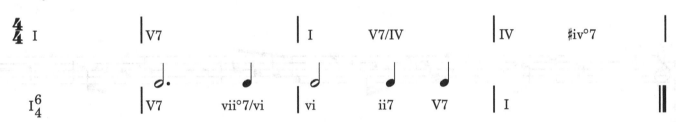

8. Add the melody to *Auld Lang Syne* and play in keyboard style.

Go to the PDM Web site for additional help with items 6 and 8.

TRANSPOSITION

1. The following examples are to be transposed an interval of a tritone.

   a. Transpose *up* to A major.

C. MORENUS

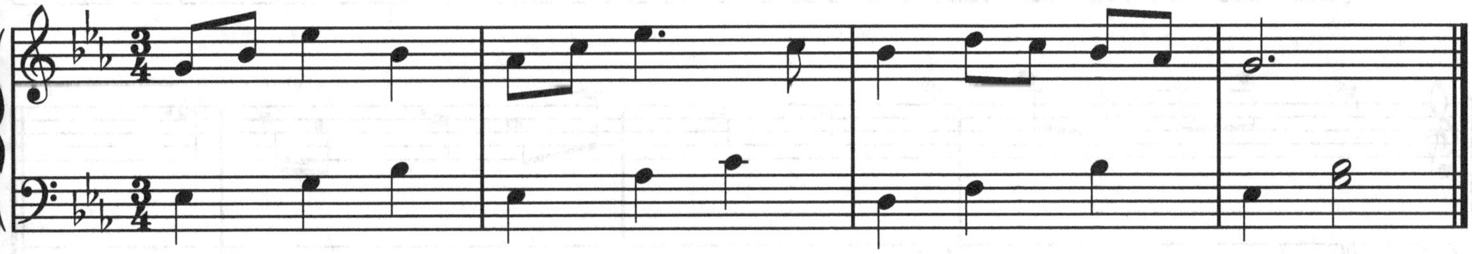

   b. Transpose *up* to E♭ major.

C. MORENUS

2. Transpose the following.

a. Careful in measure 5.

b. Notice chord shapes within the melodic line.

c.

d.

3. Transpose the *Etude in* D to A♭ major.

Etude in D

LUDVIG SCHYTTE, Op. 108, No. 7
(1848–1909)

Go to the PDM Web site for extra assistance with this transposition and for additional clarinet and horn examples.

IMPROVISATION

1. Create improvised music for the following technique exercises in classical ballet.

   a. At the barre: *Petite battements sur le cou-de-pied* (moderately fast $\frac{4}{4}$ meter; 2-bar introduction and 32 bars of exercise).

   b. In centre floor: *Port de bras* and *révérence* (slow $\frac{3}{4}$ meter; 2-bar introduction and 32 bars of exercise with the appropriate *révérence* conclusion).

Use the following form for each:

Intro.	—	2 bar
A	—	8 bar
A	—	8 bar
B	—	8 bar
A	—	8 bar
Révérence	—	2 bar

2. Return to the progressions you created in Chapter 12 (page 340). Choose a partner and create improvisation duets—one plays the progression, the other improvises a melody. As before, clearly demonstrate harmonic content, meter, and two four-bar phrases. We have given you some of the examples created by group piano students and graduate teaching assistants.

   a. From the MWF, 11:00 class, Spring 2004:

$\frac{3}{4}$ I | iv | V | vi |

V7/IV | iv V/V | V7 | I ‖

   b. From the TTH, 11:00 class, Spring 2004:

$\frac{6}{8}$ I ___ | ♭VI ___ | iv ___ | V ___ |

V/vi ___ | vi IV | ii V7 | I ___ ‖

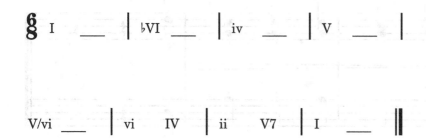

Pick some keys and "away you go!"

Go to the PDM Web site for ballet tutorial and 2. a. & b. tutorial.

(This page has been left blank to avoid a difficult page turn.)

3. These are a few of the two-bar scat patterns created by Alan Swain in his book, *Improvise, A Step by Step Approach*. Choose two for the A section of 12 bar blues—one for the idea, repeat, then a bit of poetic license as you let the other work for the second repeat and the extend. Choose another two for the B section. Pair with a classmate and try your melodic improvisation while your classmate plays tritones and a walking bass. Switch parts at the turn-around.

   My choice might look something like this:

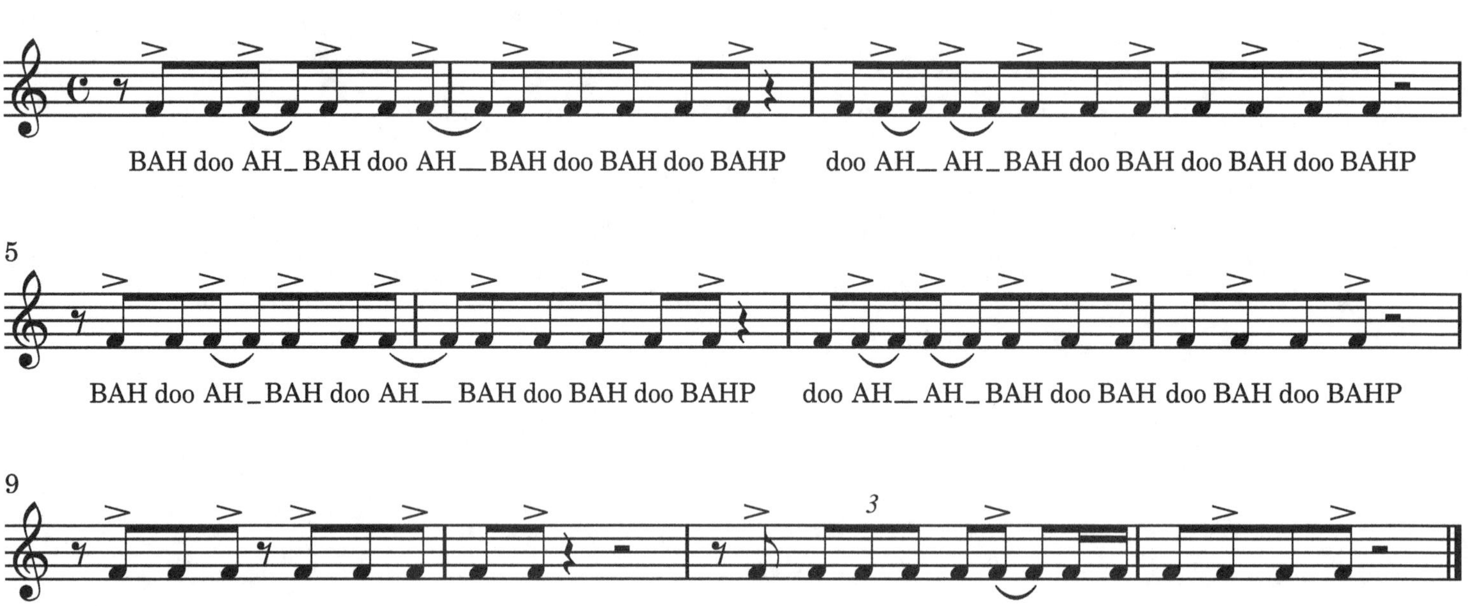
BAH doo AH_BAH doo AH__BAH doo BAH doo BAHP
doo AH__ AH_BAH doo BAH doo BAH doo BAHP
5
BAH doo AH_BAH doo AH__ BAH doo BAH doo BAHP
doo AH__ AH_BAH doo BAH doo BAH doo BAHP
9
BAH doo BAH BAH doo BAH doo BAHP
3
BAH doo-dle yah doo EE_ dee bee doo BAH doo BAHP

From *Improvise, A Step by Step Approach*, by Alan Swain (Jasmine Music Publishers, 1980).

ENSEMBLE

Tears

Secondo

ANTON ARENSKY
(1861–1906)

Andante con moto *(in Phrygian mode)*

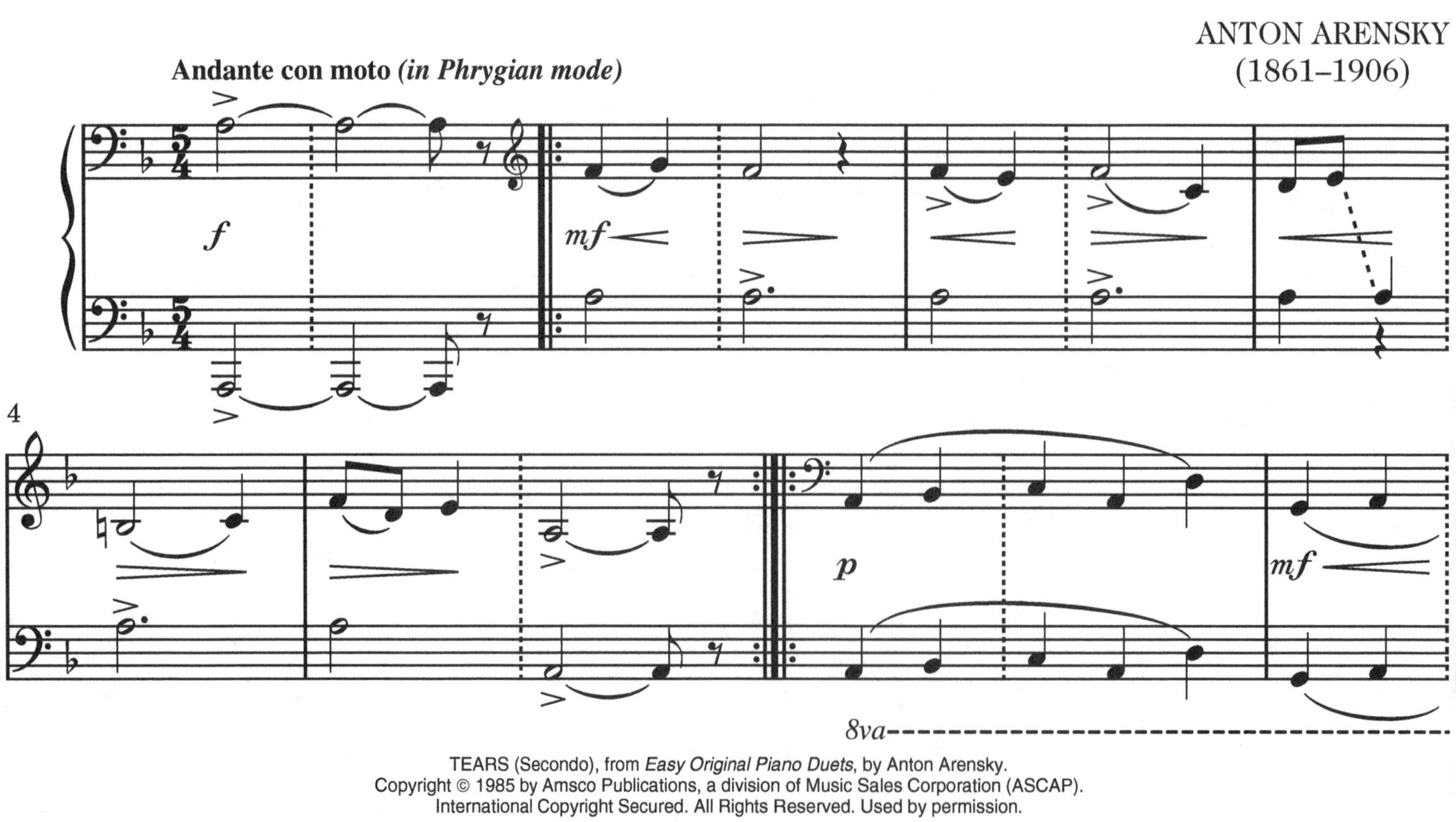
f
mf
4
p
mf
8va

(Secondo)

Tears

Primo

ANTON ARENSKY
(1861–1906)

Andante con moto ***(in Phrygian mode)***

COMPOSITION

Create a rhythmic invention. In the composition, have at least two voices with clear entrances of the "subject." Assign particular sounds (clicking a pair of pencils together, dragging a bench, slamming a book on a desk, rattling a set of keys, etc.) to particular note values. You might refer to the rhythm drill on page 64 for sound ideas. Your title might include the word "invention" if written for two parts or the word "sinfonia" if written for three parts. After distribution to your classmates, become the composer/conductor and lead the class in a performance. Go the the Web site to see examples.

SUBSEQUENT REPERTOIRE

1.

Dreams

WILLIAM CATANIA

Tranquilly, feeling in one (♩ = 48)

2. The A section of *Bright Orange* is divided into the following groups of measures: 3 + 3 + 3 + 6.

- Divide the class into four groups and *patsch* the rhythm of this section in a round-robin fashion.
- Determine the sections and groups of measures for the balance of the piece. *Patsch*.
- Play left-hand triads while tapping the right-hand rhythm patterns on a flat surface.
- Play as written.

Go to the PDM Web site.

Bright Orange

from *Sketches in Color*

ROBERT STARER
(1924–2001)

21
27
f
32
ff
mf
38
f
43
ff
sfz
8va

3. Beat subdivision must be exact, particularly at the indicated tempo.

Comfort in Solitude

DANIEL GOTTLOB TÜRK
(1756–1813)

4. Practice left-hand descending octaves and mordents. Practice bars 13 and 14 and let them determine the overall tempo.

Short Prelude in C

JOHANN SEBASTIAN BACH
(1685–1750)

Altered Seventh Chords/ Extended Harmonies (Ninth, Thirteenth)

EXEMPLARY REPERTOIRE **Folk Song** Fred Ziller

INQUIRY

1. Scan *Folk Song*. Observe:

    - range of left hand
    - balance between the right and left hands
    - harmonic progression
    - mixed modes
    - augmented sixth chord
    - pedal marking

2. Pedal releases are very important in this piece. Be very aware of what the composer wants from the piano.

PERFORMANCE

1. These dynamic levels and the low range of the left hand at times are going to demand a lot of control to maintain the proper balance between melodic content and the accompaniment. Just as you must listen carefully to the effect of the pedal, you must listen carefully to the balance of melody and accompaniment and adjust accordingly.
2. A quick harmonic analysis will help you understand the direction of the music. The page appears to be quite simple but the musical demands are anything but!

Folk Song

Andante FRED ZILLER

TOPICS TO EXPLORE AND DISCUSS

- Fred Ziller
- Norman Dello Joio
- William Gillock
- Ted Cooper
- Christoph Graupner
- Lynn Freeman Olson

SKILLS AND ACTIVITIES

TECHNIQUE

1. The following are traditional fingerings for B♭ and E♭ major scales. Note the left hand.

B♭ Major

RH:	4	1	2	3	1	2	3	4	1	2	3	1	2	3	4
LH:	3	2	1	4	3	2	1	3	2	1	4	3	2	1	3

E♭ Major

RH:	3	1	2	3	4	1	2	3	1	2	3	4	1	2	3
LH:	3	2	1	4	3	2	1	3	2	1	4	3	2	1	3

Away from the keyboard on any flat surface, play these scales ascending and descending. Then play slowly on the keyboard as you watch the finger numbers.

2. Review the white-key major scales. Start with C and repeat in the keys of D, E, F, G, A, and B major.

3.

Prelude in G Minor

MUZIO CLEMENTI, Op. 43
(1752–1832)

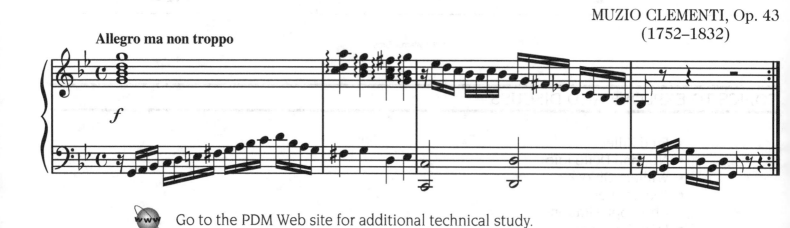

Go to the PDM Web site for additional technical study.

READING

1. Play these combinations: Vln II/Cello, Vln II/Vla, Vla/Cello, all three.

a.

SCHUBERT

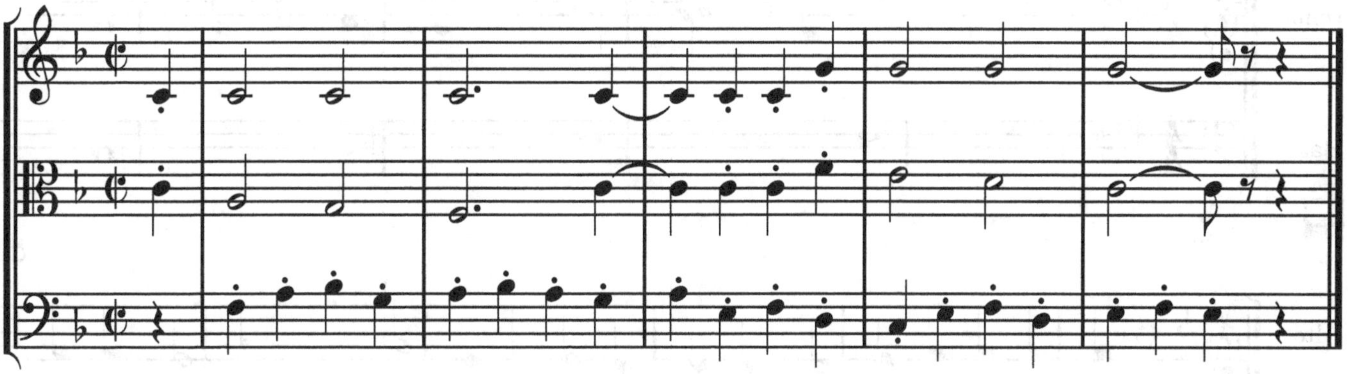

b.

HAYDN

c.

MOZART

2. Play these combinations: AB, AT, TB, ATB.

a.

PURCELL

Go to the PDM Web site for additional instrumental and vocal score reading.

b.

VERDI

c.

di LASSO

3. Once again, play a variety of combinations.

Ave Verum Corpus

W. A. MOZART

KEYBOARD THEORY

1. Altered 7th chords fall into one of two categories—those that are borrowed from the parallel minor and those that tonicize a chord diatonic to the key (secondary dominants—V7 of iii and so on). The following example shows both types.

Play the following progression in the key indicated. Move to the closest chord possible.

D major

3/4 I | V7/IV | iv | iiø7 | I^6_4 | V7 | vii°7 | I ‖

E♭ major

4/4 (rest) V7 | I | I7 | vi7 | iiø7 V7 | I ‖

2. Augmented 6th chords fall into a category of altered 7ths. The Italian is actually a triad, but in first inversion the sound is that of a dominant 7th chord. The German, Italian, and French augmented 6ths all contain a ♯4 of the key, and this tone acts as leading tone to the dominant.

♯iv	Italian	(♯6)	contains ♯4, ♭6, tonic
♯iv7	German	$(^{\sharp 6}_{5})$	contains ♯4, ♭6, tonic, ♭3
ii7	French	$(^{\sharp 6}_{\substack{4\\3}})$	contains 2, ♯4, ♭6, tonic
♯ii7	German	$(^{\sharp 6}_{\substack{\sharp 4\\3}})$	contains ♯2, ♯4, ♭6, tonic (doubly augmented resolves to I^6_4)

Go to the PDM Web site for additional work with.augmented 6ths chord

Spell augmented 6th chords in the keys given; then play in the proper inversion and resolve. The doubly augmented 6th is the only one resolving to I $\frac{6}{4}$; the others resolve to V.

Example: Key of F, German

Spell: B♮ D♭ F A♭ / Play: Spell: G♯ B♮ D♭ F / Play:

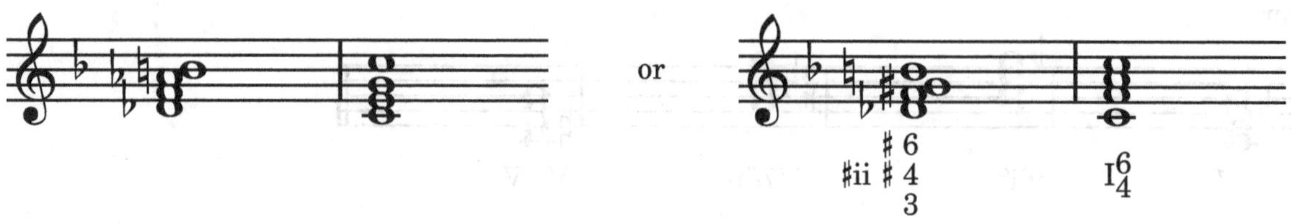

The sound is identical until the chord of resolution.

Key of A major—German Key of D major—French Key of G major—French

Key of B♭ major—Italian Key of E♭ major—German Key of A♭ major—Italian

3. Extended harmonies add a new dimension to blues improvisation. In the example below, notice which chord members are included with each harmony. This voicing is standard for blues when using harmonies that go beyond triads and 7ths.

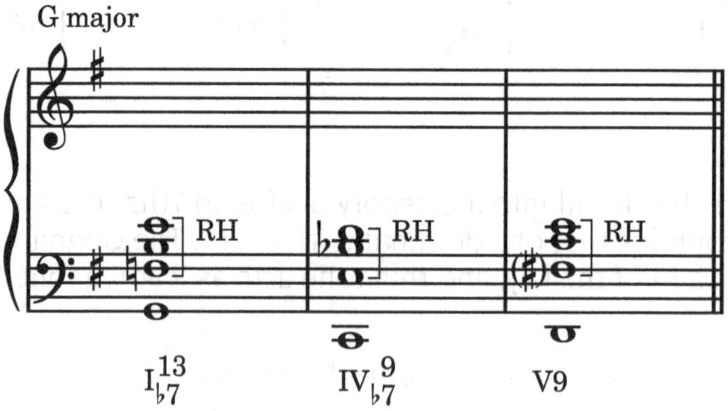

Keyboard players often omit roots of chords when improvising in a blues style. The following chords are referred to as "non-root" voicing.

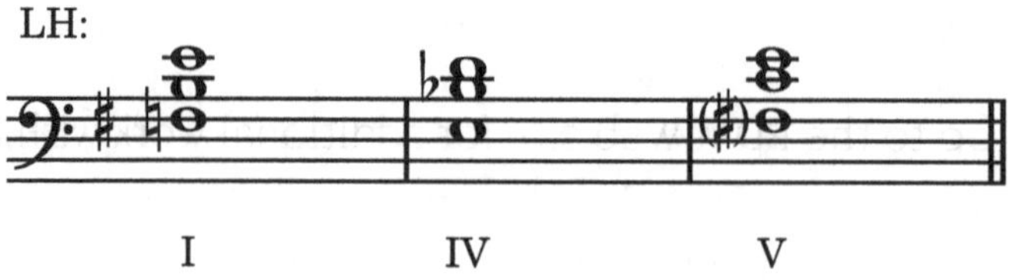

HARMONIZATION

1. For each of the melodic excerpts below choose what you feel would be an appropriate accompaniment style. Plan for changes in harmonic rhythm.

   a. Swing the eighths!

   b. Perhaps a two-handed "boom-chick?"

   c. Modified keyboard style?

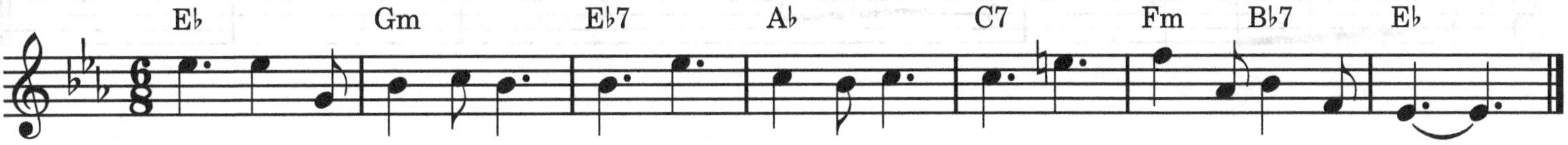

   d. Definitely calls for keyboard style.

   e. Modified keyboard style.

Irish

   f. Parts of this should look familiar.

GEORGE M. COHAN

2. Use non-root chords to harmonize. Refer back to page 382 if necessary.

St. Louie Blues

W. C. HANDY
(1873–1958)

3.

4. Use a modified keyboard style.

Amazing Grace

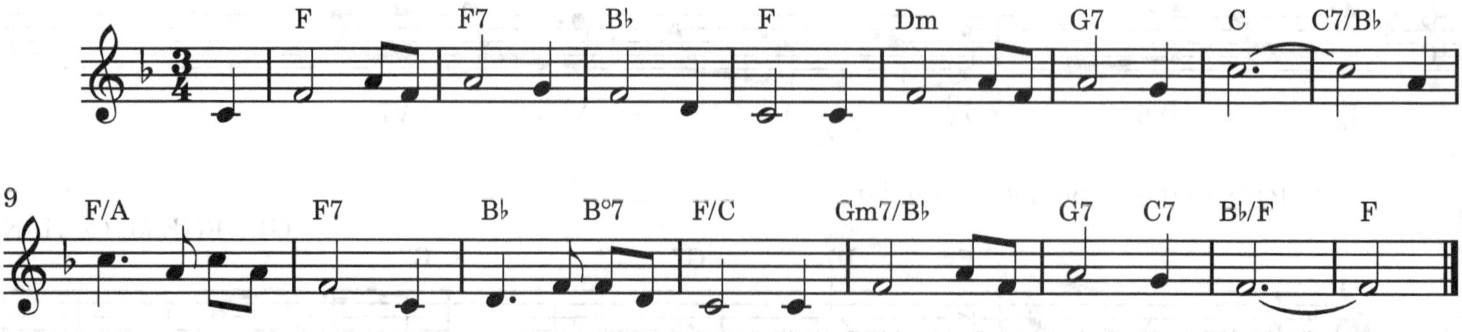

5.

America, the Beautiful

SAMUEL A. WARD

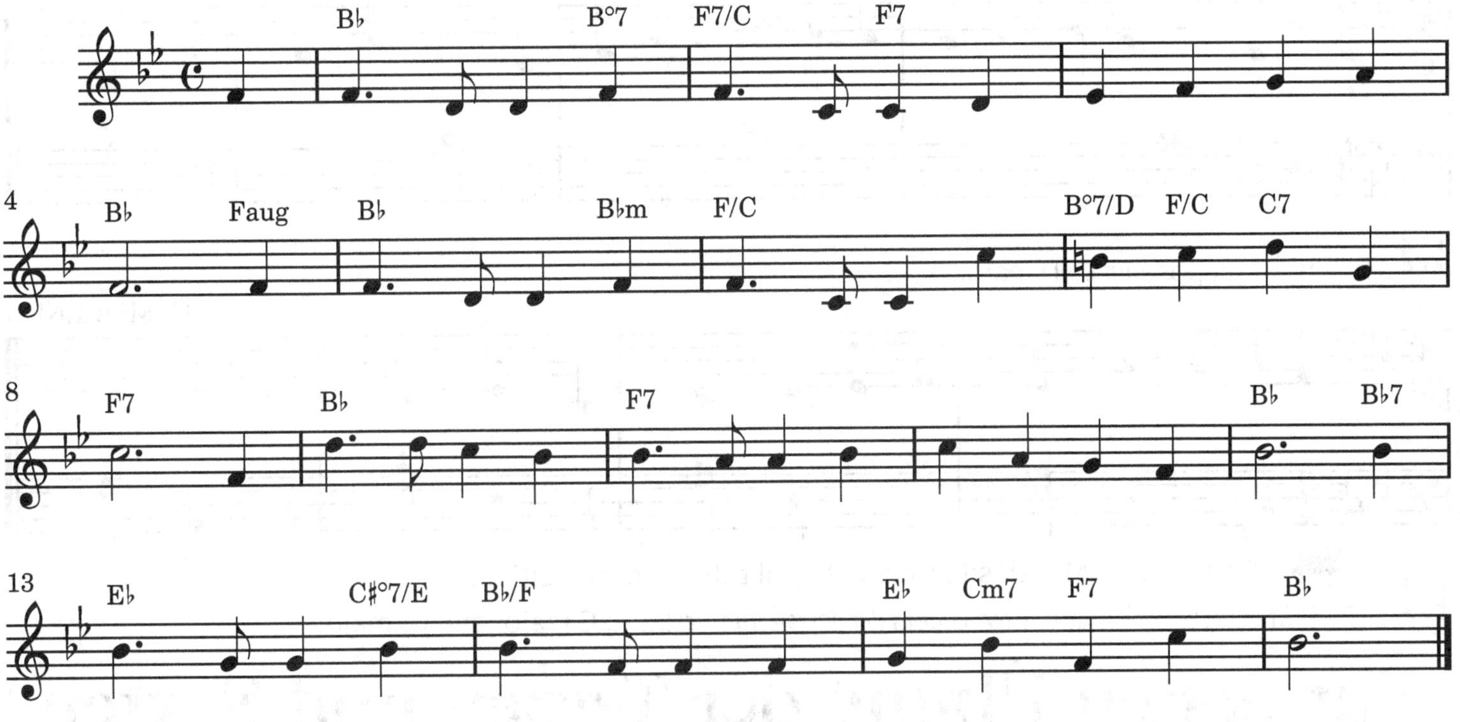

6. Accompany in keyboard style.

Eddie's Tune

MARTHA HILLEY

Go to the PDM Web site for additional help with items 2, 4, 5, and 6.

TRANSPOSITION

1. The following examples should be transposed an interval of a tritone.

   a. Transpose *up* to B♭ major.

C. MORENUS

   b. Transpose *up* to D major.

C. MORENUS

Go to the PDM Web site for additional tritone transposition.

2. Transpose Türk's *Zur ersten Übung der Terzen und Sexten* to C major and B♭ major.

Zur ersten Übung der Terzen und Sexten

DANIEL GOTTLOB TÜRK
(1756–1813)

Andantino

3. Play this excerpt as an ensemble: Part 1—clarinet, Part 2—violins I and II, and Part 3—viola and cello. Then play all string parts together as a classmate plays the clarinet. Compare the key signatures. How does a clarinet in A transpose?

Quintet in A Major

(Excerpt)

WOLFGANG AMADEUS MOZART, K. 58
(1756–1791)

Go to the PDM Web site for additional Clarinet in A.

4.

FRANCESCO GEMINIANI
(1687–1762)

5.

MOZART
(Adapted)

6.

7.

BEETHOVEN
(Adapted)

IMPROVISATION

1. Improvise three choruses of blues in F.
    - Chorus 1: RH non-root 13th and 9th chords with LH walking bass
    - Chorus 2: LH non-root 13th and 9th chords with RH blues scale melody
    - Chorus 3: RH non-root 13th and 9th chords with LH walking bass

Go to the PDM Web site for more help with blues improvisation, movement improvisation and ball improvisation.

2. Develop the following fragments into 16-bar segments to use with basic movement by 7-year-old children.

    a. Walking

    b. A puppy chasing its tail over and over!

    c. Jogging

    d. Dancing with goblins

    e. Playing leapfrog

3. Return to the *Ballad* progression on page 332. Using the recorded background as a stylistic guide, place 7th chords in your left hand as you improvise in the right hand. The melodic improvisation should consist of chord tones, passing tones, neighbor tones, etc. Remember, simplicity is a strong characteristic. Background 1 contains more of the harmonic content while background 2 is more sparse. Therefore, your improvisational style for the two should probably differ.

COMPOSITION

1. Discuss the compositional techniques used in II (page 351). Write a short work "in the style" of the Schuman. What characteristics should you include?

ENSEMBLE

Cortège

from *Five Images for Piano Four-Hands*

Secondo

With majesty (♩ = 63)

NORMAN DELLO JOIO

(Secondo)

Cortège

from *Five Images for Piano Four-Hands*

Primo

NORMAN DELLO JOIO

(Primo)

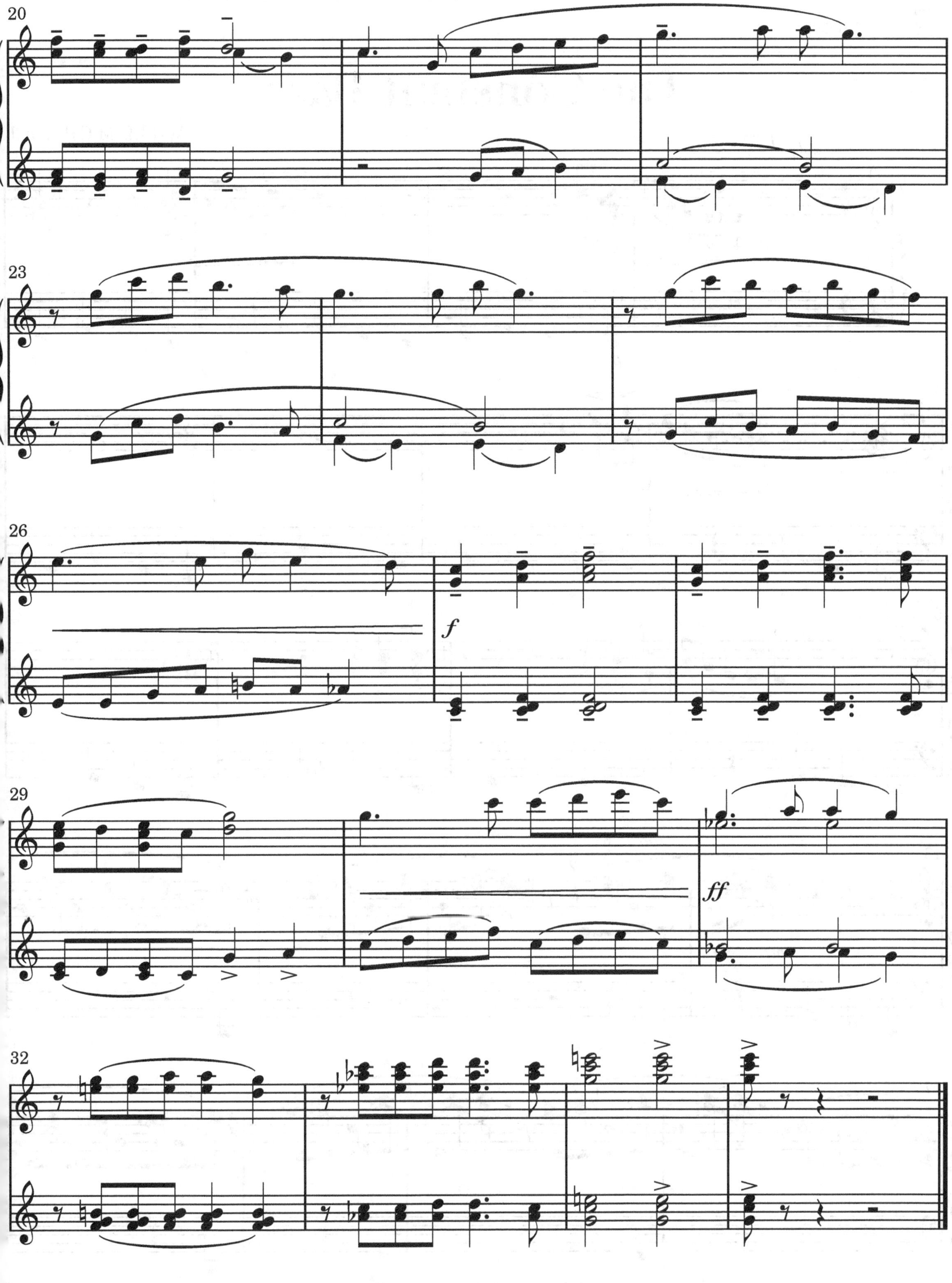

1. Enjoy!

The Constant Bass

WILLIAM GILLOCK

Steadily

21
p
25
f
29
8va
33
loco
decreasing
37
mf
f
8va

2. What is the tonal center for measures 1–10? The actual key signature? Modal implications?

Etude

TED COOPER

Allegro giocoso

17
f
22
mf
accel.
26
8va
30
(8va)
p subito
L.H.

3. Discuss appropriate articulation and mark your score accordingly.

Allegro

CHRISTOPH GRAUPNER
(1683–1760)

19
22
25
29
33
1.
2.

4. Play twice. On the repeat, sing as you play.

The Water Is Wide

British Isles Folk Song
Arr. Lynn Freeman Olson

16
20
mf
24
p
28
rit.
mf

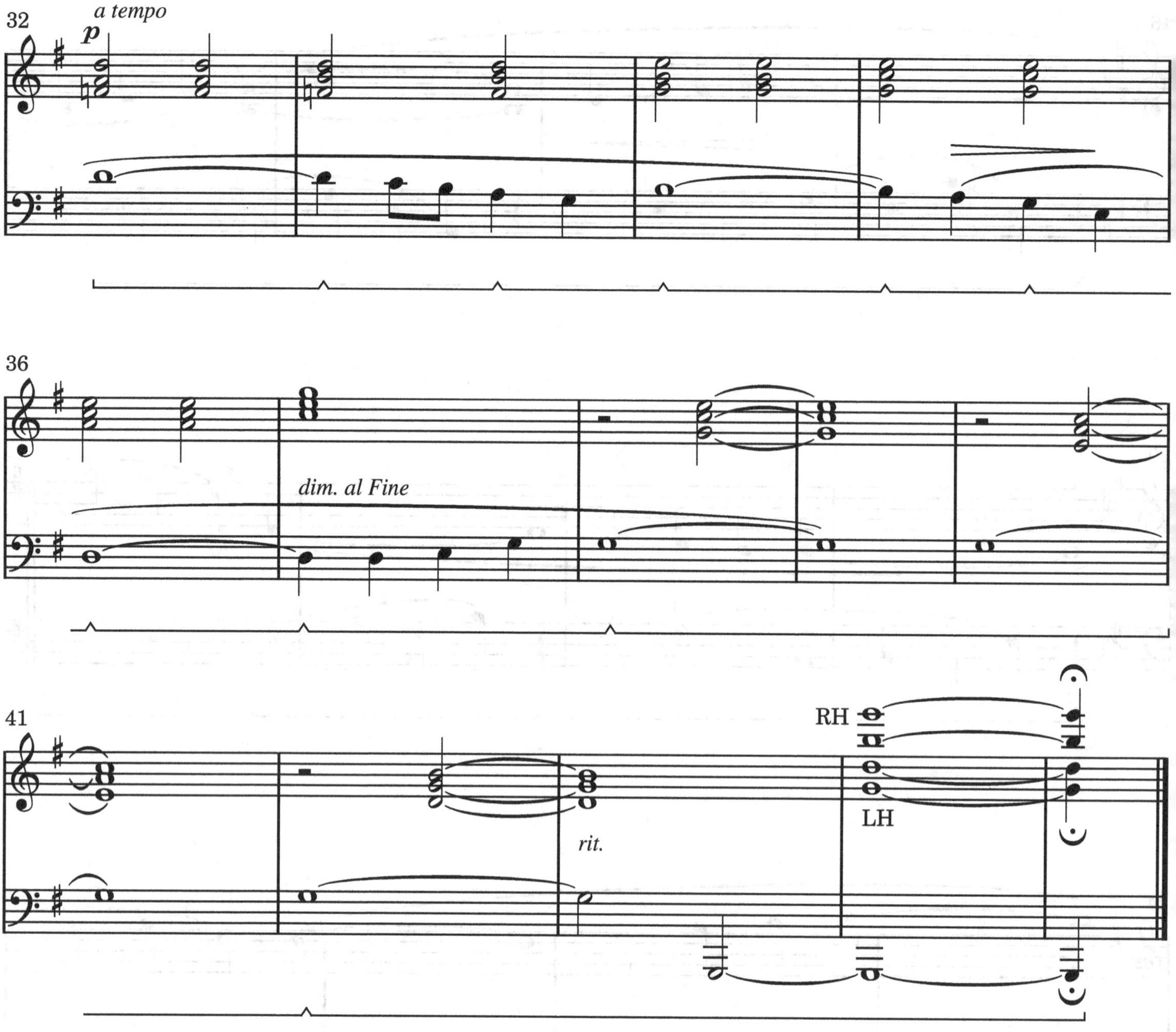

The water is wide, yet I must go.
Oh, would that I had wings to fly!
Is there a boat that will carry two?
Then both may go, my love and I.

A ship that sails out on the sea
Is loaded deep, deep as she can be,
Yet not so deep as the love I'm in—
I know not if I sink or swim.

Appendix A, B, and C from previous editions are now found on the PDM Web site.

Glossary

A bene placito at the pleasure of the performer
A tempo return to original tempo
Accelerando (accel.) gradually faster
Ad libitum (ad lib.) at your pleasure
Adagietto rather slow
Adagio slow
Adagissimo very slow
Agitato restless
Al fine to the end
Alla marcia in a march style
Allargando getting broader
Allegretto slightly less than Allegro
Allegro in a lively manner
Andantamente smooth
Andante a moderate tempo; leaning toward slower
Andantino moderately slow
Appoggiatura nonchord tone occurring on a strong beat
Ardito in a spirited manner
Authentic cadence dominant to tonic

Behaglich easily
Bewegt in an agitated manner
Breit broad, stately
Brioso vigorously

Cantabile to make the music "sing"
Cédez to go slower
Celere swiftly
Cesura (//) a complete break in sound
Chorale style 4-part texture, usually voiced "two and two"
Coda ending of a passage or piece
Come primo as on the first playing
Come sopra same as above
Comodo at a relaxed or leisurely pace
Con brio with spirit
Con dolore with sorrow
Con forza with force
Con grazia with grace
Con moto with motion
Con pedale (con ped.) with pedal
Con riposo in a calm, tranquil manner
Con spirito with spirit
Continuo bass line with figures to indicate harmonies to be played on a keyboard instrument
Crescendo (cresc.) gradually louder

Da Capo (D.C.) from the beginning
Dal Segno (D.S.) from the sign
Deciso decidedly
Decrescendo (decresc.) gradually softer
Diatonic pertaining to the key
Diminuendo (dim.) gradually softer
Dolce sweetly
Dolente sorrowful

Einfach simply
Espressivo (espr.) expressively
Etude a study; exercise or composition with a particular technical problem presented

Feuerig with fire

Gavotte a dance from the French usually written in 4 and beginning with a strongly accented third beat
Gemächlich leisurely
Geschwindt quickly
Getragen slow; sustained
Giocoso playful
Giustamente with exact precision
Grazioso graceful

Hemiola rhythmic relation of three notes in the time of two

Intenzionato with purpose
Intimo from the heart
Invention contrapuntal writing; a short piece usually consisting of a theme (subject) and a counter-theme (countersubject)

Keyboard style in harmonization, "3 & 1" voicing; melody is the highest sounding voice and determines the shape of the right-hand chord
Kräftig strong

Langsam slow
Larghetto slow; not quite as slow as Largo
Largo slow; in a broad manner
Leading tone 7th degree of the scale
Lebhaft animated
Legato in a smooth, connected manner
Leger line short line used to extend above and below the normal five-line staff
Leggero (leggiero) lightly
Leichtlich lightly
Lento very slow
Lesto lively
Liscio smoothly
Loco play as written
Luftig light
Lunga sometimes used in conjunction with a fermata; long
Lustig happy; merry
Luttuoso mournful

Ma non troppo but not too much
Maestoso stately
Marcato emphasized
Mässig moderately; may be used with other terms (i.e., mässig langsam—moderately slow)
Meno Allegro not so fast
Mesto melancholy
Mezza voce half voice
Misterioso creating a mood of mystery
Mit viel Kraft with much force
Moderato at a moderate speed
Modes in early music history, the collective name for scales
Molto much
Morbido soft, tender
Mordent in Baroque ornamentation, refers to an alteration of the written note with the note immediately below it
Morendo gradually dying away
Mosso motion
Motif subject
Munter lively

Neighbor tone upper or lower second of a harmonic tone that returns to original harmonic tone
Nicht zu schnell not too fast

Obligato an essential instrumental part
Ostinato a short musical pattern that is repeated persistently

Pastorale an instrumental piece depicting a feel for rural scenes
Pensoso pensive
Pesante heavy
Piacevole pleasant; free from strong accents
Piangevole mournful
Piú more
Pizzicato plucking a string
Poco little
Poco a poco little by little
Portato indicates a nonlegato tone; not as short as staccato
Posato dignified
Preciso with marked precision
Prestamente rapidly
Prestissimo the fastest possible

Quasi in effect; approximately

Rallentando (rall.) gradually slower
Retenu to hold back
Risentito vigorous
Risoluto in a resolute manner
Ritardando (rit.) gradually slower
Ritenuto (riten.) held back; slowed down
Robusto boldly
Rondeau a genre of music popular in French monophonic songs of the 13th century
Rondo a particular form of instrumental music which uses a recurring theme
Roulade as a florid vocal phrase
Rubato as a means of expression, to extend the duration of one note at the expense of another
Ruhig calm

Scat syllables used to verbalize blues and jazz rhythms
Scherzando in a lighthearted fashion
Scherzo a composition in a lively tempo
Schwungvoll in a swinging fashion
Scorrendo flowing
Semplice simple
Sempre always
Sentito with emotion
Senza without
Sequence a compositional technique employing transposition of a motive to different scale degrees; the transposition may be literal or diatonic
Serioso grave
Sforzando (sfz) giving a strong accent

Simile (sim.) in a similar manner
Smorzando (smorz.) dying away
Sostenuto usually equivalent to slowing the tempo
Staccato detached; usually an upward motion
Stretto typically in contrapuntal music, to overlap the subject in two or more voices
Subito suddenly
Svegliato animated

Tempo I original tempo
Tempo primo first tempo
Tonal center the tone or harmony that represents the tonic of a given key
Tranquillo quiet
Tritone augmented 4th or diminished 5th
Troppo too much

Un poco a little

Vistamente animatedly
Vite fast
Vivace quite fast
Vivacetto less lively than vivace
Vivo very lively

Wiegend swaying, rocking

Zierlich delicately, gracefully
Zeitmass tempo

Index of Titles

Index of Composers

Aural Skills - SS quiz #2 material

6
7
8
9
10
11
12
13
14

Harmonic Minor in 3rds (any key)
15
Climbing minor triads
16
(Ti)
etc.
i V64 i6 iv vii°7/V i64 V i
17
Beethoven Violin Conerto
18
*
From Mahler, Symphony No. 1
19
20

Maj7

D	Bb	G	Eb
Bb	Gb	Eb	B
G	Eb	C	Gb
Eb	B	Ab	E

7

Db			Eb
Bb		Eb	
G	Eb		
Eb			

m7

Db	Bb	Gb	Eb
Bb	G	Eb	
Gb	Eb		
Eb	C		

m7b5

Db			Eb
Bb		Eb	
G	Eb		
Eb			

°7

Db	Bbb		Eb
Bbb		Eb	
Gb	Eb		
Eb			

m(maj)7

D			Eb
Bb		Eb	
Gb	Eb		
Eb			

Maj7

			G
		G	
	G		
G			

7

			G
		G	
	G		
G			

m7

			G
		G	
	G		
G			

m7b5

			G
		G	
	G		
G			

°7

			G
		G	
	G		
G			

m(maj)7

			G
		G	
	G		
G			

Due Fri

Chord Dictation

1 Dm7
2 Gm7
3 Edom7
4 F#o7
5 Emaj7
6 Dm7
7 Fdom7
8 Amaj7

My Funny Valentine

Rodgers / Hart

Do Me R F Me S F Le S T L D T R D

1 D Dom^7
2 Gm^7
3 B^{o7}
4 F maj 7
5 C# Dom^7
6 Dm^7
7 C m (maj)^7
8 G maj^7
9 D^{ø7}
10 G Dom^7
11 C# maj^7